NOT BY CHANCE

THE TRUE STORY OF
WORD OF LIFE'S FIRST MISSION
IN COMMUNIST HUNGARY

SECOND PRINTING

PAUL BUBAR

Not By Chance

Author, Paul Bubar

Copyright 2010, Second Printing

ISBN 1-885273-17-7

First Century Publishing

PO Box 130, Delmar, NY 12054

1.800.578.6060

www.firstcenturypublishing.com

TABLE OF CONTENTS

Dedication

Foreword

Introduction

DEDICATION

Daniel Ray Bubar

July 29, 1966 – May 10, 1996

Daniel Bubar was the son of Paul and Shirley Bubar of Word of Life Fellowship in Schroon Lake, NY. He had one older brother, David, one younger brother, Jonathan, and a little sister, Sarah.

Dan grew up in the Word of Life family and spent summers on Word of Life Island from the time he was born until the time he entered the mission field. He accepted Christ as Savior when he was a boy and surrendered his life to be a missionary as a teenager. Knowing the great need of evangelism in missions, Dan completed two years of study at the Word of Life Bible Institute and continued his collegiate studies in Bible/Missions at Tennessee Temple University, graduating with honors in May 1989.

In April 1989, God led Daniel to be part of the team preparing to serve in Hungary, a country with new freedoms and opportunities. He helped begin the camping ministry in June 1990. He also started the Bible Club ministry in that land. There were 18 clubs in operation with curriculum and quiz teams.

Dan was best known for his fluency in the Hungarian language and for his love for the Hungarian people. He was also known for his great enthusiasm, for his encouragement to others, and for his commitment to the job God called him to do.

God chose to take him Home to Heaven through an auto/ truck accident in Erd, Hungary on May 1, 1996. A heavily loaded tandem tractor trailer broke away from its hitch and came out of the night directly into Dan's side of the auto. His special friend, Kinga Kovacs, was with him and walked away from the accident with no injury. It was obvious to all that it was Dan's appointed time to go Home to Heaven.

Dan Bubar's story is a wonderful one of God's plan and one man's commitment to doing what God called him to do.

You may be thinking, "What a sad story!" But it is not sad at all. Dan lived his life to the fullest. Paul, the Apostle, said, "I have run the race..." For some, the race is a marathon and we get the full track, but God chooses a short race for others. They are sprinters, and they win with a fast start. Dan loved to run and he ran life's race well – he ran to win!

Each of us run the race of life, and how far we run is God's business. He gave us life, but how we run is our responsibility before the Lord. Often young people do not think of themselves as those who are able to do much for the Lord, but Dan's story proves what one young person can do if they are willing to serve. We must all do what we can for the Lord today, while we can.

Shirley Bubar

Dan's Mother

DEDICATION

As we approach the second printing of *Not by Chance*, there are two other people, besides Dan Bubar who are worthy of the dedication of this great story of God's sovereignty and grace. They are, Alex Konya and Pastor Geza Kovacs. I want to add their names in dedication of this second printing of *Not by Chance*.

Alex Konya

It was Not by Chance that years before Alex Konya was born, his Godly Hungarian immigrant-grandfather would pray, often publically, that God would raise up someone from his family who would be led of God to go to Hungary and tell his family there about Christ.

It was Not by Chance that full-blooded Hungarian grandson, Alex, would be saved and feel led to the ministry, pursuing college and seminary in preparation for the pastorate here in America.

It was Not by Chance that in the 1980's he would pick up a news letter from Paul Bubar telling of the opening doors to reach youth with the gospel in then communist Hungary. Alex, then Pastoring a successful church in Indiana was drawn to go to Hungary on a Word of Life tour so he could "look and see" for himself.

It was Not by Chance that God would break his heart and call him to serve with Word of Life in Hungary as a teacher of Bible and Theology. His grandfather's prayers were being answered.

It was Not by Chance that Word of Life wanted to start a Bible Institute in which to train young Hungarians for the work of the ministry, and Alex was the right man at the right time and it was the right fit in every way.

Alex is a very self-effacing, enthusiastic, scholarly, preacher/teacher, who is "more Hungarian" than most Hungarians in his personality. He arrived, along with another great staff member Dave James and helped establish one of our great Bible Institutes under the Word of Life name. Having the ability to pull a team together, motivate, encourage, instruct and build up his Hungarian staff they are now moving out into other countries around Central Europe, building a base of future ministries.

It is very fitting that since Alex has been such a significant part of that wonderful ministry, that we dedicated this marvelous story of God's grace to Alex Konya and…

Pastor Geza Kovacs

Pastor Kovacs is one of the most notable pastors in all of Hungary. He has been a soul-winning, focused, visionary pastor for the last sixty years. It was Pastor Kovacs with whom Chuck Kosman and Bob Parschauer first had contact in Hungary. It was Pastor Kovacs who kept on preaching the gospel message even when ordered not to do so under communist rule. He traveled by train, bus, auto, and bicycle all over the country preaching, preaching, preaching. He became a "bone of contention" in the throat of the communist government, and to many in the church governments. He was always smiling and always articulate in "pushing the limits of change" in a godless society and a greatly restricted church.

It was Pastor Kovacs who listened to this "sometimes naive American" who (fortunately), knew nothing about living and trying to minister under communist government rule and limitations. He and his sons would listen to Bubar, Kosman and Parschauer dream of what might be. He would say, "You cannot do those things here…but, maybe in the future, if God should open doors."

It was Pastor Kovacs who quietly advised, encouraged, warned and would allow us to dream. He was the first Chairman of our Board of Directors when we finally were able to form a foundation that would permit us to exist legally. He was our official representative to the churches and government before we were legally allowed to exist.

He has remained on our Board, advising, guiding the hands of our directors to this day. He still continues to take churches with little chance of succeeding and through his leadership and strong preaching, build them into great churches. He was a very close friend and advisor to our son Dan, until God took Dan home. Thank you Pastor Kovacs. You will be our friend now and through eternity. Only God and heaven will reveal the total impact you have made on the church in your homeland.

FOREWORD

by Jack Wyrtzen

From our very beginning days, God has given direction to the ministry of Word of Life. Often it has been in areas we never planned on being involved. That was true in our first radio broadcast, evangelistic crusades, camps, clubs and overseas ministries. Yet, God led in such a way that we always seemed thrust into something without great advance warning.

This certainly was the case with Hungary. Paul Bubar found himself caught up in something from which he could not seem to extract himself. God was opening doors faster than we could go through them. It became very obvious to me that Hungary was a part of God's appointed plan for Word of Life.

This story is one of Word of Life on the cutting edge of change in Eastern Europe.

INTRODUCTION

How does God give direction to one's life? In the beginning of time God spoke to men audibly. Later in time, He directed men through Moses and the Ten Commandments, then the Old Testament prophets – they were never wrong because God told them what to tell people. God eventually sent His Son, Jesus Christ, who taught, preached, and raised up the disciples and apostles who spoke the Word of God. When Christ left the earth, He promised to send the Holy Spirit, who would lead, guide and instruct those who would follow Him.

Today our Lord still guides and directs our footsteps. He has promised to give light to our pathway to keep us from stumbling (Psa.119:105). He has given us clear direction through the writings of Holy Scriptures, if we will but read and believe it (II Tim. 3:16). The Bible was given for our direction and holds within it the answer to every one of life's perplexing problems, if we will but obey it. Our God has given us the Holy Spirit who lives within every person who has received the Lord Jesus Christ. He has also brought people and circumstances into our lives, which, under His masterful control, opens and closes doors before us.

Yes, there is a wonderful, loving God who wants to lead and guide you if you will but listen to His voice through those avenues.

My first thoughts about Hungary were in 1956 when most Americans had a "lump in their throats" as they helplessly watched TV shots of Hungarians dying under the heel of Stalin's Communist army.

Like most Americans, the horrors of 1956 faded from my mind until 1982. In April of that year God began directing my steps when I got "bumped" off an oversold Lufthansa flight out of Munich, Germany, and was scheduled through London, where I boarded

Pan Am Flight 301 to New York – a flight where I was to meet a Holocaust survivor who would focus my attention on Hungary. My fellow passenger would also use great influence in opening doors in Hungary that were closed to Westerners.

At the same time, a burden for Hungary began to come alive in the hearts of men such as Chuck Kosman and Bob Parschauer who would begin making preaching trips to the churches in Hungary.

It was obvious that it was God who was directing the circumstances of our lives to bring about the ministry of Word of Life in Hungary several years later. He would use men such as Kosman, Parschauer, the Kovacs family of Budapest and the London Kovac, along with me – and my God planned it all in advance.

Dear reader, your life is not a pointless series of happenings. Our God is aware of you and your needs. He is interested in the details of your life. He has a detailed and good plan for your life. But, you must respond positively to the great master plan our God has for you. You must consult the rule book – the Scriptures. You must follow these directions given to us by God in His Word. If you are willing to do that, He will certainly direct your very footsteps.

This story begins in April of 1982 and is a record of events that led to the opening of Hungary to the ministry of Word of Life. The story continues with significant happenings in the sovereign plan of God to this day.

Through this wonderful story, you can see how your life is neither an accident nor a vacuum. It is not by chance.

Paul Bubar

NOT BY CHANCE

CHAPTER 1

SORRY

WE ARE

OVERBOOKED

We were up early that April morning in 1982 at the beautiful Wort Des Lebens castles in Starnberg, in what was then West Germany. Having just finished a glorious and very successful leadership conference with about 250 German young people, we were all on a spiritual high...tired, but excited. I had to catch a flight back to the United States, and my good friend, Chuck Kosman, was at the door calling me to breakfast. His small blue eyes were bright with the excitement of that weekend. Kosman, a veteran missionary for the ministry of Word of Life Germany, and his team have been in the business of sharing the gospel through evangelistic meetings, music, camps and crusades in Germany and much of Europe since 1963. They thrived on the happiness of bringing young people to Christ.

God had given the team this magnificent set of castles on the long and lovely Lake Starnberg, just 20 minutes outside of Munich. With the help of many of God's people in Germany, the castles and land were transformed from ruins and squalor to stately beauty. The castles were constructed out of cut stone and had old copper roofs that had turned green from age. One castle had turrets and a courtyard, and the other was more square and resembled a villa. We always felt so very blessed to have them.

After a delicious breakfast, Kosman and I left for the Munich airport. There were many things waiting for me back in the States. First, there were 38 full-time men in the Word of Life Club ministry for whom I was responsible. The Bible Club ministry was growing. My second concern was Word of Life Island and the hiring of the entire staff for the upcoming summer. Uppermost in my mind, however, was Youth Quest '82, a youth conference conducted at the Word of Life camps in Schroon Lake, New York. We hoped to attract some 1,000 to 1,200 teens and planned 120 separate seminars dealing with the issues of life facing young people today.

I had already designated the time spent flying to New York for arranging the seminars into a logical system, one that would keep the speakers and seminar locations from being double booked. This was necessary to keep the three-day conference flowing in an orderly manner. I had three different notebooks in my briefcase, and as soon as we were airborne pulled them out and began working. Detailing the conference schedule was sure to require many hours of concentration. The schedule would be turned over to the printer upon my arrival at the Schroon Lake office.

Monday morning traffic delayed our travel on the Autobahn. Nevertheless, we arrived at the Munich Airport with plenty of time before flight departure. However, once we reached the Lufthansa counter we were in for a surprise. Checking and rechecking my ticket, the agent informed me they were very sorry, but this particular flight was overbooked and no seat was available for me.

I reminded them of the ticket in my possession, of my reservation and of the fact that they would find me a seat on that flight!

Checking the computer once more the agents told me in broken English, "We are very, very sorry, Mr. Bubar, but there is no seat available for you."

I jokingly remarked that I'd be willing to fly in the lavatory — I knew there was a seat there — if they allowed me to. With more apologies they explained that, of course, they could not permit anyone to do that. Such was my attempt to add some levity to the tense situation.

My next strategy was to ask to see the supervisor. When he arrived, I reminded him of the contract Lufthansa held in the form of the ticket that had been officially stamped by the airline. If they would read the fine print on the back of the ticket, they would determine, as I had, that this was indeed a contract requiring Lufthansa to deliver me to New York within so many hours of the stated time, even if they had to charter an airplane to get me there.

"Mr. Bubar," they responded, "of course we cannot do that, but we will try to get you there on another airline."

"Fine," I said, "that is perfectly all right. I don't mind what airplane I fly on as long as it doesn't have faded paint on the nose reading *Spirit of St. Louis.*"

They again keyed into the computer, and in a matter of minutes, arranged a Lufthansa flight to London where I would connect with Pan Am flight #301 to JFK. I happily agreed and my luggage was tagged for JFK via Heathrow.

The flight to London was uneventful. I had even decided against pulling out the notebooks since the flight was a short one. Flying from London to New York, however, allowed me a full six hours to pull together all the details for Youth Quest '82.

Arriving in London I hurriedly moved to the Pan Am gate and soon found myself aboard a Jumbo 747. I stashed everything in the overhead compartment, keeping under the seat my thick salesman's case holding my many notebooks, a couple of Bibles and everything necessary for detailing the schedule of this conference that was so important to me. I carefully chose an aisle seat giving me plenty of elbow room in which to work. The aircraft took off precisely on time. As soon as the wheels lifted, I pulled down the tray in front of me and the tray for the vacant seat beside me, arranged my notebooks and was hard at work.

Twenty minutes into my flight and my task, I noticed the man two seats to my left. He stared at me without breaking his gaze. I judged him to be about 50 years old, well dressed, and a foreigner to me. He had a trim build and sandy gray hair, which was thinning a bit. He continued his stare while I worked. Now I don't know about you, but when someone is staring at you all the while you are trying to work, it becomes a little distracting. I glanced over at him and met his gaze, smiled and said, "Hello."

He responded with a thick accent, "How do you do?"

My eyes turned back to my work. Deeply engrossed in completing my project, I had no time for conversation.

Another ten or fifteen minutes went by before the man began peering at what I was writing in my notebook. This bothered me a bit and so I looked over at him and decided to introduce myself.

"Hello, I'm Paul Bubar," I said cordially. "I am an American from upstate New York. And your name, sir?"

He responded in his heavy European accent, "I am Michael Kovacs. I am a Hungarian Jew. I am from London and Budapest. You must be a workaholic because everyone around us is sleeping, drinking or listening to music, and you are working. What do you do for a living?"

I responded, "I am a preacher."

"Oh," Michael Kovacs replied, "I see."

"Don't you believe in preachers or priests?" I asked.

He thought for a minute and then responded with, "No, I do not believe in agents. If I have a problem, I go directly to God. But exactly what is it that you do as a priest?"

I thought, *Oh no! How do I explain Word of Life? This man is from a foreign country. I've just met him and he obviously is not familiar with the United States or with Christianity. How do I explain to him Word of Life, what it is and what we do? Not only that, but I don't need this hassle right now. I have all of this work to finish in barely five hours and this man wants to talk.*

I soon learned that I was not talking to just another bored airline traveler. I discovered I was engaging in conversation with a most unusual person. In the following minutes, as we learned about each other's backgrounds, I learned I was not only talking to a Jew but one who was a World War II Holocaust survivor. How well I remembered my father's grief during WWII over the atrocities committed against the European Jews. This stranger was one of them.

My father, who was an old-time Baptist, evangelist and pastor, had taught his children to love the Jews, as they were God's special and chosen people. I learned to respect them and to care for their souls. I can remember a sermon my father delivered in 1938, when I was a boy of just five, titled, "The Jew: God's Time Clock of the Ages." Father taught us that throughout the ages God would judge the nations that raised their hands against the Jew. Here was a Jew who survived the black horror of the Holocaust. You bet he had my attention!

Michael continued, "And you, what do you do as a priest?"

"Well sir," I said, "I work for a Christian organization in America. We are Christians, not as Jewish, Muslim, Christian, but we are Christians in the sense that we are followers of Jesus Christ who take a literal interpretation of both the Old and New Testaments."

I paused for a minute, but Michael waited patiently to hear more, so I continued, "Word of Life works with young people all over the world in some 23 countries around the globe. Our philosophy is that young people all over the world have an emptiness within them which causes them to search for the meaning to life. They want a reason to live and a reason to die. We give young people hope for their life in the here and hereafter."

"We believe men and women were created by God and for God. Without God in their lives there is an emptiness that can be filled by nothing except God Himself. First of all, we believe when a young person, or anyone, comes into a right relationship with God through Jesus Christ, his thinking is changed. His thinking changes about himself. He realizes he is a sinner and has broken God's laws. His thinking about others is changed and so is his thinking about his God. His changed thinking in turn changes his attitude towards life. Because he thinks differently about himself, about others, and about God, all his attitudes that are reflected in his likes and dislikes are changed. This changes his lifestyle... how he chooses to live so that he, literally, becomes a different person because of his right relationship to God through Jesus Christ. This, in a nutshell, is what we seek to tell young people all over the world."

"Our approach in our camping program in 23 countries is that all young people share a common denominator called *fun.* They want to enjoy life. They like fun activities, so in this worldwide camping program we seek to have fun and enjoyment in their activities. We have a high-profile sports program and good music, and that attracts the youth. In the midst of this great fun and activity, each day for one hour in the morning and one hour in the evening, we open the Scriptures to them and explain to them the teachings of Jesus Christ."

My friend interrupted me at that point and said, "That is beautiful, that is beautiful. But tell me something. I have spent a lifetime searching for an answer to the question, 'Why? _Why_ did my family all perish? They were all more brilliant than I. They were all better than I.' _Why_ did they all perish and I alone survive?"

It was obvious this was an unanswered question representing a void in this man's life. He went on to tell me the story of his experience in the Holocaust. Michael Kovacs and his family, including his aged grandfather, were put in boxcars at a rail station in Szolnok, Hungary, in 1944. His grandfather could not get up over the high threshold of the boxcar, so his 16 year-old grandson jumped out to help his grandfather. At that point, a Gestapo officer stepped forward and stopped him.

"Enough," he said, "the car is full. You go to the next car."

So the two were separated from the rest of the family. The long ride to the Jewish death camp must have been a nightmare. How many times I have thought about it. Only in recent years have such films as the _Holocaust_ and others chronicled the agony and tragedy of these millions of Jews put to death. They are God's special people, loved by our Lord Jesus Christ and, yet, they have paid a terrible price. Every time I hear the story of the Holocaust I get a lump in my throat, as do millions of sincere people around the world.

Michael's story continued. He wondered how his folks were and how they were surviving the trip in the boxcar. He described what it was like as they approached the death camp, the cold and damp in the air and the coldness in the face of the Nazi officer who stood behind the rain-spattered plate glass window in the railroad siding station that day.

As the cars rolled past, the officer stood there and waved his hand back and forth. When he brought his hand forward, Michael later learned, it meant the people in that car would survive and be taken to the work camp section of the compound. When he moved his hand back, that group would go immediately to the showers and to their death by poison gas.

My Jewish friend went on to explain, "As our car rolled by, the officer brought his hand forward. That meant life. As the car carrying my family passed, the animal had to bring his hand back and that meant death. Why? *Why?* Tell me if you can, why did this happen? Why did I live, and my whole family perish?"

With a lump in my throat the size of an apple, I remember the compassion and sorrow I felt for this man that I did not even know. I looked at my life. God had been so good. I quickly thought over my background. I was born into a godly Christian home where both my parents loved the Lord Jesus Christ. I was raised to love the Lord, to seek His forgiveness and to walk with the Lord. I have been blessed with my own family, and they are all in step with the Lord.

I did not suffer the tragedies Michael had. My life in ministry and with family has been very blessed. At 26 years of age I found myself leading a Bible study group in D.L. Moody's hometown of Northfield, Massachusetts. The Bible study grew, people started finding Christ and we formed the Northfield Baptist Church. I was single then, into automobiles and airplanes, and had not planned to pastor a church. The people there were wonderful and gracious to this young, immature, still-learning pastor. The church continued to grow, not because of me, but in spite of me, I'm certain! It was at Northfield that I would discover that God had called me to minister to youth. At Northfield, I met Jack Wyrtzen and learned about Word of Life. Little did I know that a few years later I would leave the pastorate and join with Word of Life to give birth to a new ministry: Word of Life Bible Clubs. Soon after joining the staff of Word of Life, I met the most beautiful woman I've ever known, Shirley Swanson. At the time, Shirley was working as a secretary for Jack Wyrtzen.

In 1963 we were married at Northfield Baptist Church among the people I loved so much. God gave us four wonderful children over the next few years: David, Daniel, Jonathan and Sarah. Our children were all very dear to us, and they all came to trust Christ as their personal Saviour at an early age. As I was away in ministry during much of those years, Shirley must take the credit for the special character and good spirit of our children. Shirley has always been a constant encourager to me and to our children. I have been such a blessed man through all these years!

I have also known many advantages by living in America. I could remember the words of my dear gray-haired Dad who, when I was young, would say, "Son, have you thanked God that you live in America...that you don't live under some dictator? Have you thanked God that you are born free?"

My Jewish friend interrupted my thoughts with the word, "Why?"

I responded as gently as I could. "Oh, my friend, I can tell you why."

Suddenly I forgot all about the work I had to do and that I had a conference schedule to assemble. All I could think of was the hurt I saw in this dear man's face and that he didn't have an answer, but I did.

I remember reaching for my Schofield Bible, pulling it out of my briefcase and saying, "Sir, I can give you an answer to your question." We then started through the Scriptures, beginning with Genesis 3. We talked about the fall of man, of sin's entrance into the world through the first man, Adam, and what makes man do the awful things he does. We talked about how that because sin came into the world, man fell from a sinless state and became a lawbreaker. Because the first man, Adam, became a lawbreaker, every man born into the human race has had, deep within him, this yearning to break the laws of God. It is because of this fall that sin rules in the world.

Because of this evil nature, when man is left to his own devices and the idea that he will never be brought to accountability, he can sink to any level. It is this sinful nature that has produced the Hitlers, the Eichmans, the Stalins and the other arch murderers of history.

Together we turned to Genesis 6. There I read, "And it repented the Lord that He had made man on the earth and it grieved Him in His heart." In other words, man became so awful in God's sight that God was sorry he ever made man to begin with.

From there we turned to Isaiah 53, and I read the Scriptures to Michael of how Isaiah, the prophet, foretold our Lord's Coming. Isaiah wrote, speaking of the Messiah who was to Come:

> *He is despised and rejected of men a man of sorrows, and acquainted with grief: and we hid as it were our faces from him; he was despised and we esteemed him not. Surely he hath borne our griefs, and carried our sorrows: yet we did esteem him stricken, smitten of God, and afflicted. But he was wounded for our transgressions, he was bruised for our iniquities; the chastisement of our peace was upon him; and with his stripes we are healed. All we like sheep have gone astray; we have turned every one to his own way; and the Lord hath laid on him the iniquity of us all. He was oppressed, and he was afflicted, yet he opened not his mouth; he is brought as a lamb to the slaughter, and as a sheep before her shearers is dumb, so he openeth not his mouth. (Isaiah 53:3-7)*

We went quickly from Isaiah to the New Testament, and I shared with my new friend about our lovely Lord Jesus. I told him how Jesus was falsely accused and rejected of men; how He was oppressed and condemned. I talked about how He was scourged and the significance of the scourging. I told how Jesus was nailed to a cross, all without opening His mouth and protesting, because Jesus knew His mission was to come to this earth, to die and to shed His blood to rescue men from their sins.

From the book of Romans, I explained how that if man would confess Jesus with his mouth and believe in his heart that God raised Jesus from the dead, man can be saved (Romans 10:9-10).

This dear, sincere, sensitive, very smart man, with tears in his eyes, said, "Oh, that is the most beautiful story I have ever heard. Is it _really_ true?"

"Yes," I told him earnestly, "it _is_ really true. It is the gospel truth." I reminded him that our Lord Jesus wanted to be his Messiah.

We turned to Revelation 3 where Jesus speaks to every man and says, _"Behold, I stand at the door, and knock: if any man hears my voice, and opens the door, I will come in to him, and will sup with him and he with me."_

I pointed out how this is a promise straight from the mouth of Jesus, and that if any hungry-hearted man wants mercy and forgiveness, all he has to do is open the door of his heart and the dear Lord Jesus will come in to live with him. "Sir," I remember saying, "Will you allow this wonderful Jesus to be your Messiah?"

This newfound acquaintance of mine, who had experienced so much grief, pressure and hurt in his life responded, with, "Oh, I am that close," as he held up his fingers a half inch apart, "but, I cannot...I absolutely cannot."

By now, in our conversation, I had learned that after this kindhearted Jew had been liberated from the death camp, he and a friend had started back toward Budapest; yet, he had no family to welcome him.

Camping out one night on their trek to Budapest, they came across an old Russian army officer to whom they offered a cup of coffee by their campfire. The officer asked where they were going. When they told him Budapest, the old soldier stood erect and said, "No, no young men. Don't do that, whatever you do. Flee to the West. Run tonight. Go to the West. Go as far as you can and don't stop until you get out of the Communist Bloc."

That army officer apparently knew what would happen in Budapest and in all of Eastern Europe. But Michael and his friend couldn't comprehend what the old Russian army officer was trying to tell them. In their youthful determination to go back home, they thought, "He's crazy. He doesn't know what he's talking about." And so, they continued on their way to Budapest where, exactly as the old Russian officer had warned, they became trapped. Michael would not escape Communism until 1949 when, following a very daring plan, he would flee to the West via Vienna. From Vienna, he went on to Sydney, Australia. At the end of 1968, he traveled to London with his family when the Labor Party came to power in Australia.

Over the years in London, this very bright, savvy, kindhearted, and benevolent Jew made his mark on the financial world. Getting involved in a very special line of business, his markets span the globe today. I have no idea of his wealth. I can only guess.

As we approached JFK Airport, I remember feeling that this unplanned meeting on Pan Am flight #301 had a much deeper purpose and reason than I could understand that day. I felt I had been in the presence of a most unusual person and that God, in His sovereignty and marvelous plan for both of our lives, had brought us together.

Looking back, I remember I did not want to talk to this man. I did not want him to interrupt my work, which was to be accomplished before we landed in New York.

I did not know it then, but Michael Kovacs was to be a very important figure and friend in my life. He had determined in his heart that he did not want to sleep away the entire flight to New York. He wanted to talk to someone. He has since told me he couldn't understand why I didn't want to talk to him. If I didn't talk to him, he was going to sit with a person who would. I had the distinct feeling this meeting had been foreordained by a wise and holy God.

Landing in New York, Michael and I exchanged business cards as the aircraft taxied to the gate. I wrote down the phone number of my new friend, and we parted company.

Does God order our steps? Every step? Does our God put significance even in the strangers we sit next to on an airplane? Is there a divine purpose in everything we do in life? Is it really true as stated in Psalm 139:16, that before each of us is born, our God scheduled every day of our lives?

CHAPTER 2

LEARNING
THE LANDSCAPE

In 1972 Word of Life's team in Germany made an evangelical trip to Hungary, Yugoslavia and Bulgaria, which revealed to them firsthand the restrictions under which Communist governments placed their people and especially the Church of Jesus Christ.

At that time, the Bulgarian Communist government was the most restrictive of Christianity and evangelism. And although there could be no advertising of public meetings, every church our team entered was filled to capacity as the route of their itinerary spread through word-of-mouth.

The team made many friends in Bulgaria, including one young pastor who decided to travel with them from meeting to meeting. In the midst of their travels, this young Bulgarian pastor lost his traveling documents, and to be found without them in a foreign district would result in his immediate arrest and imprisonment.

As they approached one of the churches, they encountered a police roadblock. The Bulgarian pastor, realizing that he was without his papers, began to weep. Turning to Chuck Kosman, the leader of our team, he pleaded, "Please, Chuck, see that my family is provided for. Somehow promise me you will get funds through to the East to ensure my family has enough food to eat. Promise me, please, promise me." It was too late to reverse the car and avoid the police, so they did the only thing they could; they prayed. "Lord, blind the eyes of this officer. Lord, spare our brother in Jesus' name."

An officer approached the car and asked the occupants for their passports. He took the passports from our team, looked at them and counted, "One, two, three, four."

He then looked at the five occupants and counted them one, two, three and four.

"Yes, you may go." he said, "Here are your documents."

But wait a minute; there were five men in the automobile. Did he not see one of them? Or did he, in fact, see all five, and sensing he should not report them, count only to four? Or did our Mighty God blind his eyes to this Bulgarian pastor? We will not know the answer until we get to heaven. On their way to Bulgaria, our German team stopped in Budapest and met a wonderful pastor, Geza Kovacs, who led the small, struggling Budafok Baptist Church and would eventually become a very special friend.

Until 1985, citizens of Communist-Bloc countries could not leave without an exit visa. A letter of invitation guaranteeing the financial means of passage and a guarantee of return were needed in order to obtain this elusive document. Until 1986, an entire family would not be allowed to leave the country together; one or two members would be refused an exit visa, guaranteeing the return of the rest of the family to the Communist Bloc.

Realizing that Pastor Kovacs was no ordinary Baptist preacher but one upon whom God had placed His blessing, Chuck Kosman invited him to spend several weeks at the Wort des Lebens (Word of Life) Castle at Lake Starnberg. Special efforts were made and Pastor Kovacs and his wonderfully-talented church choir were permitted to leave Hungary for several visits.

Camp Tahi: A Place of Refuge

Hungary had its own youth camp, owned by the Baptist Union, which had existed since 1928. The facility was extremely primitive, a little more than one hectare (less than three acres) in size. A barn-like structure with a concrete floor served as the auditorium and on either side were two attached sheds containing six-foot shelves that served as bunks. Young people would climb onto these shelves with their sleeping bags and lie next to each other, the boys on one side of the building and the girls on the other.

The kitchen was in the basement of another building, and a slab of concrete with a corrugated fiberglass roof served as the dining room. There were only two toilets, which ran off into a small brook on the edge of the property.

If I described only the physical aspects of Camp Tahi, you would miss its significance. Camp Tahi, for generations, had been the place of evangelism. Thousands of Hungarian Christians can trace their salvation to that small piece of ground.

It was here that Evangelist Billy Graham had first conducted public meetings in Hungary. Because the government would not permit him to rent any public facility, and because no Baptist church was large enough to accommodate those who would attend, he held his first crusade at Camp Tahi in 1978. About 10,000 people gathered for that meeting.

This was the only youth camp in three Communist-Bloc countries that our team visited. It is what everyone in Hungary, including Pastor Geza Kovacs, thought of when they heard mention of a Christian youth camp.

When Pastor Kovacs arrived at our beautiful castles at Lake Starnberg, he could hardly believe his eyes.

"You mean Christians can have something this nice? How is it possible?" he asked, shaking his head. "Only in the West. Nothing like this could ever happen in my country — could it?"

It was during this important visit to our castles in Starnberg that Pastor Kovacs invited Chuck Kosman and Bob Parschauer back to Hungary to conduct evangelistic meetings.

Janos Kadar

Meanwhile, very slowly, changes were beginning to take place in the Hungarian government. Janos Kadar, chairman of the Communist party, was not a hard-liner. As a matter of fact, he had led the revolution against Moscow in 1956, when Russian tanks rolled into Hungary to put many of its young men in unmarked graves atop Buda Hill. Kadar was imprisoned and tortured for his disobedience. A rebel of sorts, Kadar was trusted by the Hungarians, none of whom had any great love for the Russians, because of his involvement in the revolution.

As a child, Kadar attended a Christian school run by the Reformed Church. It was not a Christian school as we know such academies in the West, but it was not a government-run public school either, so religious instruction was available in the school. I am told that Kadar's stepmother was a godly woman who belonged to the Seventh Day Adventist Church.

As the new Communist government under Kadar began to stabilize, small freedoms emerged. In 1975 Kadar made a public statement that would profoundly affect the future of Jesus Christ's Church in Hungary.

"Hungarians are basically a religious people," he said. "We have made a grave error in trying to ban religion from our society. Therefore, we will change. In the future we will permit religion under culture."

Very slowly, the pressure began to ease on the churches of Hungary.

The Deviant Problem

At this time, a very serious problem existed in Hungary. Under their Communist system, a child born illegitimately would be taken from its parent and placed in a government-run orphanage. This would happen regardless if the mother wanted to keep her child or not. Under the Communist regime, all adults had to work, and daycare was provided. But, it was not provided for people who were unmarried. Thus, the children were taken, and it was against the law for the parents to visit them. Those children now belonged to the government.

These orphanages were awful. They were huge, cold, stone buildings with plaster walls, often painted pea-green. They would sleep about 20 in a room. More like Alcatraz Island than Boys' Town, and holding three or four thousand children each, these institutions were primarily staffed by matrons, there only by government mandate. There was education but certainly no religion. There was no God there, no love, only discipline.

A male visitor to one of these places would be mobbed. Since women staffed the orphanages, and no visitors came, the children almost never saw men. Tiny three, four, and five-year-olds would crowd around, embracing the visitor's leg, crying, "Papa, Papa," hoping that he was their father coming to take them away from that terrible place. It was a heartbreaking scene.

Thousands upon thousands of children all over the country were raised in these institutions until they were 18, when a Communist Party official would summon them to the office and tell them that the government could no longer afford to feed them and that they must leave.

"But where will we go?" the children would say.

The government officer then would tell them, "You will report to such and such a place where there will be a position for you. It will provide you a salary. You must live on the salary provided for you by the government."

Often, these 18-year-olds would respond, "But we know no one out there. Where will we stay? Where will we live?"

"Well, that is up to you." the officials told them. "You must fend for yourself."

"But we don't know anyone."

"Then get to know someone. You must leave now."

And so these hordes of young people, these young men and women who had been raised with no God and no love, had to leave, with no place to go. Because they had been raised in a moral vacuum, when they hit the streets, usually of Budapest, it was said, "If bad breath should walk by, these poor youths would follow it." Because they were valueless and amoral, they would follow anything that appeared interesting to them, good or bad.

These hordes of young people, believed by some to total 200,000 in a country of only 10.2 million people, would often become the deviants, the drinkers and druggies, the punks and perverts of Hungarian society. The government freely admitted they did not know how to deal with these youth, and it became a growing problem in a Communist society that did not make allowance for people and which, in any event, could provide no answers to their valueless existence.

Geza Kovacs had for many years been an evangelist at Camp Tahi, conducting prayer meetings wherever he was allowed, even while under intense personal scrutiny by the government. This was during the hard years in Hungary, following the 1956 uprising of the people against the Communist regime, an uprising that had led to much slaughter and, sadly, no success for the people. At around this time Pastor Kovacs approached several government officials and said to them, "The Church of Jesus Christ in Hungary can help with your deviant problem, but you won't allow us to. Give us our freedom and we will show you that we can help."

So the Kadar government, finally seeing the light, began to alleviate some of the pressure on the churches and grant them some small freedoms.

I will never forget the celebration at Budafok Baptist after they were finally allowed to hang a sign on the outside of their church. Something almost every American church takes for granted, this two foot by two foot glass case was the cause of great rejoicing, because the parishioners would finally be able to let their neighbors on this small suburban side street know of upcoming events.

In the spring of 1984 I was invited to our Castles in Germany for a youth leadership conference, during which Chuck Kosman told me of his invitation to visit Hungary. He asked me, "Paul, how would you like to go along? How would you like to go behind the Iron Curtain and have an opportunity to preach the gospel in one of the churches in Budapest?"

I just about jumped out of my shoes!

"You bet!" I said, "When can we go?"

Chuck told me that they were still making arrangements and that he would try to make contact with Pastor Kovacs and schedule something for October of that year.

As the date of the Hungarian trip drew near, it appeared that the necessary funds might not be made available. I remember dejectedly phoning Kosman and telling him that the trip looked very doubtful.

His response was very definite and typically Kosman: "Bubar, you are coming! Everything is arranged. These people are expecting you. You are not going to get out of this one even if I have to send the money myself!"

I knew we had to find the funds. I talked with my superiors and finally convinced them of the trip's importance. The financing was somehow approved.

I have often reflected on what might have happened had I not gone on that trip. Perhaps our difficulties were Satan's attempt to keep Word of Life from winning Hungarian young people to Christ. I am sure now that it was part of God's perfect plan that I should go to Budapest in October of 1984, for I would soon learn that our lives are ordered by a wise God and the days of our lives are not by chance.

First Border Crossing

I will never forget my first trip to Hungary. I invited my friend and pastor, Roger Ellison of Mountainside Bible Chapel in Schroon Lake, New York, to go with me; a pastor of great wisdom whom I felt could make a real contribution to our mission in Hungary. I had known him since his days as Professor of Theology at Tennessee Temple University in Chattanooga. Ellison was about 45-years old at the time of our trip, with wavy brown hair and a slim build. He was always neatly dressed with a very pleasing personality. He was jovial, upbeat and very well educated, although he would never flaunt it. He was a modest, honest man, with a lovely family. Flying into Vienna, we were met by Chuck Kosman, Bob Parschauer, and other members of the German musical team. During the four-hour drive to Budapest, I experienced my first border crossing at the beautiful little town of Hegyeshalom, along the border of Hungary and Austria. This was a country town, and the people there worked on the cooperative farms (all government jobs, of course) which produced wheat and corn throughout the lovely, rolling hills.

I had been told of the mine fields on the Hungarian side and how the checkpoint was set back from the Austrian side. This was done in the event anyone decided to make a break for it — there would still be one half mile of Hungarian territory upon which to pursue and apprehend them. As we drove, I saw the curves in the road that were banked the wrong way to prevent speeding and the guard towers and the large steel gates across the road. There, the heavily armed, stone-faced soldiers stopped each vehicle for inspection before they were permitted to proceed through the checkpoint.

Tension was high. I remember thinking, *What am I doing here? I could be home with my family. So many things could go wrong: What if they discover I'm not a tourist? Will they find something wrong with my papers? Will they inspect my luggage and find the Bibles?*

We went through the checkpoint with no troubles. Eventually, even these seemingly dangerous border crossings would become routine with the inner knowledge that I was on God's business and that He would go before me and make the crooked places straight. This knowledge eased my troubled mind. I was not there by my own choice but by God's. The things that were unfolding before me were not by chance but by the plan of a sovereign God. He was slowly introducing us to people, places, perplexities, and His absolutely incredibly wonderful plan.

CHAPTER 3

FIRST DAYS
IN HUNGARY

Kosman, Pastor Ellison and I arrived in Budapest around 11:00pm on Saturday. We drove immediately to the Budafok Baptist Church in the suburbs of Budapest. It was late, so our greetings to the Kovacs family were brief.

Since it was very difficult to communicate with people in Hungary either by phone or letter at that time, we were not quite certain where our meetings would be the next day. Very few Christians had telephones in their homes, and there were none in the churches. If you wanted to communicate by phone, you would have to write a letter and set up a specific time when the pastor would be at a known telephone location to receive a call at a predetermined time.

Consequently, it happened often that we would go to Budapest for meetings not knowing the exact time or location of the meetings. We would learn of the arrangements only after arriving in the city. This trip was no exception.

We learned our meeting the next morning would be at the Buda Baptist Church on the Buda side of the Danube River in Budapest. That night, Chuck Kosman and I stayed in a Budapest hotel, not wanting to put any pressure on the Kovacs family. After breakfast the next morning, we drove Kosman's car to the address we had been given for the church service.

The Buda Baptist Church is a beautiful church, with black marble floors, simple, stained wooden benches, and newly plastered walls. When we entered the building it was already filled with believers. There were families and people of all ages. Everyone, as it was throughout Hungary, was poor. The mood was somber and quiet. This was not Sunday School, though it was at the hour known to Americans as the Sunday School hour. There were no Sunday Schools in Hungary – under Communist rule, churches were not allowed to conduct organizations, and this included Sunday Schools. Instead, it was a prayer meeting. The auditorium was nearly filled and, one after another, people would stand to their feet and singularly pray to the Lord. Although I could not understand what they were saying, it soon became obvious to me that they knew the One to whom they spoke. Their prayers were not short, and many seemed to be laying their hearts bare before God. It was a great experience for me.

The prayer meeting went on for approximately 45 minutes. After that, I was introduced to Pastor Szakacs. This man, who was an amputee, walked with a supporting crutch. He seemed quite nervous at meeting this American, and I was nervous being in a new situation. I had been in Hungary less than 12 hours. There was no briefing as to what kind of a situation to expect in the churches. I knew my message would be a gospel message, and I needed to be very careful not to mention anything political whatsoever. I had been told that there would be secret police and informers in every service and, therefore, I needed to choose my words wisely. This explained a little bit of the tension I was sensing.

My previous preaching experience in Germany taught me that one should not just preach a gospel message and extend a public gospel invitation at the close as was usually practiced in America. Instead, one should tell his audience at the start that he wishes to present to them the claims of Jesus Christ and will, at the end of the message, give them an opportunity to respond to that message by publicly receiving Jesus Christ as their personal Lord and Savior. In this way, I was told that the German mind would be more conducive to listening to the gospel. Otherwise, they would feel they had been tricked or trapped into a response.

Since this was the first time I had been in Hungary, I assumed, however incorrectly, that the Hungarian mindset was much like that of the Germans.

After I had been introduced in the service, I brought greetings from the Christians in America. I assured Hungarian believers that there were many Americans who prayed for them and told them the Hungarian people had a special place in the hearts of American Christians. The audience seemed to respond, and were warmed by that greeting.

Then, preparing to launch into my message, I informed them that I wanted to speak about the suffering of the Lord Jesus Christ, how He came to this earth to redeem man and save him from his sin. I told them that at the end of the service I wanted to extend a public invitation, inviting them to trust Jesus Christ as their Savior. Upon announcing this, I suddenly noticed a change in the expressions on the faces of the people packed into the church that morning. I very quickly lost all eye contact with my audience. I didn't understand why.

As I continued on in my message, telling of the love of the Lord Jesus Christ and of His suffering and His death on the Cross, the people emotionally seemed to distance themselves even further. They would look down at the floor and up at the ceiling. I couldn't understand what was happening. The further I went on, the more difficulty my interpreter had. He was now struggling with many of the words, though I knew he was an experienced interpreter. As I approached the end of the message, I knew it would be time to give the invitation. The closer I came to that moment, the more I felt estranged from my audience. *Why was this happening?*

Could it be that they did not give gospel invitations in Hungary? I wondered as I continued to preach. *Could it be that to respond to a gospel invitation meant being called in for questioning, loss of job or potential imprisonment? Certainly, this has happened in the past.*

All of this raced through my mind. *Should I give a public invitation? I have come* to *preach the Gospel of Jesus Christ. Is there anything the authorities could do to me or to the pastor of the church if I gave an invitation?* I had no answers. Yet, I knew in my heart, whatever the consequence, I not only had to preach the straight Gospel but also extend an invitation.

I invited those who wanted to receive Jesus Christ to pray to the Lord and told them I would lead them in a sinner's prayer. As I came to that part of my message, I found it nearly impossible to speak. It was as though I had to literally drive the words out of my mouth. I could never remember, in all the years of my ministry, sensing such resistance to a Gospel invitation. I turned to the pastor and asked if he would step down to the front of the church with me to meet any who chose to respond. Of course, I had to speak to him through my interpreter, but it seemed as though the pastor hardly knew what to do. I thought that surely a Gospel invitation was not foreign to this brother, but it was.

I asked them to choose a hymn of invitation since I did not believe they knew Western invitation-style hymns. They selected a hymn with about six verses in it. It was in a minor key and sounded to me like some Gregorian chant. Nobody moved and hardly anyone sang. The organ boomed out the minor chords of the hymn and we waited. The minor chords reflected the mood of the people. How I wished we could get through the invitation quickly, but no. In Hungary when you sing a hymn, you sing every verse. So the organ boomed on, playing all six verses.

Then, between the verses, I heard a step, slide, step, slide sound over to one side of the auditorium as suddenly, along the right-hand side of the room, came a young man. I judged him to be about 18-years old. He was crippled with a paralyzed leg. He would take a step and then drag the paralyzed foot along behind him. Every eye in the room focused on him. Then, suddenly, on the other side of the room, another young man of about the same age stepped forward, and then a third young person started down the center aisle.

I would not have missed those next few seconds for the entire world. The entire atmosphere in that church was dramatically changed. The first thing I noticed was the old men. They had their handkerchiefs out, blowing their noses and wiping their eyes. Next, I noticed many of the ladies took the kerchiefs off their heads or from their purses and they, too, had their faces buried in them. The mood had changed from tension to high emotion and tears of joy.

The old people were overcome with emotion and joy, remembering when pastors in Hungary gave public invitations. The young people who responded were too young to remember such things and responded in ignorance that it was not normal to do so.

It was all confirmed in my mind. They do not give invitations in public meetings in Hungary, and I had done something not done at that point in time. I had done this in ignorance. These young men who responded to the invitation could be identified and possibly called in for questioning.

Things were changing in the country. Some small freedoms were starting to be felt in the churches. Everyone seemed so uncertain of the reality of these new freedoms. The first young man, who had come down the aisle with his paralyzed leg, I am told, had recently been released from one of the government orphanages and was considered a deviant.

As soon as the service was dismissed and we made certain that someone who spoke Hungarian would be dealing with these young people, we went into the Pastor's study and met with some of the church leaders. There we tried to explain to them what Word of Life was and how we would like to be involved with the young people in Hungary. The reaction was mixed.

Leaving the church that morning, I walked up the street to where Kosman's car was parked. As I approached the car, I saw an old man waiting beside the automobile. He knew it was our car by its West German plates. As he saw me approaching, he walked quickly toward me, waving both arms in the air and speaking rapidly in Hungarian. He threw his arms around me in a Hungarian embrace and said, "Koszonom, koszonom."

I pulled back from him a moment and said, "Sir, English, English. I only understand English."

At that, he switched his language to one I did understand a little. He started speaking in the German tongue, "Danka, danka."

About that time, Chuck Kosman arrived at the scene and spoke to the man in fluent German. It seems this old man had a daughter who had given birth to a child illegitimately. Eighteen years earlier, the infant had been placed in an orphanage. The grandfather kept contact so he would know where the child was. When it came time for the young man to be released from the orphanage, the old man was there to help him. The grandfather brought the young man to the church service that morning. His grandson was the first one to respond to the gospel invitation. The grandfather was happy beyond belief, so much so that he could not control his tears of joy. I felt this indicated God's stamp of approval on what the Lord had put in our hearts to see happen in Hungary.

Kosman said, as we got into the car that morning, "Paul, I think this is only the beginning."

The Prodigal Son

That night we were to be in the evening service of the great Budafok Baptist Church. This church has a great history. For a number of years during the 1960's and 70's, Geza Kovacs had his license to preach suspended. He had not been allowed to preach in any of the churches. However, many of the churches wanted him to come anyway. He had the reputation of being a good evangelist and a fiery preacher. So, he continued his preaching every time he had an opportunity. Sometimes he would travel by train and sometimes by bicycle. He would preach, as the Scripture says in II Timothy 4, "in season and out," or whenever he had opportunity.

This was much to the dismay of the authorities. They could not contain him. One day, I am told, they came to him and said, "Kovacs, would you like to have your license back to preach again?"

"Of course," he said.

"If you will stop running all over the country," they told him, "maybe we can give you a church."

The church they gave him was at the very top of an extremely steep hill in the suburbs of Budapest. It was accessible alright, but a person would have to put his car in low gear to climb the cobblestone hill. The church, I am told, had a small congregation of German settlers. I am also told that probably the average age of the believers in the church, prior to his coming, was 60-years. There were no young people.

It is safe to assume the authorities thought they would stonewall Pastor Kovacs in this almost inaccessible location. But that was not the way it was to be. He was faithful in preaching and teaching the Word of God. He loved young people and they loved him. People began to be saved, and the remote little church began to grow. Kovacs was determined, and he was loving and gentle. In his family, and among friends, he was known as "Geza Bacci," or Uncle Geza.

Pastor Kovacs continued to find success in his ministry. He contacted pastors and people from the West who helped them significantly with gifts, and as this little congregation grew in size, permission was finally granted for them to build a new building at the foot of the hill. The Budafok Baptist Church is now a beautiful new structure.

It has a beautiful auditorium, not large in size, but with a very high ceiling. So high, in fact, that there are two balconies. As we prepared for the evening service, the auditorium was nearly filled to capacity. The wonderful German music team had performed well, and it was time to preach.

A Hungarian lady by the name of Ildiko Kovacs translated that evening. Ildiko is the wife of Pastor Kovacs' oldest son, Dr. Geza Kovacs. What a special and lovely lady and a very spiritual person, what I would call a Proverbs 31 woman. She is the daughter of a well-known Hungarian pastor who faithfully crisscrossed the country preaching the gospel of Jesus Christ during years of persecution. Ildiko had learned English the hard way, not through language school, but by studying it in books. There were no English language schools at that time in Hungary. One was permitted only to learn Russian or other Eastern European languages. In spite of this, Ildiko learned to speak English very well. She had a modulated voice, and she spoke precisely.

That night I felt led by God to preach on Revelation 2, about a church that had lost its way. Why I decided to preach on that subject, I do not understand because certainly this would not be that sort of church. Yet, I remember the burden on my heart was very definite to preach on that subject.

During the course of the message, I spelled out the story of the Prodigal Son, taken from Luke 15. I told how this son, far from home, far from family, and far from God, found himself in the hog pen of the world and he made a choice. He said, "I don't belong here. I will go back to my father and home." He made a deliberate choice to turn around and go back.

I painted a picture of the father looking down the valley and praying, "Oh, Lord, would you today perhaps bring my son home again?" I painted a picture of the son coming back and being locked in an embrace with his father, telling him how sorry he was, admitting to his father that he had sinned and was no longer worthy to be called his son, requesting only to be made a laborer on his father's farm. The father's response was to say, "But, you are my son. You will always be my son. I don't care where you have been or what you have done. The important thing is that you have come home."

At this point in the message, God broke the heart of this sensitive translator, and Ildiko began to weep openly. Her large blue eyes filled with tears, and yet she was my voice, so she continued.

"Some of you have wandered away from the Savior. You are wondering if maybe your sin is too great and that the Savior won't welcome you. I am here tonight to tell you that our Heavenly Father knows everything about you, and he is waiting with open arms for you to come back to Him. He says to you, 'I remember the day you were born. You are my son. You will always be my son. All that matters is that you have come home.'"

The invitation was opened then, and people began streaming down the aisles. Fifty people flooded the front of the Budafok Baptist Church that night. There was not a dry eye in the entire place. God had done a great work. Through the interpretation of Ildiko Kovacs, I asked who had come to receive Jesus Christ as

Savior for the first time, and who had come because, though they had trusted Christ at an earlier time, had wandered away from the Savior and now wanted to come back to Him.

We separated them into two groups. Pastor Kovacs' son, Geza, took the group of those who had come to receive Jesus Christ, and they went into one room. Pastor Kovacs and I took the larger group of about 35 downstairs to a large, open room. There, for nearly an hour, we allowed each person, who wished, to pour out his heart to the Lord and tell the Lord he was coming back to Him.

That was probably one of the highlight meetings of my ministry. The "after" meeting went on for nearly an hour. That night, the entire meeting, from beginning to end, lasted two and a half hours. Nobody seemed to mind. I knew this was God's stamp of approval on our ministry in Hungary. Though it was only the first day that we had been permitted to minister there, I knew God was saying to us, "This needs to be repeated over and over again from one end of the country to the other."

The First Contact with the Church Leadership

I had been asking my friend, Chuck Kosman, if he felt it would be possible for us to one day start Word of Life camps in Hungary. He had told me about the very small camp owned by the Baptists, but he did not think they would permit us to run a Word of Life camp there. Nevertheless, he felt it would be worth trying.

Chuck had been in touch with Pastor Kovacs to see if we could get a meeting with the Baptist leadership. The Baptist churches of Hungary were a part of a larger group of churches known as the Free Church Union. The Free Church Union is separate from the Catholic Church and the Reformed Church. All of the smaller denominations are lumped together under the Council of Free Churches.

The President of the Free Churches was a man by the name of Szakacs. Dr. Joseph Szakacs was a member of the Seventh Day Adventists. Included in the Free Church Council would be all of the Baptists, Methodists, Evangelical churches, Plymouth Brethren, Seventh Day Adventists, and Pentecostals. This man represented all of these churches. He was a tall man with a large forehead and a full head of black hair. He was about 50-years of age at the time of our first meeting. The President of the Baptist Union was a man named Janos Viczian. Viczian was also about 50-years old at this time, with a stocky build, blue eyes and a neat appearance. Both of these men were in positions where the government tightly controlled them. We would have to be in touch with both of them to proceed with our hopes and plans for Word of Life. Pastor Kovacs got in contact with these men and was able to arrange an invitation for us to appear before them.

The meeting was set at the denominational headquarters on Aradi Street, not far from the Budapest Opera House, on the Buda side of the city. It was to be held on September 28, 1984.

When we realized we were actually going to have a meeting, I finally dared to allow myself to verbalize some dreams for Hungary. We sat down with a pad of paper and began to formulate the proposal we would present.

It appeared to us at that time that there was only a slight possibility of our being permitted to do anything. If we could, it would have to be tied to the government's problem of deviant youth. It seemed impossible, at that time, for anyone from the West to ever go into Hungary and live and be able to minister to these young people. Hungarian men and women would have to be trained to do that for us. Kosman and I spent hours dreaming and writing a proposal. Monday finally arrived and along with Pastor Kovacs we made our way to the denominational headquarters.

I remember my impressions as we entered the offices of the Council of Free Churches. It was in the same location as the denominational headquarters. It was old, drab, and colorless, so different from American architecture. At least that is how I saw it through my American eyes. We went through the formal introductions and then were seated at a long, narrow table with the Hungarians on one side and Chuck Kosman, Pastor Ellison, Bob Parschauer, Pastor Kovacs and me on the other. We decided it would be best if I read our proposal, since we wanted it to be accurate. We were not really sure of the reading abilities of our interpreter.

Following is a copy of the verbal presentation given to the head of the Free Churches and the head of the Baptist Union on that memorable day of September 28, 1984, in Budapest.

A Brief and Proposal Read to the Directors of the Free Church Union and Baptist Church Union of Hungary

September 28, 1984 in Budapest, Hungary:

Introduction

The government (Communist) of Hungary is concerned with the spread of juvenile delinquency in their country. There are more than 250,000 "Deviants" on the streets. These are orphan or illegitimate children raised in government (Communist) orphanages. They have been raised by an *it* (state) — no love, no morals, no absolutes, no Bible, no parents. At 18 years of age, they are turned out onto the streets. With no moral foundation, they go the way of rebellion, alcohol, drugs, and sex perversion. The government does not know how to deal with the problem. The state cannot help. The government has turned to the Free Churches.

The Free Churches have said, "Yes, we can help if you will relax your restrictive and repressive laws and allow us the freedom to help." The Free Churches have turned to WORD OF LIFE to help them. The Free Churches have used the call to help with the "Deviants" to reach out to *all* of Hungary's youth.

The Presentation

by Paul Bubar

Hungary is a beautiful and exciting country. Its people are gracious and caring. There is excitement among the church people over new freedoms within their churches, and yet it would appear to me that many are learning how to deal with those freedoms.

Man is composed of three parts: body, soul and spirit. When one part of man is neglected, man is in conflict with himself.

There is an inborn part of man that cries out to satisfy the emptiness of his soul. That emptiness is only filled when a relationship with God has been established through Jesus Christ. That is why youth (or adults) who have established these relationships are among the worlds happiest in every land. Those who have neglected this relationship or who have tried to replace that relationship with God with other things are among the most *troubled* in soul and spirit.

Word of Life Fellowship is an interdenominational Christian ministry that ministers in twenty-three countries of the world. Its primary objective is to *assist* churches that preach the Gospel to prosper and grow to great numbers. Word of Life specializes in assisting a local church to reach out and bring in the youth of their respective communities. Their objective is to introduce them to a life-changing relationship through Jesus Christ.

The youth of Hungary will not be reached through an *external* organization. They will only be reached effectively from an *internal* source that is exclusively Hungarian. That source already exists *in the Gospel-preaching churches of Hungary.*

However, it is my opinion that many of these churches lack in *methodological direction and motivation.* It is similar to a broken arm just released from a cast. The arm has been unused for many months. The arm is weak, due to a lack of consistent use. The arm must be given therapy and "shown how" to operate again. It must be exercised in order to regain its strength.

Word of Life Fellowship, as an interdenominational organization, wants to help the Gospel-preaching Free Churches of Hungary. It wants to assist the churches in effectively reaching out to the young people wherever Gospel churches exist. It wants to help the Hungarian Free Churches by showing them effective methods of reaching this part of society, and it wants to show the church how to become an exciting and integral part of the life of Hungary's youth. Then youth will look to Christ and their churches to resolve the conflict problems of their soul and spirit.

Word of Life Fellowship has been doing this effectively for nearly *50 years.* Its methodology has not been to bring a team of "professional outside leaders" into a country but to train local church leaders to more effectively do this work.

As an example:

BRAZIL: Over the last 20-years, Word of Life has invested millions of dollars into Brazil. It has built two Bible schools, one with a seminary. It has built five Bible camps. There are more than 100 people on their staff, with only five workers being American. The director is married to a Brazilian citizen. Their Board of Directors is all Brazilian.

ARGENTINA: In the last ten years, more than 200 churches have been helped in building a dynamic youth ministry. Some churches have increased their size by four to five times in numbers. It has started a university-level school with more than 200 students, plus has built camps that in 1984 accommodated more than 5,000 youth. At the school, a multi-classroom building, a library, and an 800-seat auditorium have just been completed.

A second property (a resort hotel) has been purchased in southern Argentina. This was sold to Word of Life by the Argentine government. More than 70 Argentines are employed with only two being American.

WEST GERMANY: Beautiful castles, *leased* from the Bavarian government, are used as youth camps. More than 3,000 youth attended their 1984 camping season. More than 50 people are employed with only *one* musician who is American. More than 1.5 million dollars has been invested in Germany from the U.S. and Canada, and we own no property there.

PHILIPPINES: Word of Life has camps and a school.

AUSTRALIA: Word of Life has youth camps, Bible study groups and a seminary. (In Hungary, a Bible school is called a seminary.)

CANADA: In Canada, an already developed youth camp facility is being negotiated for, costing us over *one-half million* dollars over a ten-year period. Word of Life has been helping Canadian churches for many years. Only *one* American is on our staff there. All others are Canadians.

How Can Word of Life Help the Churches of Hungary?

It is very difficult to pass on methodology and style from a written manual. We learn better by seeing and hearing than by reading. Therefore:

1. Because your government will not allow Americans to have residence in Hungary, we would like to select two Hungarian

young couples to come to America at our expense to spend two years in specialized study in church youth work. We will underwrite their education and living. While there, they will see one of the most dynamic youth ministries in North America in operation. They will actually experience it so they can return to Hungary and "Hungarianize" it.

2. We would like to bring successful youth workers and pastors to Hungary who will share their successes with your pastors. Is it not possible that new methods, without betraying old Biblical principles, need to be considered?

3. We would like to consult with the leaders of the Hungarian churches in the establishing of a "Coffee-House" ministry in Budapest. If it is successful, many Hungarian churches can duplicate it. This would be a means of reaching out to Hungary's "deviants."

4. We would also like to help the church in Budafok (since they already own a property with great potential) renovate and prepare a "Halfway House" for transforming "deviants" back into society as respectable, law-abiding Christians and citizens. (This suggestion is to satisfy the *government's* request.)

5. We would like to show local churches how to prevent youth from becoming future "deviants." You can develop the greatest "deviant-rescuing" operation in the world, but unless you keep youth from going into that culture, you *will always* have the problem.

6. We would be interested in establishing and operating a Family Retreat Center* for the people of Hungary, as we have done in many other countries.

7. We want to help the local Gospel-preaching churches grow. We can do that with proven curriculum, leadership training and coaching to local church leadership teams of

adults who will operate a dynamic program that will cause their youth membership to double and triple in size in many cases. This is achieved in other lands through the Youth Bible Study groups.

None of these things can be achieved unless there is a desire on the part of pastors, parents and youth. Therefore, if you would invite us, we would like to *return for a week of meetings that would include a conference for pastors, parents and youth.* This conference would be carried on in three locations (three churches) simultaneously, on a Friday, Saturday and Sunday. At that time, we would communicate some methods of evangelism. We would bring pictures of our activities in other countries, plus a wide range of curriculum. Hopefully, this will be used to create a greater desire on the part of pastors, parents and youth.

We are ready to help you where and when we are able.

*In Hungary, you do not use the words "youth camp," or "youth clubs," since this is indicative of politicizing youth.

–End of Statement–

–Postscript–

This meeting was held with Hungarian church leaders on one side of a long table and Bubar, Kosman, Parschauer, Ellison and Pastor Kovacs on the opposite side. Kosman and Bubar were directly facing the Free Church Union President and his interpreter, who is President of the Baptist Union. The proposal was warmly received. There was protocol and pomp, but there was genuine interest on their part. As a matter of fact, there was excitement. The President of the Council said to me through his interpreter: "Mr. Bubar, you are a very fine salesman. Let us discuss it together and we will get back to you. We want help."

After this, the lesser "Politicos" and the President of the Baptist Union, Janos Viczian, took us to dinner. It was Viczian to whom Kosman and I asked very direct questions when we were alone. We asked him about the possibilities of a Western organization being allowed to function in an Eastern Bloc country such as Hungary.

Summary

(Given, one week later, to the directors of Word of Life)

It appears that a door is open for Word of Life to minister directly and openly in Hungary.

It appears that there are limited freedoms.

We have the organizational machinery already in Europe (Germany).

We have some extremely mature, sharp, educated and dedicated young Hungarians who will come to America to be trained in Bible and youth work by Word of Life.

We have a wise and experienced man (wise to the ways behind the Curtain) directing our work in Germany (six hours away).

We have opportunities in Hungary (inviting churches – potential camp properties).

All that is restraining us is:

1. an affirmative formal invitation by the Baptist Union of Hungary to "umbrella" Word of Life into the country,

2. an affirmative response by Word of Life leadership, and

3. the funds to do all of this.

We do not know how much longer the door will remain open, but it does appear to be open now. Underground people feel the cloud is on the horizon. All it takes is the wrong man in Moscow who would *tell* Hungary to tighten up.

May God give us wisdom in how we respond.

Prayerfully submitted,

Paul Bubar

Additional Information and Recommendations

(Given only to the directors of Word of Life)

1. Do not use the words "youth camp." Call it "Family Training Center, Family Saving Center, or Family Conference Center." DO NOT CALL IT "Bible Clubs," call it "Youth Bible Study Circle." (The words "clubs," and "camps," are political words.)

2. There is an underground church in Hungary. I can speak of this rather than write it.

3. The Baptist Union is made up of men who are playing a game of "Christian politics." It reminds me of Baptist Conventions in America or Canada. There are some sincere men in the Union, or perhaps I should say they are all sincere. They sincerely believe they are right in doing things the way they do. They will say they have great liberty, just not great liberty as we know it.

4. Be prepared to gain ten pounds while in Hungary. They shove delicious food in your face to show their hospitality. It is endless.

5. Almost anything can be done in evangelism on the church property. You can advertise and invite. All preaching must be nonpolitical.

Wondering What the Future Holds

What an exciting time it was for all of us, but especially for Kosman and me. We had read the report over and over. Everyone had a hand in making suggestions, including Pastor Ellison and Bob Parschauer. It was only a dream of possibility at that time. I don't believe that any of us really thought our proposal would receive a positive response. We were just dreamers putting our dreams down on paper.

After the formal meeting and the informal dinner meeting, we made our way back to the Budafok Baptist Church and prepared to return to the West. Driving from Budapest back to the border, Kosman and I spent a couple of hours trying to evaluate the meeting. What did they mean by the statements they made? We were learning that Hungarians, as most people in Eastern European countries have had to do for survival, give the kind of an answer that could be interpreted two or three different ways. In that way, if they were ever quoted, they could say, "Well, yes, that is what I said, but what I meant was... "

We recounted the many words that were said by Dr. Szakacs and Dr. Viczian. We were looking for a glimmer of encouragement or hope. Was it there, or wasn't it? Their statements could have been taken to mean almost anything to us. We believed they were encouraging us, but they did not really dare to offer us much hope until gaining permission from the Minister of Religious Affairs for the Communist government, Dr. Miklos.

All the way to the Austrian border, we kicked these statements and questions around. What was said and what did it really mean? I had been allowed to be a part of something so exciting I could hardly stand it. Now we had to return to our ministries. Kosman and Parschauer were to go back to Germany, and Pastor Ellison and I to Schroon Lake in upstate New York. Pastor Ellison would return to his church and I to the ministry of Word of Life. The big task ahead of us now was to be able to accurately relay to the leaders of Word of Life what we had seen and experienced.

The Return to Budapest Four Weeks Later

Arriving back in Schroon Lake, I read my report to Jack Wyrtzen. Jack is the founder of Word of Life, and his story is an extraordinary one. In his early seventies at the time of this tale, his blue eyes shone as brightly as ever, and his personality was still as upbeat and lively as it was when he was in his twenties. He was as excited to hear my news as though he had been there himself. Over and over he said, "Praise the Lord. Isn't the Lord good? Maybe God will allow us to do something there." It was a very positive response.

However, not everyone in our organization felt the same way. There were some who felt it was only a trick to get our money and that the Free Churches were tied to the World Council of Churches. The World Council of Churches is an organization that is worldwide, and they are very liberal; they do not hold to the deity of Christ, nor do they hold to the belief in the virgin birth. Their main reason of organization is to support political and liberal causes. We all felt that Word of Life should have no part in any kind of venture that would give approval to the World Council of Churches. I argued that, to the best of my knowledge, the Free Churches in Hungary were *not* tied to the World Council of Churches. However, a member of our staff had information which I learned later came from the Carl McIntyre Organization and was twenty-five years old and that indicated there was a close tie to the World Council. This was old information and not necessarily reliable. The Carl McIntyre Organization was created as a response to the World Council of Churches, and is the Council's antithesis. The Carl McIntyre Organization is also political, but with views to the extreme right. Thus, with conflicting reports, the only way we could possibly move ahead demanded that I return to Budapest and investigate more deeply.

The first week of November 1984, was the anniversary of the Free Church Organization in Hungary. I had been invited to return along with our Founder/Director, Jack Wyrtzen. This would be an excellent opportunity.

Jack and I returned, along with a Hungarian friend of Jack's by the name of Joe Steiner. A tall Hungarian with a long face and blue eyes, Joe had escaped from Hungary in 1956 and was working for Trans World Radio, involved with the Hungarian broadcast that beams short-wave into Hungary. Joe, with a deep bass voice and an excellent translator, would be our interpreter.

I remember upon that second arrival in Hungary how I was filled with questions. Was the information I had been given in the States accurate? If so, we could have no part of this entire venture. Or was it just bad information? Do they even know of the World Council of Churches in Hungary, or is it just a mechanism by which some of the leaders could get exit visas to leave their country and spend a few days in the West?

Jack and I were met again by Kosman at the Vienna airport, and we made the three-and-a-half hour drive to Budapest, putting up at the Inter-Continental Duna Hotel downtown.

The next evening I was to speak at a youth meeting at the Budafok Baptist Church. I noticed a very large, muscular, and fully bearded man standing in the back of the room. He had a full brown beard and small blue eyes, and he was listening intently. I thought probably he was Hungarian, but after the meeting he immediately came to me and, speaking with perfect American-style English, he said, "I want to thank you for that message, Paul. God blessed my heart through it."

I knew then he was not Hungarian, but American.

"Who are you," I asked, "and where are you from in America?"

His response was, "I am Brother John."

I knew that was a dead giveaway of someone working with the underground church. They would never speak their last name, but only call themselves Brother Andrew, Brother John, Brother Bill, or whomever.

He did not tell me where he was from except to say, "My wife was saved in one of your Word of Life Bible Clubs many years ago."

For some reason it clicked in my mind and I responded with, "Yes, it was in Phoenixville, Pennsylvania, and you are John Peterson, the former gold medal weight lifting champion in the United States Olympics."

He said, with a twinkle in his eye and a smile on his face, "I am Brother John." I knew he would not tell his last name nor confirm it, but I knew who this dear brother was.

I knew also that he was working underground in that country trying to strengthen the Church of Jesus Christ and doing a good job. There were a number of men such as him who had given their lives to come into the country as tourists and businessmen on an irregular basis. They would contact cells of pastors who would meet in small groups. These men worked with an organization known as BEE. They were carrying on an education ministry among the pastors teaching them Bible doctrine and theology. I believe The Free Church Union knew of their existence, but also knew they were doing a job that needed to be done. The Union, consequently, always looked the other way.

The BEE men would enter the country and meet with these small cells of pastors who would never meet at the same place twice, nor would there be any rhythm to their calendar. They would always be certain to meet never on a Tuesday each month or never the same part of the month or the same place, and yet I want to say that these dear men and this great ministry were used mightily of God in all of Eastern Europe.

I invited John to come to our hotel so he could meet with Jack. He was very nervous about talking in the hotel room, so we turned the radio on and up to a loud volume. It was safe to assume that any of the rooms where Westerners stayed were bugged. Our Brother John was so nervous about talking in the room that we went for a long walk. He reminded me that the only safe place to talk was walking down the street.

I salute men such as Brother John and many others who for years carried on a clandestine ministry of teaching Bible doctrine and theology to pastors who had not had the opportunity to be fed in this way for many years.

The official pretense of our being in Budapest was for the fortieth anniversary of the Free Churches. Jack Wyrtzen brought along Joe Steiner who, as I mentioned, escaped from Hungary in 1956. This was his first time back into the country, and though he was an excellent interpreter, it was obvious he was very, very nervous, even was a little fearful. Sometimes we would glance over at him and see his blue eyes looking around at our surroundings, as if he were searching for someone who might be following us.

As Jack Wyrtzen and I sat with him in the Nejipest Baptist Church where the celebration of the Free Churches was being conducted, Joe, our interpreter, was seated in the row behind us, and would lean forward to speak between the two of us. He would quietly interpret everything being said on the platform.

That afternoon, Dr. Janos Harmatta, who is both a Christian psychologist and psychiatrist, was speaking. He was a tall man of German origin, though from Budapest. Sitting before him on the platform were some Communist ideologists from the University in Debrecen. Dr. Harmatta was discussing the deviant youth problem in Hungary, and he was sharing with the Communist leaders how that society absolutely needed what the Church of Jesus Christ had to offer.

As Dr. Harmatta spoke before the ideologists in public, our interpreter stopped translating, and he said, "Oh, oh my, this is a very brave man. He is very, very brave indeed." Then he went on to tell us what Dr. Harmatta was saying. "The deviant problem in Hungary is not first of all a social problem, but a sin problem. The youth of Hungary need a reason to live and die. They need a foundation for life. Their lives are crumbling, and they need the foundation of Jesus Christ, the only One who can give them a sure foundation."

I remember thinking at that time, as Joe Steiner was translating, that Dr. Harmatta, indeed, was not only very intelligent, but also very brave. He had a commanding presence, standing at about 6'1", about fifty-years of age, with brown, curly hair. If by God's grace Word of Life would be allowed to do something in that Communist country, I wanted to make sure we had such a brave, honest man on our Board of Directors. Though I did not fully realize it then, that desire would one day become a reality.

Throughout the rest of our week in Hungary, Chuck Kosman, Jack Wyrtzen, and I had many meetings in many churches. We had been scheduled primarily in the Baptist churches throughout the country. There were no restrictions placed on our preaching, much to our surprise and great pleasure.

We freely gave Gospel invitations for people to publicly receive Jesus Christ; and there was what I would call, aggressive evangelism taking place. People would respond when the gospel was presented clearly. They would appear to be a little fearful at first, but the young people especially responded because they didn't know that you weren't supposed to. They just knew that nobody had ever done that before. So, in our various meetings across the country, we preached in some twelve different churches in one week. The Gospel was freely offered, and young people responded along with some of the elderly in meeting after meeting after meeting.

While we were there we went back to visit a very special place, Camp Tahi. The camp is located about a forty-five minute drive from downtown Budapest, right near the famous Duna bend in the Danube River, in the village of Tahi. This was the three-acre piece of property that, for many years, had been owned by the Baptist churches. It had been taken away from them by the government and then given back because it was such an insignificant piece of property. Yet, to the Hungarian Christians, it was holy ground because it was a place where the Gospel could be preached to young people.

As Jack Wyrtzen, Chuck Kosman and I walked over the land, we prayed, "God, in your grace, either give us this piece of land to be able to minister to the youth of Hungary, or give us some place where we can freely preach the gospel and run an exciting program that will attract hundreds of Hungarian youths, that they might be saved. Lord, will you please open the doors so we may have an opportunity to minister to the youth of Hungary with your gospel of grace?"

Driving back to Budapest, Kosman and I let ourselves dream out loud. We were to meet with the Free Church Council for the second time. We would request permission to run a youth camp at Tahi. At the first meeting, a month earlier, they had refused.

We met with Dr. Szacacs and John Viczian again before this trip was finished, and they were not so resistant. This time they said, "Maybe it can be arranged." We were encouraged that matters had gone from a definite "no" to a "maybe."

Dared we dream of being able to run a youth camp in a

Communist country? All three of us, Jack, Chuck, and I, were dreamers, dreaming of God's willingness to allow us to do what was seemingly impossible at that point in time. If the church leadership would only allow us to conduct camp, it would be the beginning.

Kosman and I made a third trip to Budapest and met directly with the leaders of the Free Church and the Baptist Union. We again requested permission to operate a camp and, at that time, in February or March of 1985, they agreed to allow us to do just that. To God be the glory!

Each time we were in Budapest, we visited the home of Dr. Geza Kovacs, the eldest son of Pastor Kovacs. We were to become great friends. Geza, Jr. had a stocky build and brown wavy hair, and like many Hungarians, he took everything he did in life very seriously. This highly educated Doctor of Agrobiology was not only exceptionally brilliant (he had two earned doctorates and was one of the leading Agrobiology scientists in the country), but he was also one of the most warm and tenderhearted believers I had met in a long time. It was refreshing to be with Geza and his dear wife, Ildiko, who had translated for me that special night I told the story of the Prodigal Son. They were a loving, gracious family with three lovely children.

I so much wanted to have Dr. Geza Kovacs learn about Word of Life camps and how we operate. I dreamed of a way we could get him out of the country legally and bring him to Word of Life, or at least almost to Word of Life. During the second trip, I discussed the whole plan with him.

When I returned to Schroon Lake, I contacted the Agro Department of the University of Vermont in Burlington, one and a half hours from my home. Going directly to the chairman of the department, I walked into his office without an appointment. He knew little about my background or about Word of Life. So, I used the names of a couple of local, highly respected Christian medical doctors, Dr. Tabor and Dr. McGee, who had been a part of the University system at one time. They had given me their seal of approval, and the man in the Agro Department was interested. I tried to explain to him about this brilliant Hungarian Agrobiologist. I asked if there was any way they might give him a scholarship so he would be allowed to come to the University of Vermont to study or to conduct scientific research.

The University could not fund the whole venture and wanted Word of Life to join hands with them and provide half of the funding.

At that time no one could leave Hungary without an exit visa, and it was not easy for anyone to obtain such a document. Usually one could get an exit visa for an individual, but not for an entire family. Dr. Kovacs, if he came to America to be indoctrinated in the methodology of the Word of Life ministry, wanted to come for a period of two years and be able to bring his entire family. He wanted his children to learn to speak English and for this to be a great educational time for them.

I took all of my findings and the plan we had put together to get Dr. Kovacs out of Hungary and put it all down in a letter directed to him. Unfortunately, in my haste, I neglected to warn my good secretary concerning proper procedure for sending such a letter to Communist Hungary.

One day as I was leaving my Schroon Lake office, bound for a flight out of the Albany airport, my secretary said to me, "On the Kovacs letter, do you want it to go on regular letterhead or plain paper? Do you want it addressed directly to Dr. Kovacs? How do you want me to handle this?"

Without thinking at all about what she was really saying, I said, "Look, just put it on a letterhead and send it, the way you would send a regular letter." That, I learned later, would be a great mistake.

Some weeks later, I received an envelope addressed with a lead pencil. The envelope had been stamped in Basil, Switzerland. I opened it and as I read, my heart sank very quickly. The letter was unsigned, anonymously rebuking me sternly.

The writer reminded me that I had done something terribly wrong. I had written a letter on letterhead stationery. Any letter entering Hungary from any organization in the West would be opened by the government, scrutinized, and used against the person to whom it was addressed. This letter reminded me that when I need to communicate with anyone in Hungary, I should do it on a postcard (they do not scan postcards) or on plain paper with a plain envelope as personal correspondence. I had violated these rules in my ignorance.

The letter went on to remind me that, at best, the letter I sent to Dr. Kovacs was in a government file and would be later used against him. At worst, the letter could lead to his being brought to the police for interrogation and possible arrest.

"For Interrogation and Possible Arrest!"

I was stunned. What had I, as an American, completely naive to the methodology of a Communist system, done to my new friend? I confess to you that I closed the door to my office and cried out to the Lord, "Lord, blind the eyes of the postal workers to that letter. Allow it to pass through without any delay or interrogation." I went to my home and shared the news with my wife, Shirley. I well remember the feeling of helplessness. I telephoned Brother John in Vienna, knowing he would be very familiar with how things operated in a Communist system. I shared with him long distance the true feelings of my heart. He agreed that the sender of the letter of rebuke was very possibly correct in his estimation, that I had acted naively, and that we would just have to wait and see what happened. After my phone conversation with Brother John,

I again dropped to my knees in my study asking God not to allow my ignorance to bring harm to my newfound friend.

Many months went by, and Dr. Kovacs eventually did receive the letter. I assumed, however, that a copy was in a government file somewhere, waiting to be used against the doctor at a later time.

I figured out, later, that the letter of rebuke came from one of my translators who moved freely in his position working for the government as a doctor of chemistry. He often traveled to the West and had written me this letter from Basil, Switzerland. Dr. Bukovsky, the sender, later became one of our closest allies and friends, and a member of our Board of Directors.

Although Dr. Kovacs suffered no negative consequences, the matter served to make us realize we were in a country where the Communist government was not friendly to Westerners and we became very sensitive to Hungarians and their fears.

CHAPTER 4

THE MOST
NAIVE MAN
I HAVE EVER MET

Following my return to the States from Budapest in November of 1984, I had many photographs of the meetings we had held in churches. I was tremendously impressed by the fact that in every service a full 40 to 50 percent of the audience was comprised of young people, and that the churches were filled to capacity. I thought this was a good sign.

I decided to place a phone call to my Jewish friend in London, whom I had met on the Pan Am flight two years before. I remember telling him "I've been in your country three times. I have many pictures I would like to show you. Will you be coming to America any time soon?"

"Yes," he replied, "as a matter of fact, I am coming in about six weeks. I will be visiting my son, Stephen, in New York. He is a businessman there." I immediately made arrangements to meet him in New York.

The date finally arrived in January of 1985. I drove to New York and to the newly established office of Stephen Kovacs. As I rang the buzzer, my Jewish friend from London came to the door and greeted me warmly. He immediately turned and shouted to his son, "Stephen, Stephen, come quickly. This is the man I told you about. This is the man I met on that flight two years ago who almost converted me. Stephen, it was that close," he said, holding two fingers barely a quarter of an inch apart. "I mean it was *that* close."

He invited me into the office and we renewed a very young, two-year old acquaintance. I couldn't wait to show him the photographs of the Hungarian young people's faces. I told him, "Michael, I have been to your country and fallen in love with your countrymen. They are the most sensitive and wonderful people of any in the world. Look at these pictures, taken in churches all over Hungary. The churches are filled to capacity, and look at the ages of those filling them. They are young people."

My London friend responded, "Yes, you are right. The youth of Hungary have realized that the Utopian dream is only a nightmare. The Utopian dream has failed them. It had turned to ashes in their mouths and they are turning away from Communism in large numbers. Communism is broke. It is the failure of the century. It is worse than broke, and young people are searching. They are turning to religion of all kinds. Why, even in my synagogue, empty just a few years ago, it is filled to capacity, largely with young men and women. You are doing the right thing. You must keep doing what you are doing at any price because one day, in the near future, things will change. There is a great light on the horizon. You must keep doing what you are doing so when great change comes, you will be in on the ground floor. What is it you really want to do in Hungary?"

I began painting a picture of our dream. I told him of Word of Life starting our Bible Clubs for young people and owning a youth camp where we would play sports and share the teachings of Jesus Christ. As I began describing the dream for him, he interrupted and said, "Paul Bubar, you are the most naive man I have ever met in my life. You are incredibly naive. Don't you realize they are Communists? It is a Communist government. You cannot do any of these things there without permission, and they are not going to grant you permission. You are naive to think that way. They are Communists, and they are bastards, every one of them."

"Yes, I know what you are saying is true," I told my friend, "I know I am naive. After all, what do I know about living under Communist rule? What do I know about your country? I have only been there three times, for a total of two weeks. I know relatively nothing about your country or their Communist government. But, my dear friend, you forget that you and I work for different people. The One I work for is capable of raising up governments and putting them down. He is capable of changing the hearts of kings, presidents, and dictators. If God should so choose, this dream will one day come true in your country."

As I spoke these words my friend's countenance seemed to soften. He looked out the window and said, "Yes, you are right. I know you are right. You need much help. You will need a good attorney. Here are some names I want to give you. Write them down and tell these people that I sent you. Tell them what you want to do in our country. You be sure and talk to them just like you talked to me on that airplane."

He began to give me the names of some of the most prominent people in business and government in Hungary. He gave me names of men high up in industry and in banking. These were all highly educated men. I was to contact one of the top attorneys in that country. Michael Kovacs said, "You talk to these people and tell them exactly what you want to do. See if they can help you. You remember that there is a great light on the horizon. "

I questioned him as to what he meant by this great light. He answered, "Well, it is only a rumor in my circles."

"What kind of rumor?" I asked, "What can you tell me?"

"I do not want to tell you anything," Michael said, "because it's too early to tell you anything, except that Russia is broke. She is worse than broke. She will come to the West asking for financial help. She will come to the United States asking for massive loans."

I laughed. "Just a minute, you said that I was naive. I am not the naive one; it is you who are naive. Russia approaching the United States to ask for financial help? Maybe under a President like Carter, but certainly not under Ronald Reagan. There is no way that could ever possibly happen. What can you tell me about this rumor?"

"It is only a rumor in my opinion," he said.

"Well, what is the rumor?"

Michael finally responded. "The freedom of Hungary and Poland, this is the first step with the coming collapse of communism."

Again, I laughed. "My friend, Russia will never cut loose Hungary and Poland. She needs them to protect her borders."

Michael Kovacs responded with a slight chuckle. "To protect her borders? Ridiculous. The missile ended that twenty five years ago. She doesn't need them. As a matter of fact, they are a tremendous drain on Russian resources and finances."

I had to admit he was right. I pressed Michael further so I might know more about his opinion. I did not want Word of Life to become involved in any way if we would have to layout large sums of money to buy property only to have it confiscated later. The more I pressed him, the less he would tell me. All he would say was, "It is only my opinion. I can tell you no more. However, you must keep doing what you are doing because when this freedom of these countries comes, you will be in on the ground floor."

I recall leaving my friend and thinking that I had been in the presence of a very wise and, what I would call a street-smart person. Here was a man who was Jewish in birth, a member of God's chosen race. I had the strange feeling that right then, in his encouraging words, he was being used of God.

As I drove back along the New York State Thruway headed to Schroon Lake, I wondered what the rumor was. It was too much to believe that possibly Hungary and Poland would be free one day. Upon my return to Schroon Lake, I thought I would inquire in Washington, DC to see if there had been any rumors about the freedom of Hungary and Poland floating around in political circles. I called a senator, who had been a good friend to Word of Life over the years, a man who dearly loves the Lord, Senator Charles Grassley from Iowa. Grassley was a Republican Senator who had been in position for about ten years at that time. I told the senator about this rumor that I had picked up from Europe concerning the freedom of Hungary and Poland and asked if he had heard anything about it.

"I have not heard anything like this anywhere in Washington," he said. "It seems too far out to accept as truth. I can tell you I have heard nothing."

I wondered if anyone in the Pentagon would have heard such a rumor and I called another old friend of Word of Life who was stationed at the Pentagon at that time. I shared with this man, Colonel Vaughn, the rumor I had heard. He, too, had heard nothing of it in military circles.

"However," he said, "if there is any truth to it at all, there is a man you can call. His name is Colonel Joseph Porter."

"Who is Colonel Porter," I asked, "and how might he know?"

Colonel Vaughn replied, "He is in charge of all military intelligence on the Eastern tier of Europe."

I thought to myself that *means he is a top military intelligence agent. Should I call him? What would happen if someone in Hungary discovered that I had contact with someone in military intelligence at the Pentagon?*

About that time several things were happening. First, on three or four occasions when I would pick up our home telephone to make a call, the line would be open. On two occasions there were subdued voices in unstructured conversation. I began to suspect my telephone line had been tapped. I convinced myself I was just becoming paranoid, though I couldn't convince my wife of this.

Secondly, two men had come to the home of my mother-in-law, Ebba Swanson, claiming to be conducting a tax survey. Only one man spoke, and he did so with a foreign accent. After a few general questions, he began questioning my mother-in-law about me! He asked what I did, whether I traveled much abroad and other personal questions concerning me. Ebba suspected that this was a strange way to conduct a tax survey and suggested the men talk directly to me for any other information. They never did contact me, and as near as we could determine, there was no tax survey being conducted in our town. Because of these and other incidents, I was hesitant to have any contact with persons in Washington, D.C., especially in military intelligence, and especially from my telephone. However, at that time, I was driven to know the conclusion of this rumor. My friend, Colonel Vaughn, had forcefully told me, "Be certain that you tell Porter that I have suggested you call him, otherwise he won't talk to you."

I called the Pentagon again and was put through to Colonel Porter. I remember saying to him, "Sir, allow me to introduce myself. You don't know me. My name is Paul Bubar, and I work for a Christian missionary organization by the name of Word of Life."

The man responded, saying, "Did you say your name was Bubar, Paul Bubar?"

"Yes, sir," I told him.

"You work for an organization by the name of Word of Life? Would that have anything to do with a place called Word of Life Island, in the Adirondacks? Have you had anything to do with Word of Life Island?"

I was surprised that he would know about Word of Life. I said, "Of course, Word of Life Island is the camp for high school and college age youth, in the Village of Schroon. It is one of many Word of Life camps around the world. I have had something to do with Word of Life Island for more than twenty-five years."

"Well, Paul Bubar," Colonel Porter exclaimed, "I am so glad to talk to you. I have intended to telephone you at least once a year for the last ten years."

Curious that he would know who I was, I asked, "Sir, you mean that I know you?"

"Well," he said, "you may not know me, but I certainly know you. Do you remember when there was a group of West Point cadets on Word of Life Island some fifteen years ago?"

I told Colonel Porter I remembered that time very well.

"Well," he continued, "I was a brand new Christian, and I remember being in a meeting in Pine Pavilion on a Monday night when you were preaching."

Monday was the night that I always preached at Word of Life Island.

"You preached on such and such a subject," Colonel Porter told me, and he proceeded to give me the outline of my message.

I thought, w*ith a memory like that, no wonder this man is in Intelligence and Surveillance.*

"God so dealt with me that night as you were preaching,"

Colonel Porter said, "that I could hardly wait until the Wednesday night campfire when I would give my life to serve the Lord. I told the Lord then that He could have my life. I wanted to serve Him. I would even be willing to leave the military and become a missionary if that was what He chose for me. Every time I have a spiritual birthday I think of you and I am moved to call you, but I never have done it. I am grateful to the Lord for you and the ministry you had in my life. Now, how can I help you?"

By that time, I was stuttering and stammering in my surprise. I again reviewed for him the incidents in the Hungary story and the rumor that my friend had heard.

Colonel Porter replied, "Paul, if I had any information for you, it would probably be kept classified. But I can honestly tell you that I have not heard this rumor, and I know nothing about it. I can tell you where every missile is located. I can tell you where every tank is parked. But I have heard no such rumor."

It seemed to be a dead end street. So, I decided at that point to let the rumor ride. (More about this rumor later.)

By now, I had a compelling urge to chase this Hungary thing further. I knew I must return to this Communist-dominated country. There were so many wonderful people there. So many people that were so open to the preaching of the Gospel. So many young people were searching for the answers to life. Something inside told me I must return.

Jack Wyrtzen had become convinced that there was every possibility in the world that Word of Life would get an opening in Hungary. So, he began encouraging me every time he had the opportunity. I now had the names of many influential people in Budapest, and so I returned again. I needed to find a less expensive hotel, preferably one that did not cater to people from the West. I made a reservation at the Taverna Hotel on Vaci Utca. It was located on one of the first "walking streets" in Budapest, not far from the other hotels. Of course it was Communist built and run, but it was fresh and new and very convenient. We were very happy to have made the switch.

The morning after I arrived in Budapest, I decided to call one of the men on the list given to me by my friend Michael Kovacs. I called Dr. Faye. He was the Deputy of the National Bank of Hungary at that time. Although he was living in a Communist country, he was, like most of the Hungarian residents, truly a Capitalist.

When I reached his office by phone, I introduced myself and told him I was a friend of Michael Kovacs.

Whereupon he replied, "Oh, oh, you are a friend of Michael Kovacs. Come, come, come to my office."

When I asked when would be a good time to meet with him he said, "Right now, as soon as you can come."

I couldn't believe the warm and immediate response I received. I took with me a gift of a Ryrie Study Bible. This is a King James Version of the Bible, complete with the study notes for difficult verses, put together by Dr. Charles Ryrie, a brilliant scholar. I took it along because of my friend Michael's advice to talk to Dr. Faye as I did to him. I planned to do just that.

Arriving at the Hungarian Bank Building in downtown Budapest, I walked inside the old, gothic structure to a guard post just within the main doors. I presented the guards with my business card and told them I had an appointment with Dr. Faye. After checking with his office, I was escorted by an armed soldier up onto the second floor and down a long corridor to the office of Dr. Faye.

Dr. Faye was a slender man, of average height, with very white hair. He smiled broadly at me and received me cordially. As is the usual custom in Hungary, he asked if I would like some coffee, and his secretary began preparing some.

I sat down across the table in his office and he said, "Now, how can I help you? Why have you come?"

I began by telling him what Word of Life is and why we were there. I told him of our involvement in twenty-three countries around the world with camping programs, youth programs in local churches, and even with Bible Institutes.

I explained our philosophy, that when a young person comes into a right relationship with God through Jesus Christ his thinking is changed. This changed thinking changes his attitudes about life, and his changed attitudes about life change his lifestyle, therefore, becoming a brand new person on the inside. I shared with him our goal of presenting Jesus Christ as the only sure foundation for a person's life. I told him how I thought we could do so much good for the youth of Hungary.

The man listened very intently. At the end of the conversation, he said thoughtfully to me, "Mr. Bubar, I have never heard anything like this before. It cannot be that simple."

"Dr. Faye," I told him earnestly, "it is that simple. But, because you are an influential banker for your government, you are accustomed to buying anything that you want. You will think that you can buy your salvation, but you cannot, sir. Salvation is a gift from God. It cannot be purchased at any price. It is a free gift from our Heavenly Father. You can receive it or reject it."

"Well, yes," he said slowly in response. And then, changing the topic, "We will talk about something else."

I soon left his office, but before leaving I presented him with a Ryrie Study Bible with a Word of Life shield embossed on the front cover. He seemed very grateful to receive such a beautiful gift.

I was never to meet Dr. Faye again, but this was my first

experience at expressing the Gospel of Jesus Christ to a Hungarian government banker. We were to have the privilege of doing this many times in the coming months. It was a great opportunity, and I was very pleased to have made the acquaintance of this man.

I was thrilled with the doors that were opened to tell about Word of Life and our dream for Hungary. It seemed everyone I talked to wanted to listen. Doors were opened for me to talk with many top leaders in the following months. I often asked myself, "Why? Why has God given me these opportunities? Will all these separate pieces of this amazing puzzle fit together one day? Were all of these events just coincidental?"

I knew in my heart that this was not coincidental; and I trusted in God that our mission would continue to move forward, and move forward is what we continued to do, with great excitement of what could be in Hungary.

CHAPTER 5

A RYRIE STUDY BIBLE
AS A BARGAINING TOOL

By now, we had been allowed to conduct a youth camp for teenagers at Camp Tahi. Bob Parschauer, my good friend from Wort des Lebens (Word of Life) in Germany, directed the camp. Bob was a natural choice; he was wonderful with the youth, with his hearty laugh and vibrant personality. Tom Mahairas, pastor of the Manhattan Bible Church, a man who had been saved years before through the ministry of Word of Life Island, was also on hand to conduct this first youth camp. He too, was a great inspiration to youth, and an excellent pastor who was always true to God's word.

That first youth camp at Tahi was one of the most exciting adventures our men ever experienced. The opportunity to reach out to the Hungarian youth and impart the joys of finding spiritual communion with Christ was one for which they were very grateful.

The camp was basic, very rustic and secluded except it was surrounded by the summer homes of some Hungarian military officers and other VIP's. Those staying at the camp could not make any noise or the neighbors would complain to the government about the commotion coming from the camp, disturbing their vacations. Nevertheless, Tahi provided great excitement for Hungarians, young and old alike.

Our team from Germany provided good music for that first camp in 1985. Both Bob and Tom are both fiery preachers who will hold anyone's attention. My, how the Lord worked! The camp was filled to capacity with about two hundred campers each week. It was a wonderful time, and a great success.

And not just for the campers: on Sundays, believers came from all over Hungary to Tahi with their families, toting picnic baskets, to spend the day. During the afternoon, there were so many people that the auditorium was filled to capacity, so they sat out on the hillside. A rustic pulpit was moved down to the foot of the slope, and our team would conduct an evangelistic rally outside. In addition to the two hundred campers, there were approximately 1200 people who made their way into Tahi. What excitement!

After the preaching, a Gospel invitation was given and people flooded to the front of the hillside meeting to publicly confess Christ as Savior. There were literally scores and scores of young people and adults embracing Jesus Christ as their Lord and Savior. If ever we were looking for an indication from the Lord as to the future of Word of Life in Hungary, this was the sign.

The following year when we sought permission to conduct camp again at Tahi, we met with much resistance from the denominational leaders. We were told we made too much noise. We had to tone things down considerably, but eventually permission was granted. That second year, 1986, Bob Parschauer and I were back, along with some of the German musical team, and camp was a repeat performance. Camp Tahi was filled, and on Sunday we had an unbelievable meeting out on the hillside. Again we were reinforced that the Lord wanted us to be in Hungary.

In 1986, after our second camp, I decided to phone my Jewish friend, Michael Kovacs, in London to tell him of the success of our camp.

"Yes, I know," he said, "I have heard all about it." I wondered how Michael had heard, and who he knew who would have been apprised of our having had this very successful youth camp.

Again, he reminded me, "You must keep doing what you are doing, at any cost." Then he said, "I have been working very hard for you in Hungary."

"What have you been doing that is so special?" I asked him curiously.

He said, "Do you remember that I told you I had house guests from Hungary? People very high up in Hungary?"

"Yes, of course I remember."

"Well, do you know who those house guests were?"

"No," I said, "how would I know who they were?"

He replied, "It was Mr. Grosz."

"Who is Mr. Grosz?" I asked.

"What! You do not know who Mr. Grosz is? He is the number one Secretariat in Hungary."

By number one Secretariat I knew what Michael Kovacs meant. In a Communist country, the entire country is divided into districts. The number one district is the most populous and largest district in the country, and then the districts would be numbered down to, say, District 26, which would be the least populated.

This meant Mr. Grosz was the "secretary" over that largest district, which was Budapest.

My dear Jewish friend continued, "When I was in Budapest a couple of weeks ago, I took one of your Ryrie Bibles with me. I made an appointment with Secretariat Grosz. When I went to his office, I took with me this beautiful Bible and gave it to him as a gift."

Michael went on to tell me what happened. When he had presented the book to him, Secretariat Grosz had asked, "Why would you give me a Bible as a gift? I am not a religious man. I am not a believer in the Bible or God."

"But you are a good man," Michael had answered, "and before you joined the Communist party you were a printer by trade. This is a beautifully printed Bible, such as they do not print here. I knew that, as a printer, you would have a special appreciation for this Bible."

After some small talk, Grosz looked at my friend and said, "Michael, what is the real reason you have given me this Bible? What can I do for you?"

My friend answered, "Hungary is full of confused young people out there on the streets. There are young people on drugs, young alcoholics, homosexuals, and perverts. They are young Hungarians you could not bring under one roof of Marxism. The man who gave me this Bible works with young people all over the world through his organization. It is called Word of Life. Why not allow these people to help you with your youth problems here? I would like for you to telephone your man in charge of all religions and tell him to meet with my friend, Paul Bubar, the next time Bubar comes to Hungary. He will bring a proposal of how he can help your society with your youth problems."

Grosz immediately picked up the phone, called Dr. Miklos at the State Office of Religious Affairs and requested Miklos to send him the file on Bubar. At that point, Michael thanked Secretariat Grosz and left his office, eventually returning to his home in England.

Dr. Miklos was the Minister of Religious Affairs, a cabinet level post in the Kadar government. He was a Stalin-era hold over. Miklos was an atheist and a hard-line communist who, in my opinion, did not want the Church to succeed and grow. He wanted it to die. That is why he was placed over the churches. He was a student of Church History who wanted to stifle the churches in Hungary any way he could. Nevertheless, because Kadar decided to give the Church some freedoms and allow it to exist, Miklos had to be in concert with the mandates given by the Chairman of the Communist Party.

Miklos was a powerful, political man. You could often tell his demeanor just by looking at him. He had graying hair and icy blue eyes set in a square face. His nose was sharp, and he had a straight mouth, which often frowned. Miklos was short and stocky, and was originally brought up on a farm. He was a highly educated man, and one that we were going to have to deal with often.

Thankfully we also had good friends on our side helping us. Michael had put his reputation on the line for our sake. His talk with Grosz was incredible. Here was a Jewish capitalist from London meeting with a top Communist leader in Budapest on behalf of Word of Life, seeking to open closed doors so Word of Life might have a spiritual impact and bring young Hungarians to Jesus Christ. I have to ask you, is God creative? The answer to that is a resounding, "yes!"

Michael Kovacs told me, "You should not contact Miklos, but wait and see if he contacts you. I want to see if Mr. Grosz has any real clout with the government. If he does, we will know he is on the way up, and may be the one who will one day replace Communist party chairman, Janos Kadar."

In the same phone conversation, I reminded Michael that I had met with a top attorney in Hungary whose name and phone number he had supplied to me.

Michael said, "He was very impressed with you."

I was surprised to hear this, since at the time when I met with this attorney, Dr. Gayer, he seemed to be very unimpressed with me.

"Do you know what impressed him most?" Michael asked.

"Well," I said, "it may have been when he asked me a difficult question, and I think I gave him a very good answer."

"No," Michael told me, "that was not it at all. It was when you prayed."

"When I prayed?" I asked, "I don't remember praying with this man."

"Yes, you did," my friend said.

So, I ended the conversation on that matter because I felt there might be confusion on Michael's part as to whether or not I had even met with Dr. Gayer.

After we finished our phone conversation I sat, deep in thought, trying to remember praying with Dr. Gayer. I told my wife, Shirley, of the conversation I had just had with Michael and confessed that I could not remember praying with the lawyer at all, and that Michael was confused. At least someone was confused.

Suddenly, I remembered something, but it was so insignificant to me that I had dismissed it from my mind. Evidently, it was not insignificant to Dr. Gayer.

Dr. Gayer was a dear friend of Michael Kovacs and a brilliant attorney — probably one of the best legal minds in the country. He had worked for years under the Communist system, most likely hating it every minute of every hour. My friend in London told me to contact him because I would need a good attorney, and he was the best I could find anywhere in Hungary.

I had been very busy in meetings all over the country and didn't have the opportunity to call him from Budapest. It was not easy at that point in time to make phone calls from the country into the city.

Finally, we arrived at the university city of Debrecen near the Russian border and stayed in a hotel overnight. It was there that I made the call to Budapest trying to set up an appointment to meet Dr. Gayer. I had told him I was a friend of Michael Kovacs. That was always the key that opened doors instantly.

Dr. Gayer was very cordial over the phone and asked where and when we could meet. I told him when I would be in Budapest, and we made arrangements for me to meet him at his office, and then go out and have dinner together.

In his office, I tried to explain what Word of Life is about and what we wanted to do in his country. I told him our philosophy of ministry, and that we wanted to tell young people about Jesus Christ because when a young person comes into a right relationship with God through Jesus Christ his thinking is changed. Dr. Gayer seemed unimpressed with our philosophy. He seemed very cold, indifferent, and almost uninterested. It was my opinion that we would not even have had dinner together had he not already invited me to do so. Hungarians are very gracious.

We spoke very little as we walked from his office down to the Continental Duna Hotel along the bank of the Danube River. The Danube was brown and it's slightly unpleasant odor wafted up to us. There was not much to say at the moment, but despite our lack of conversation, this wonderful Hungarian was a very gracious and polite man. I could tell from the conversation we did have, that he was well bred, well educated, and had a very kind spirit.

Arriving at the hotel for dinner Dr. Gayer sat nervously looking at me. It was as if he were pondering a question. Finally he spoke and said, "Paul Bubar, for twenty-five years the deviant youth of Hungary have been my avocation. I have never in my life heard this approach before. I have a question for you. How do you *know* you are right?"

I replied, "That is a good question, sir. That sounds like an attorney's question, but I do know I'm right. You see, where do you go when you have to make a judgment on a legal matter? The answer is, you go to your statutes and your laws that have been enacted by your government. That is your absolute authority in matters of law. I know I am right because I also have an authority. Do you know where our laws in civilized society originate? Where did they come from in their original form? The answer is, they came from the Mosaic Law. My authority comes not only from the Mosaic Law, but also from the One who gave it, Jehovah God. The Word of God is my authority."

There was a long pause before this brilliant, kind attorney said, "Yes, that is very good. That is very good. I have never heard that before. That is very good. Well, we will talk about something else."

On that note, he changed the subject of our conversation. At about that time the food arrived at our table and Dr. Gayer started to eat. Something inside of me said, *Aren't you going to pray over your food?* All of my life, since childhood, I always prayed and thanked the Lord for my food before I eat. I could not compromise my convictions, no matter whose presence I was in. So, I interrupted my host and said, "Sir, pardon me, but I am a Christian. As such, I'm a follower of Jesus Christ. All of my life I have been taught that everything we have comes from the hand of the Lord. It has always been a practice of mine, before I eat, to thank the Heavenly Father for the food. Would you be offended if I thanked Him for this food?"

He looked at me rather startled and then said, "Well, no, of course not. You do that." He immediately folded his hands and bowed his head.

I started to pray, "Dear Heavenly Father, I want to thank You for this gift of good food that we are about to enjoy. I accept it from Your hand. I want to pray for Dr. Gayer. I pray, dear Lord, that You will make him very wise. He has to make many very important decisions on a daily basis. Give him, I pray Thee, wisdom that comes from Heaven above, from the very Throne of God. Help him to make right choices. In Jesus' Name, Amen."

We then went on and enjoyed our meal. That brief prayer of thanks for the food was so insignificant to me that I had totally forgotten it. Yet this is what my friend, Michael Kovacs, referred to when he said Dr. Gayer was impressed when I prayed.

Dr. Gayer had said something like this to Michael, "When he prayed for his food, I knew he was a good man. And, Michael, he prayed for me. I have never heard anyone pray for me before."

It was this man who, as the result of a seemingly insignificant prayer, would become our good legal friend and would give us much excellent advice in the thorny road ahead.

For this, I thank you, Lord, for arranging the insignificant little things in our lives that tell others who we are, much louder than any of our words.

In the meantime, some weeks had gone by after my telephone conversation with Michael Kovacs regarding Dr. Miklos, and still I heard nothing from Dr. Miklos, the government's Minister of Religion.

I had prepared the proposal for the Hungarian government with a slant toward reaching the deviant youth. But it was now time to go to Hungary with the proposal and I had heard nothing from Miklos.

I sent a telex to Budapest but received no confirming response. When we left Schroon Lake, I still had not received a positive response, and consequently, felt that prospects for success were shaky at best. It appeared that Michael's efforts were wasted, or that perhaps Grosz had not contacted Miklos.

My mind was filled with questions. *Did Grosz not contact Miklos? Had my telex not gone through? Had Miklos unsuccessfully tried to contact me? Should I contact the Minister of Religion's office, assuming he had received my telex?* Because our time in Budapest would only be over a weekend, I had just Friday and Monday when Miklos' office would be open.

Upon our arrival in Budapest, we met with George Theis, Executive Director of Word of Life International, and his son, Steve. We jumped into our meetings immediately. More than 120 workers attended the Christian Workers' Conference despite the fact that it was a national holiday.

Sunday was filled with meetings all day long in three different directions. What a joy it was to mix and mingle with these wonderful Hungarian churches and Christians. People trusted Christ in almost every service through public, open invitations. When George Theis spoke at the Baptist church in Kiskorish on Sunday evening and gave the invitation, many responded. One of the women that came forward was the wife of the local Communist Party Chairman, the most important political figure in the city.

Following instructions from my friend, Michael Kovacs, I had not directly been in contact with Dr. Miklos. I had prepared the proposal in such a way that a Communist government could give permission. For example, I did not propose Bible Clubs, but rather "Deviant Saving Centers." However, to this point I had received no contact from Miklos and, therefore, had no set opportunity to present our proposal. If the appointment with Miklos did not develop while I was in Budapest it would mean another costly trip from New York at a later date.

Should I phone Miklos and risk raising his anger? I decided to do as Michael suggested I not do. On Friday I phoned the State Office of Religious Affairs and asked for anyone who could speak English. There was no one.

It was Monday morning. It weighed heavy on my heart that we were scheduled to leave on Tuesday morning, which meant if I was not received by Dr. Miklos today, I would not see him at all on this trip. It became obvious that Miklos did not want to meet with me. Once again I questioned my thoughts, would my phoning his office force his hand or anger him? Upsetting him would be counter-productive. I decided there was nothing I could do but wait — and pray. I did plenty of both.

I decided to make one last attempt at scheduling an appointment with Dr. Miklos. If I failed, I would know that the proposal was not of God.

As I opened my Quiet Time diary early that morning in Budapest, I turned to read Ephesians 1:15-23. Paul says here that his prayer for the Christians at Ephesus is that they would realize how incredibly great God's power is to help those who believe in Him. He said, "It is the same mighty power that raised Christ from the dead."

As I read those words, at that moment, I knew in my heart that God was going to make things come together that day. I made telephone contact with Dr. Miklos from the hotel at 9:00 a.m. At 11:00 a.m. I was received by Dr. Miklos and was given the opportunity to tell him what Word of Life was doing in twenty-three countries around the world.

I presented a formal proposal to Dr. Miklos that explained what Word of Life wished to do in Hungary.

The Proposal

I asked the Hungarian government to allow Word of Life to do the following:

1. Enter the country on an official interdenominational basis;

2. Establish a base of operation there;

3. Help the free Gospel-preaching churches learn how to become "Deviant Saving Centers" so that they could train their pastors and laymen in "deviant prevention;" and

4. Lease property from the government, upgrade it and use it as a "Deviant Prevention Center," (that is what Word of Life Island and Ranch are) plus a training center for adults who are interested in deviant prevention (that is what Word of Life Bible Institute is).

Dr. Miklos accepted the proposal with what appeared to be an open mind and seemed very happy that I was interested in the youth of their society. The man was actually smiling at me. It was obvious that word had come along the chain of command. Miklos had heard from Grosz.

Miklos told us that he planned to study the proposal and then meet with us for negotiations on June 30 — another trip — in only four weeks.

To lighten the conversation a little, I presented Dr. Miklos with a gift of a personally autographed Word of Life Ryrie Study Bible. He responded by asking if a Baptist would read a Catholic Bible and then gave me a copy of a Catholic Bible printed in Hungary. He also stated that Word of Life may be able to operate within the country if what we were doing was for the betterment of Hungarian society, we obeyed their laws, and we invested financially in their country.

I learned later, of course, that his last condition was really the bottom line. At that time, the government was seeking to get everyone, including church groups, to invest hard currency in Hungary.

Before leaving Dr. Miklos I took off my Word of Life lapel pin and pinned it on his lapel. As I did, I told him, "Dr. Miklos, I want to temporarily make you an honorary member of our staff. I won't expect you to wear this pin at your formal state functions; in fact, what you do after I leave is your business. But, for the moment, I invite you to become a part of Word of Life."

He smiled and thanked me and said, "Good. We will meet again in June."

This contact and action did not mean we were in the door, it only meant that we were received at the doorstep. It did mean, however, that I had met and had a positive experience with the Cabinet level official who alone could let us in the door.

I met with the Free Church leaders after our meeting with Miklos. I learned they had heard rumors that I had sent Bibles to the top Communist officials in Hungary, and they were terrified. They feared what might happen to both Word of Life and themselves, since they had invited us into the country. Their fears changed to joy when I relayed the facts to them.

They said, "If Miklos gave _you_ a Bible, it means he likes you. The way this has happened could only be arranged by God. It is good. It is a miracle in Hungary. Praise the Lord!"

When we met with our friends, Pastor Geza Kovacs and his family, there was much rejoicing. No one, to their knowledge, had ever gotten that far in bringing in a Gospel ministry from the West in more than forty years.

There were thankful hearts around the dinner table that night. We knew that what we were doing was of the Lord. God would intervene whenever He needed to, in a miraculous way.

CHAPTER 6

WARNING SIGNALS,
BUT I CAN'T
FIND THE BRAKES

We had many meetings with top ranking officials from varying denominational organizations, as I have stated earlier, and we soon learned that in a Communist country everyone speaks in riddles. Chuck Kosman, Bob Parschauer, and I would always leave the meetings asking ourselves, "This was what they said, but what did they mean? Their words might have meant this or that."

Our team spent hours trying to decipher what was meant in any of these meetings with the denominational hierarchy. I do not, and did not, look at these men as being evil. They were, for the most part, good men. Many had circumstances in their backgrounds which should have disqualified them as pastors, but they were very intelligent men and, consequently, they were more or less "kicked upstairs" into administrative positions.

These men had to function directly under the authority of the State Office of Church. All of the presidents of the various denominational organizations answered directly to the President of the Free Churches. The Free Churches were all of those small denominations — those other than the Catholic, the Reformed, and the Presbyterian churches.

Dr. Miklos was President of the State Office of Church. He was the government's man over all religion. Miklos held great power and, like I said earlier, he was a Stalin-era holdover who, I felt, did not want the churches to succeed at all. I felt that he wanted the churches to die, but he did not want any kind of an uprising. He became, then, a student of Church History and was the government's iron fist over all the churches.

Everyone feared Miklos. The president of each denomination answered to the president of the Free Churches who, in turn, reported directly to Miklos. The denominational leaders, as well as the Free Church leader, all bowed and scraped before Miklos for fear of losing their positions, or fearing that his wrath could, at will, be directed at their churches.

Each man felt that he served the people in his denomination and that he furthered the cause of Christ through his denomination. But these men had to walk a very tight line, pleasing both the people and the authority over them — Miklos. One hard jerk on their leash by Miklos left them hyperventilating and gasping for air.

I believe these men very much wanted Word of Life's presence in Hungary, but Word of Life had to be tightly controlled by these men in order to satisfy Miklos. They were under enormous pressure from Miklos to know where we were and what we were doing every hour of our time in their country. Whenever we would meet in denominational headquarters, which I referred to jokingly (and for protection's sake) as "Second Heaven," these men gave us as much freedom as they dared, but never enough for us to be truly free. They sought to give the impression that there was freedom of religion in Hungary, and yet we were not free to do as we wished. Our actions had to fit within their strict guidelines. We were tightly controlled.

I knew this, but I do not know if they knew I figured this out. We knew that most of what we said in idle conversation, if it was of any significance, would be reported directly through denominational headquarters on up to Miklos. We knew that in almost all of our meetings there was someone present to serve as an informer.

The government wanted our money. The denominational leadership received instructions to obtain as much hard currency out of the western churches as was possible. Consequently, there began a steady stream of church leaders from Germany, the United Kingdom, Canada, and the United States of America through their office.

These denominational men who were on a leash to the State Office of Church gave us as much freedom as they dared, enough to get the promise of American or western money for projects, and yet they allowed us as little freedom as they felt would keep us coming. It used to rankle us that they would be so bold in suggesting how we ought to invest our American funds for their causes. These men were very clever at this. The bottom line became that they wanted to exchange dollars for the Gospel.

We referred to denominational headquarters as "Second Heaven" because the men there seemed to have the authority attributed to God in that they would determine where you could preach, when you could preach, how much you could preach, and whether or not you were acceptable for the Christians in Hungary. They were a little higher up than the churches, but they certainly did not have the attributes of God. Consequently, in our learning to talk in riddles, we referred to many of the people, places, and things using words having various meanings, such as calling denominational headquarters "Second Heaven."

Under the Communist system, one is not paid a salary commensurate with one's value. Almost everyone received basically the same salary. So the Hungarians, who are highly intelligent people, discovered ways to beat the system. They contrived ways to get more than one salary coming to them if they could. Some, in lieu of increased salaries, would take perks.

The perks could be cars, or office phones. Or sometimes this just meant being given a little more authority to exercise, or the possibility of moving around with the authority figures. This gave them a feeling of importance and respect. It is difficult to blame some of these dear Christian people for wanting respect and desiring to exercise a little more authority.

One of these men from denominational headquarters was a deacon in one of the key Baptist churches in Hungary. His name was Lajos Barbarics, and his wife's name was Eva. We referred to him as the Silver Fox. There is no question that this man loved the Lord and that he wanted to see young people brought to Jesus Christ. In fact, it was quite well known that he and his wonderful wife had been used of God several years before Word of Life was on the scene in Hungary to bring in a well-known children's ministry underground.

It was done quietly through contacts in the West. On more than one occasion their house was searched by police looking for Bibles and other "contraband." They were used as a conduit of children's ministry materials at great personal risk. It is my belief that these people were greatly used of God.

I referred to this deacon as the Silver Fox because of his silver hair and his quick driving. He was often in our presence, and we knew he had been instructed by denominational leadership to be with us most of the time. We also knew the denominational leadership expected him to know everything we were doing. Yet, truly this man was a servant to us. He drove us to meetings, speeding along like a fox. He was a very clever man, much more clever than many people gave him credit. He was, I thought, looked upon with disdain by the hierarchy because they knew he was reporting information about us, yet I believe this man was truly pleased whenever he saw young people find Christ at our meetings. He reported to the hierarchy in order to be accepted in the denominational higher circles, and to gain the respect of these men. And yet, he cared very much about our work through God. In any case, we couldn't seem to break free from him.

On the other hand, from our observation, the Silver Fox was the most organized and the best organizer of all the men from Second Heaven. If we wanted to have good meetings attended by many people, and we wanted to be sure the meeting would be promoted ahead of time, we tried to have the Silver Fox involved in organizing these meetings.

It seemed everywhere we went the Silver Fox was also there. Ours was a love-hate relationship with him. It almost became a game. We loved him as a person because we knew he truly loved the Lord. He has one of the loveliest families anyone could have. His dear wife is one of the sweetest, loveliest ladies you would ever know, and she loved her man. They had good children — every one of them loved the Lord and, to my knowledge, still loves the Lord and serves Him today.

So, we would play the game. We wanted him to produce good meetings for us. He would see that they were organized well in advance, when nobody else seemed to care about helping us. Yet, we knew he was passing information directly to denominational headquarters and they, in turn, passed it on to Miklos. There was the ever-present State in control.

We would play hide and seek games with the Silver Fox, trying to avoid him in certain meetings. We would try to carry on conversations with Pastor Kovacs, but the Silver Fox was always there. His nickname was used both affectionately and in frustration.

Though we knew the Silver Fox was reporting on some of our activities he was, indeed, our friend. We consider him as such to this day.

The Breakdown with the Denominational Leaders

During our many subsequent trips to Budapest, we always had a meeting with the boys in Second Heaven early on. They wanted to know our entire itinerary in detail. They told us, "Remember, we are held responsible for you while you are in this country. We are your protection and we have to answer to the government for everything you do."

This was, indeed, a true statement. In other words, the government's edict to Second Heaven was, "Keep them in a box." That is the system used under any Communist government. They don't want you getting out of the particular box you are put in, whether it is the social box, the education box, or the religion box. Keeping the lids on those boxes, to the government, meant keeping everything under control.

Naturally, we were in the religion box. As a Westerner and as an American in particular, I have known nothing but complete freedom of operation and thought all of my life. Being categorized and restrained so strictly was not what I was used to.

I was blessed as the youngest child born into a godly family whose preacher father would tell all of his children, "Have you thanked God lately that you were born free, here in America? Because you were born in America you can do just about anything you want to do, within the law. You can become anything you want to become if you desire it enough. Why, you could grow up to be President of the United States if you should so choose." Then he would add, "Although I don't know who would ever want to stoop to become President when he could serve the King of Kings."

When you are raised in that kind of atmosphere, it is very easy to think you can do anything you feel the Lord would have you do, and that you can do it in God's power if God is in it. Somehow, I felt these principles could be practiced in a Communist country as well. I was very naive. I did not understand the Communist system, but somehow I could not help but try to pursue my dreams. So, when we met with the boys in Second Heaven, we made proposals. In these proposals we would press for the freedom to do more. We made proposals to be able to operate summer camp at Tahi, which we were allowed to do for two seasons. We proposed to obtain permission to bring pastors of great American churches to Hungary to conduct training classes in youth work and in church growth. Permission eventually was granted for that as well.

We were able to bring to Hungary godly pastors such as Dr. Dan Gelatt, Pastor of the First Baptist Church in Elkhart, Indiana; Pastor Jerry Day of Berean Bible Church in Columbus, Indiana; Pastor Wally Holder and his wife of the great First Baptist Church in Concord, New Hampshire; Pastor Herb Fitzpatrick, of Maryland; Dr. Charles Anderson, of New Jersey and Dr. Howard Bixby of Baptist Bible Seminary in Clark Summit, Pennsylvania, along with many other wonderful pastors.

These men gave instruction and encouragement to the Hungarian pastors. Most of these American men were more blessed by the Hungarian pastors than the Hungarian pastors were blessed by them. They were thrilled to see the hardy love for the Lord these men had, and how they continued to function despite the repressive control of the Communist government.

When we traveled to Hungary with these men, we sought to get them into churches outside of Budapest so they could get a feel for what God was doing in other parts of that country as well.

The American pastors became a great source of encouragement to us. Churches such as First Baptist in Concord, the Gateway Cathedral in Staten Island with Pastor Dan Mercaldo, Faith Evangelical Free Church in Trexlertown, Pennsylvania, and others became great financial encouragers in that they started investing $100 to $200 each month to help cover the cost of the many trips back and forth to Eastern Europe. We owe a great debt of gratitude to the people in these churches for the support they provided in the early days of this adventure.

It was not only Gospel preachers who invested their time and resources to accompany us on our trips to Hungary. Great musicians contributed their talents, as well. Tim Kaufman learned to sing in Hungarian in order to have a ministry to these dear Hungarian people. Dave Musselman, pianist extraordinaire, from Atlanta, Georgia, and other musicians invested their own ministry funds to be able to minister to the believers in Hungary.

The more we tried branching out in ministry in Hungary, the tighter were the governmental controls on our activities. It became increasingly clear that the church authorities wanted our Western funds but they did not want us moving around the country without their foreknowledge and prior approval. The more visits we made to Hungary, the more familiar we became with both the people and the places, and we began to move around Budapest and the country of Hungary much like we would move around the United States. This was not appreciated at all by the church authorities who had been told to control us.

Unknown to me at the time, the name "Kovacs" would become very prominent in the future of Word of Life Hungary. That name would be used at a political level as well as at the spiritual level. These men were always positive and encouraging, and would allow me to dream of what *could* be in the future.

The Great Kovacs Connection

The name Kovacs is a very common name in Hungary, much like the name Smith in the United States. I myself knew many people by that name. One was my good Jewish friend in London, Michael Kovacs. A second was Pastor Geza Kovacs. Pastor Kovacs was a godly man, hated by the government and by the church authorities. He was as independent as he dared to be, and knew his limitations quite well.

As a young man he had been an evangelist. He was graduated from the Baptist Seminary and had become an associate student pastor at the Nejipest Baptist Church in Budapest. The senior pastor at that time was a man by the name of Haraszti. Pastor Haraszti wanted to leave the country to pursue higher education and had enrolled at the Ruschlikon Seminary in Switzerland. While he was away working on his Masters degree in Theology, Kovacs became the interim pastor at Nejipest.

Kovacs, a great soul winner, during those two years saw many people receive Jesus Christ. More than a hundred people joined the church of which some forty-two were new converts.

When Pastor Haraszti returned with his degree, Nejipest Baptist was a very different church than the one he had left. There were more people in the church who loved Pastor Kovacs than wanted Pastor Haraszti. You can imagine the conflict that followed. Young Kovacs resigned when the senior pastor returned. The deacons and people said, "No, you will remain." He reminded them of his agreement with the senior pastor, and decided it was the ethical choice to resign. However, in consultation with each other, the two decided they should work together as co-pastors for two years. Pastor Haraszti was then invited to become the pastor of a sister church and Kovacs became the pastor of Nejipest.

The Nejipest church began growing rapidly. The communist leadership became irritated by the conversion of so many young people. They effectively pressured the Baptist hierarchy to stop the activities of Pastor Kovacs. In 1964, the church authorities revoked his license to preach, but he kept on preaching anywhere a pastor would dare allow him to speak. He traveled all over Hungary preaching the gospel everywhere, every time he could.

Because his license to preach was revoked, he had to work at a local factory and was listed by the government as a laborer. This happened at about the time his oldest son, Dr. Geza Kovacs, Jr., was graduating from high school. His son wanted to enroll at the State University. At that particular time, the sons of pastors were not given any opportunity to further their education, especially the son of the one who had bucked the government all along the way. It was almost impossible for a child of a pastor to get into the University.

When it came time, his son went to the university and applied to take an entrance exam. At registration time, a university official looked up the name of Kovacs on a list provided by the government. The official looked down the list for the name, Kovacs. There were many of them. Finally coming to the name Geza Kovacs, he moved his pencil over to the occupation column and discovered Geza, Sr. was listed as laborer, not pastor. Because Geza lost his license to preach, he was declared as a laborer by the government just in time for his son to enroll in the university.

Eventually, each of his sons was able to enroll in the university because of his laborer classification. Each son became highly educated in his field of service. This was another way God was taking care of this independent, godly pastor.

Pastor Kovacs continued moving across the country, preaching and evangelizing everywhere he could. This disturbed the hierarchy very much. People were asking why he was no longer a pastor, and he told them why. This made the church authorities look very bad. They did not know how to control this brother.

One day, representatives from the church authorities came to him and agreed to return his license and give him a church. This was in 1970, when Pastor Kovacs was about fifty years old.

"Will you promise not to run all over the country preaching?" they asked him.

"Well," said Pastor Kovacs, "maybe I will, but maybe I won't. I would, however, love to have back my license to preach."

As mentioned in Chapter Three, the church authorities (denominational leaders) restored his license and at that time he was offered the pastorate of an obscure little church, barely accessible at the top of a hill, in the suburbs of Budapest. I am told the church had only twenty-five or thirty people attending. With Geza as pastor, and with the Lord's blessing, in the following years the church was to grow as people were led to Jesus Christ by Pastor Kovacs.

Young people began attending the church. The mood, along with the freedom of religion, began to change. Westerners began visiting the Budafok Baptist Church. The church was permitted to purchase property at the foot of the hill and to build a new church building on that land. The church then began to receive some financial help through the World Baptist Alliance program.

The men in the congregation constructed almost all of the new building. Lojos Barbarics, the Silver Fox, was a member of the church and contributed his engineering and draftsmanship skills to the building. It was a beautiful, modern edifice with a main floor and two balconies.

Geza Kovacs was the pastor who would eventually be permitted to get an exit visa to go to Germany and visit the Word of Life Castles. He also invited Word of Life, in the form of Kosman, Parschauer, Batdorf, and the German evangelistic music team, to conduct many meetings in Hungary. Geza Kovacs and his dear family soon became friends of the heart with Word of Life. We loved them dearly.

Pastor Geza Kovacs was married to a godly woman named Olga. The couple had shared many difficult times. One of those hard times was when, because of his activities, they were given two weeks to leave the country. Special connections with someone high up in government allowed for them to stay. As many Western friends began visiting Budapest, this dear lady always had plenty of good food on the table. It was around the table in the Kovacs home that Kosman, Parschauer, and I talked about the future of Word of Life in Hungary.

From Pastor Kovacs we received godly counsel. In return, we spent much time talking with him, trying to stretch his horizons to think about the future of youth evangelism in Hungary. Many times we sat around the table with Pastor Geza and his sons Dr. Geza, Zoltan, and Peter, and I would say, "Let's dream about the things we would like to do in this country. Let's make believe there are no restrictions on the church and that we may do anything we want to do."

I wanted to stretch their thinking and broaden their horizons. We began to verbalize some of our dreams. I would tell them what Word of Life was doing in twenty-three other countries around the world, in the youth camps and the Bible Clubs in America, Canada and Argentina. I told them how the young Argentine men who would fall in love with the Lord and become almost fanatical about getting out the Gospel to the youth of their country and other South and Latin American countries.

One of the Kovacs would always say, "But you must remember, you are in a Communist country. That is not allowed here. You will not be able to do this."

"Well," I would respond, "let's do as much as we can. Let's go as far as we are able."

One day I said to Pastor Kovacs, "Why don't you allow me to be the point man? I have an American passport. They will not do anything to me but maybe throw me out of the country. You need to be careful. You are a Hungarian citizen. With my American passport and Kosman's Canadian passport the worst they are going to do is to expel us. Let us go on the offensive. You stay totally in the background."

Pastor Kovacs sat there grinning, with his blue eyes bright and mischievous, and said, "Well, we will see what the Lord has in mind."

One evening while taking a long walk along the Danube River with Dr. Geza Kovacs, Jr., the agro-biologist, I said, "Geza, let me tell you how we do evangelism in America with the Word of Life Bible Club ministry."

I then told him about our basketball, volleyball, and softball marathons. I explained how sports are used to evangelize and how hundreds and thousands of young American athletes found Christ as Savior. As we walked along in the crisp, fall air, and under a night sky filled with many stars, I painted a picture for him of what youth camps might be like in Hungary.

Dr. Geza found it difficult to understand because, for Christians in Hungary, sports had been considered a sinful activity. Sports were not taught in the public schools in Hungary. In order to be involved, one had to belong to a sports club. Within those clubs, frequented mainly by adults, was a lot of drinking and ungodly behavior. A Christian would have nothing to do with that kind of atmosphere. It was difficult for this native Hungarian Christian to comprehend how sports could be used as an opportunity to preach the Gospel to young people. But the Kovacs family was a very progressive family. They learned they can trust God. They learned to stick their necks out, which they had done many times before. They learned that with God, anything is possible.

As we walked and talked that night along the Danube, I urged Dr. Geza to stretch his imagination. We dreamed of youth camping in Hungary. Should it be at Tahi or at a totally different location, away from the summer homes of the officials? At a new location we would be able to make a lot of noise, and also have more room for athletic activities. These dreams were almost too much for the Kovacs men to envision at that time.

All the while, during our many conversations, listening quietly in the background was Zoltan, the young, married engineer son in the family. Zoltan was in his mid-twenties, a tenderhearted, quiet, strong young man with curly dark hair and a gentle smile. Zoltan had a heart for God, and he was learning to become a dreamer. He also knew what it was to take risks. He was a hard worker, and he had taken on a second job laying sewer pipe for the government, to earn extra money.

Early in our trips to Hungary, at one meeting in the city of Kaposvar, someone had come to us wanting us to look at an old castle just outside the city. He said that it could be purchased for an unbelievably low price. The villa was in great disrepair and would take tens of thousands of dollars to renovate. At that time, Word of Life was not certain they wanted to invest heavily in a country that could confiscate property after we invested a lot of money into it. We rejected the idea.

Zoltan, whom I later would refer to as the young Capitalist, was already running a business on the side while working for the government in a construction firm. We learned later that he had somehow gotten together $4,000-$5,000 and had purchased this castle property on his own.

Zoltan had a great interest in reaching deviants and drug-involved youth. The property was later to become a part of the first Christian social foundation. It was known as Menedek, which translates as "shelter." Zoltan was able to form this Christian foundation that worked under the Department of Social Affairs and which would become the first Christian Hungarian organization to get out of the religion "box."

Though the foundation was Christian in every way, Zoltan was able to get those in the social box to go along and stick out their necks to help him form the foundation. This angered the church authorities, all the way up to Miklos, very much. It was reason for them to hate the Kovacs' even more. All these things only served to anger the boys in Second Heaven because they were probably feeling pressure from the State Office of Church, which was a very formidable and fearful thing to them. The more freedoms we took, the more pressed they were to control us. By now we had conducted many evangelistic meetings in churches across the country. In all these meetings we extended Gospel invitations. Young and old alike responded to these invitations and received Christ as Savior.

There is a Baptist Seminary in Hungary that was tightly controlled by the government. They would take as much freedom as they dared. The Baptist Seminary was supported financially by the Baptist World Alliance and the Southern Baptist Convention. I believe it was a good investment on the part of these organizations as it was the only training vehicle for young future pastors in all of Hungary.

I commend the Southern Baptist Convention for their early investment in some of these Hungarian Baptist churches. Most Hungarian Baptist churches preach the Gospel. Very few Baptist churches in Hungary are liberal. A church with a liberal message could not survive under Communism.

Because of our evangelistic fervor and our extending public invitations, it was my assessment that the people at the Baptist Seminary felt disdain toward us. To neutralize that perceived feeling, I was attempting to bring recognized world scholars to Hungary under the banner of Word of Life. I was able to bring Dr. Charles Ryrie, a very dear friend of mine and Word of Life, and an early supporter of this adventure in Hungary. Dr. Ryrie was a member of Word of Life's board of directors, and he is also the man who is responsible for the Ryrie Study Bible that I had presented to so many of our new acquaintances in Hungarian government. After Dr. Ryrie agreed to travel to Hungary, we made arrangements for him to lecture at the seminary. He was well received at the Baptist Seminary. I believe he did much in giving Word of Life credibility among the theologians in the Baptist hierarchy there.

It was on one of these early trips that several things happened to grab my attention. On one occasion, Chuck Kosman was with me for an appointment with Dr. Gayer, the brilliant Hungarian attorney who had been moved by the time I prayed for him before we ate together. We shared with him what we wished to do in Hungary and how we wanted to eventually own property and run a Christian youth camp. He was not too encouraging and warned us that the laws had not been changed enough to allow for what we proposed. He felt the necessary changes would eventually come, but no one could know for certain.

One day, sitting in a restaurant, he said to us in a low voice, "I feel I need to warn you. You must never forget where you are. You are in a Communist country. Communists do not like what you are doing. They will allow you to go along so far and then, when you have gone as far as they want you to go, they will throw you out of the country.

"It will happen something like this. You will go to your hotel one night and police will be waiting in the lobby for you. They will identify themselves and ask you to take them to your room. They will do a search of your room, and somewhere in the room they will find either a piece of pornography or a map of a sensitive area. You will be put under arrest and eventually be thrown out of the country. You must never forget that everything you do..." he leaned over the table to say in a firm, low voice, "...everything you do is known! Do you understand?"

Dr. Gayer had made his point. To relieve the tension of the moment, I jokingly said to him, "I suppose they know even of the conversation in our room."

Still leaning over the table with his face directly toward us he said, "Especially in your room. Everything is known."

Kosman and I used to joke about that. Kosman could be a great kidder as it was. We would be conversing in our room and Kosman would say, "Bubar, would you make that statement over here, just a little bit closer to the microphone? We want to make sure they understand everything we're saying. Testing, one, two, three, testing."

Then we would say good things about the government, how wonderful Communism is and how wonderful it is to work under this repressive system. We would carry on what we jokingly called the Kos and Bubar show.

Whether anyone was listening at those foolish moments or not, we will never know. We felt reasonably secure in our jesting and miniature comedy hours because we knew we had an American and a Canadian passport. We felt we would not be imprisoned in this country for our private jokes.

Around this time, in Hungary, I met Dr. Akos Bukovsky. Dr. Bukovsky is a doctor of chemistry and a very wise Christian leader and interpreter. From him I received another very poignant warning.

I was invited to come to his apartment. Whenever we would visit Akos, he would ask us to speak in low tones until we were inside the apartment. He did not want others in the building to know he had Western, English-speaking guests. As we entered the apartment, he took a cassette off his desk and put it in his boom box recorder and pressed the play button. Coming out of the recorder was my own voice, a recording of a message I had given only a few weeks earlier in the auditorium at Word of Life Inn at Schroon Lake, New York. There, I had been asked to tell the Hungary story.

Although folks in Schroon Lake could not understand at the time, I often spoke in riddles. I rarely gave the real names of Hungarian people, but instead used fictitious names. For example, in my message, I referred to the men in denominational headquarters as Second Heaven. The folks at Schroon Lake probably thought I was trying to be mysterious and James Bondish. Yet, the demonstration being played out before me now made me realize more fully that it was not just fun and games. Here was my telling of the Hungary story from Schroon Lake now on cassette in Budapest, Hungary. I looked at Dr. Bukovsky in astonishment and asked, "Where did you get that?"

With a smile on his face he said, "Never mind that. But one thing you can be certain of is that if I can get a copy of this message, then anyone in Hungary, at any level, can also have one."

I admit that for a moment, I was terrified. What had I said? Had I been secretive enough? Was I careful to use fictitious names? Had I disguised things enough? I couldn't remember. Would some Christian leader in Hungary be called in for questioning because of the words contained in my message? That was exactly the point Dr. Bukovsky wanted to make.

"Akos," I said, "What did I say on this tape? Did I say anything wrong? Will anyone get in trouble?"

Smiling he replied, "No, quite frankly you did very well. I think you were very wise. Fortunately, I don't think anything was said that would be incriminating."

What a relief that was! Yet, what a burden to realize I could not say things even in the friendly atmosphere of our own Word of Life Inn at Schroon Lake without fear of my words being sent directly to government officials in Budapest. I was to be constantly on my guard.

This message at the Inn was delivered near to the time when

we sensed we were being watched even at Schroon Lake.

At that time we lived on a secluded, dead-end road just outside the Village of Schroon Lake. My wife, Shirley, began noticing different automobiles, with a single occupant, parked at the end of our road. This was unusual and started happening all of a sudden. One day, Ebba, my mother-in-law, stopped at one of these cars, looked at the driver and asked if she could help him. "No!" he replied, and immediately drove off.

These were some of the negative happenings that helped raise the tension just a little at that point in the Hungary project. There were times we believed our telephone lines had been tapped, but frankly, we never thought too much about it. Neither my wife nor I had anything to talk about of which we were ashamed or that was in any way "clandestine." If someone wanted to waste time watching our house or tapping our phone, good for him.

On the positive side, we saw signs of light on the horizon in Hungary. One bright light was an experience with Dr. Ana Gondosh. This woman was very well connected with the Social Reform Movement and with the Social Welfare Department of the Communist government. She was a petite brunette with blue eyes, in her mid-thirties at the time, and very intelligent. It was with this highly educated woman that Zoltan Kovacs had much contact as he sought to make his Menedek Foundation an independent entity.

Dr. Gondosh was very concerned about families in Hungary, especially those with working mothers who were unable to care for their children while they worked. She was concerned about the deviant situation – the young people involved in drugs and rock music. She wanted somehow to provide a social program that would keep the families together, instead of seeing them divided and devastated.

Dr. Gondosh was a personal friend of Communist Chairman

Kadar's "Girl Friday," the woman who was his executive assistant. Dr. Gondosh had many contacts very high up in government, and she was an encouragement to us.

It is my appraisal that, at the time, very few people even within the Communist government were truly Communist. They knew the system did not work. It was bankrupt and almost everyone in government wanted to see change. Dr. Gondosh was no exception.

I asked Zoltan if it was possible to meet with Dr. Gondosh so the next time we traveled to Budapest, he arranged an appointment. Dr. Gondosh was invited to the home of Zoltan and Louise Kovacs for a breakfast meeting. Since the doctor spoke limited English, Zoltan's sister-in-law, Ildiko Kovacs, served as interpreter.

I began the usual way, "Let me tell you who we are and why we are here. We are a Christian organization, not as in Jewish, Muslim, Christian, but as followers of Jesus Christ who take a literal interpretation of the Bible."

I went on to explain our philosophy of how when a young person comes into a right relationship with God through Jesus Christ his thinking changes for the better, and his attitudes and behaviors in his daily life are improved positively. Therefore, he becomes a brand new person in Jesus Christ. I told her about Jesus and how He came to pay for man's sin.

Tears began to fill this dear lady's blue eyes. I continued, gently telling her, "Dr. Gondosh, the dear Lord Jesus wants to be your Savior. He wants to take away your sins. He wants to give you a special place in Heaven. Won't you allow Him to do this by receiving Him into your life?"

By now, the tears began to flow and she could not speak. Because of the embarrassment from her tears, she turned her face away from me and I said, "Dr. Gondosh, don't be ashamed of your tears. Tears are the language of the soul. Tears mean brokenness and surrender. Don't be ashamed of your tears, but allow Christ to be your Savior."

"Oh," she finally replied, "I would like to make that choice, but I cannot. No, I absolutely cannot. Not now."

Dr. Gondosh did not receive Christ that day, but she became a friend to what Word of Life was doing in Hungary. I was to meet with her on two other occasions. Her husband was keeping company with another woman and she, in retaliation, kept company with another man. On weekends they would all join with the children and spend time together. This was tearing her apart. She could see her family coming unglued. On top of that, to receive Jesus Christ meant she would have to face her fears of being mocked by her co-workers in government; those in government positions often would put down religion.

After learning about her family situation, I felt pressed to confront her in one of our meetings.

"Dr. Gondosh," I started, "it is your sin that is keeping you from the Savior. It is the lifestyle you are choosing. God not only wants to save your soul, He wants to save your family. However, you are going to need to forsake your sin when you come to the Savior. But you will not have to do it on your own. The Lord will help you have the strength to live for Him."

But Dr. Gondosh would not address this issue with me. I wish I could tell you whether this tormented lady ever came to the Savior. I have not seen her since that time and, to my knowledge, she has not trusted Christ.

During this time, the verbal warnings from Second Heaven were becoming more and more frequent. Each time we met with the men in Second Heaven, the rhetoric grew louder and louder. They were becoming more distrustful of our goals. We were creeping out of their box, and they did not like it. They would tell me, "You cannot go out on your own and do anything. You must do everything through us."

I knew it was an attempt to control us, but I did not want to be controlled by the government. I would say, "Then you show us some property. You take us to look at a place where we can conduct our own youth camp. Find us something we can afford."

On one occasion Dr. Szakacs said, "All right, I want to take you to see a monastery that is available. It is in the village of Tura. The place is known as Tura Castle."

One very cold day we visited Tura Castle. Dr. Szakacs himself, the President of the Free Churches, took me with him and his interpreter. We drove about twenty miles outside of Budapest to a small town. On the edge of this town was a beautiful old monastery and grounds. The problem was the monastery stood in unbelievable disrepair and, without much work, was totally unusable. Also, it included only four acres of land. There was barely room enough for a soccer field.

I went through the formalities of looking at the property with Dr. Szakacs since he so graciously took the entire day from his pressing responsibilities to demonstrate his care for Word of Life. But it became evident that day that Dr. Szakacs had other things in mind. We stopped at a little restaurant for dinner on the outskirts of Tura. It was during this meal that we talked about the Kovacs connection, that is, the Pastor Kovacs connection. I had told Dr. Szakacs we were special friends to the Kovacs family. That meant we would never do anything without them, and we would never betray them. They were not just friends in a spiritual sense but had become friends of the heart. We truly loved the Kovacs family, and we stood in agreement with their philosophy and ministry. We would not abandon them.

This seemed to anger Dr. Szakacs. He went on to make wild

accusations that Pastor Kovacs was a devil, and that he doubted if the Pastor were even a Christian. He stated that he knew Kovacs took in two or three salaries and was living much better than he, Dr. Szakacs, was as President of the denominations. He tried to justify his anger as righteous indignation.

I made a mental note of all of this and decided Pastor Kovacs had most likely angered the denominational hierarchy because he would not jump at their whistle nor march to their drumbeat.

In my many meetings with John Viczian, the President of the Baptist Union, we always met at Aradi Street in the presence of several other men. I felt that somewhere, buried underneath all of the politics and administration, John was a man who once had a very big heart for things of the Lord. I knew there had been a ministry of tears in his life, and I told him so one day. I learned he had a beautiful daughter who, while traveling back from some church youth meetings, was involved in a horrible automobile accident and taken Home to be with the Lord. John and his wife were heartbroken.

I knew John deeply cared about young people and wanted to see them brought to the Savior, and yet this man constantly "beat" on me. I understood this must have been because Miklos jerked very hard on his chain. I could never talk to John alone. On several occasions I asked him, "John, the next time I come to Hungary, I want to have dinner with you alone. I want to have some hours alone with you. You speak English and you understand me. We don't need an interpreter. I want to be able to share my heart with you and to learn more of your heart."

He always assured me that would happen, but it never did. After one verbal battle in Second Heaven, John Viczian walked out to the street with me. It was raining and I had a taxi waiting. As we stood there in the rain, realizing I again had been cheated out of any one-on-one time with this brother, I said, "John, there are some things I need to say to you. You are very important to the Church in Hungary. There are men in this country who would like to do away with you and your position. There are those who, if they could, would do this to you," I said, snapping my fingers in the air, "but God has kept you here in this position for a reason. We want you to be our friend and we want to be a friend to you. I can tell you that Word of Life will help the Church in Hungary by bringing hundreds of Hungarian young people to Jesus Christ. You need us, John. Don't fight us. Let us help you in your goal of winning the Hungarian youth to Jesus."

He just stood there in the rain, his eyes welling up with tears, and said to me, "How do you know about what you have just said?"

I responded, "A friend of mine told me this, and he also said that you are a man who once had a great heart for God."

"Who told you all of this?" John asked again.

"Pastor Geza Kovacs," I answered him.

"Geza told you that?" he asked in astonishment. "Geza Kovacs told you that I had a heart for God?"

"Yes," I said, "he told me that as recently as this week."

"I cannot believe that Geza would have told you something like that."

Tears coursed down this man's cheeks. He turned and went back into his office at Aradi Street, and I stepped into my taxi to return to my hotel room.

The Monastery at Oroszlany

Zoltan Kovacs was the first to sense the loosening of controls within the government as far as their openness to business interests from the West. He heard of some pieces of property being considered for sale to hotel chains or other business development interests from the West. One of these was an old monastery in the town of Oroszlany, about an hour's drive west of Budapest on the way to Vienna.

I asked Zoltan to contact the city officials in Oroszlany to set up an appointment with us to talk about their monastery and possibly even to inspect it. This would be the first property we would look at without prior government approval, completely on our own. Zoltan very graciously arranged the meeting and on our next trip back to Budapest, Zoltan, Pastor Geza, and Ildiko Kovacs joined me in visiting the monastery property.

This was a beautiful facility. It was an old monastery that suffered severe damage from bombs during World War II. A part of the original structure remained standing as a monument. The city of Oroszlany had started investing quite heavily to renovate many of the buildings, but the entire renovation project was only about a quarter completed. Their goal was to attract a tourist hotel company to buy the facility thereby bringing Western cash into their local economy.

After thoroughly inspecting the property and taking many pictures, we went to the city chambers to meet with members of the city council. Although we had previously met with church government officials, this was the first time we had met with any civil government officials to explain exactly who we were and of our desire to see Hungarian young people brought to Jesus Christ. It was a new experience for us all.

We were amazed at the thorough attention these officials gave to us and what appeared to be their openness to our talking about the effective means Word of Life uses to spread the Gospel. We told them we were interested in their property if we could buy it at a very low threshold price, allowing us to invest all our money in renovating the buildings and grounds. They seemed to be very open and agreed to talk further about this, at least in principle.

We were excited about their open response and willingness to talk. We left the meeting in Oroszlany's city hall with great excitement in our hearts and a feeling that what we wanted to do in Hungary was within the realm of possibility. We knew we had knowingly made this approach to the city fathers without the express and direct prior approval of the men in Second Heaven and the Department of Religion. In essence, we made an attempt to bypass them. We did not know if it would really be possible to carry out this transaction or whether the hammer would fall on us somewhere along the line. The city council members agreed they would talk with the Ministry of Finance and see if they could get some kind of a deal approved for us. We agreed that we could do nothing without the approval of our Board of Directors in the United States.

Anything agreed upon that day in Oroszlany was done only in principle. However, having gotten at least this far was cause for great rejoicing and jubilation! I had the feeling that the negotiations with the officials at Oroszlany City Hall were only the beginning. On the other hand, I also felt we were up against a sleeping giant that might wake up and step on us!

CHAPTER 7

OUT OF CONTROL
AND IN THE DITCH

By now I had made many trips to Budapest. I knew the streets of that city better than the streets of cities in my own country. I knew many government leaders, the hierarchy, and many pastors and Christian leaders, and I was known to many people in Hungary as well. To this point, nothing negative had happened except for the continual reprimands from the boys in Second Heaven, who always did their best to control us. With assurances that changes were beginning to take place in the Kadar government, we began to feel freer than we really were. I paid little heed to the warning of Dr. Gayer, our attorney, "Never forget where you are."

Many of the Christian leaders in Hungary looked upon our Word of Life men, me in particular, with amazement. They did not have the liberty to take the freedoms that we did. They all had Hungarian citizenship and passports. We were, at this point in time, pushing the limits of change in our activities. We knew we were making waves, but somehow we wanted to find out just where the line was drawn, allowing the Hungarian believers to sit back and watch. We foreigners would get the ax, not them.

I remember speaking to two of the most trusted pastors I knew in Hungary, Pastor Daniel Monus of the Kiskoris Baptist Church, and Pastor Geza Kovacs.

"There are times I wake up in the middle of the night thinking about you men," I told them. "We have been in your churches and you have helped us get into many other churches where we not only preached the Gospel, but also extended public invitations. Literally hundreds of Hungarians responded to our Gospel invitations. I wake up wondering, 'Will the hammer fall?' All these people who have made public professions of faith are known to the authorities. Yes, there has been change in the government, but it is still a possibility that these believers who have confessed publicly could be called in for questioning. Will the government allow us to go just so far and then, all of a sudden, round up all these people? Will these pastors in whose churches we have preached the gospel be called in before the authorities for questioning or, possibly, imprisonment?"

I told these two godly pastors how fearful I was for them. Should we continue to invite people to receive Christ publicly at our meetings, or should we back off? Both men responded the same way.

"What can they do to us? Put us in prison? We doubt that will happen, but should that happen, it will be worth it to see these people coming to know Christ as Savior. Don't stop. Keep on giving Gospel invitations. Keep preaching hard to the young people of our country."

By continuing to conduct meetings with Gospel invitations I am certain that many in the government perceived us as loose cannons. In my strategy, I wanted to get around all of the controls placed on us by the men in Second Heaven. But I knew I could not get around the controls placed upon us by the Minister of Religion in the State Office of Church, Dr. Imre Miklos.

It was my belief, however, that the men in Second Heaven were not reporting *everything* to Dr. Miklos. My incorrect perception of Dr. Miklos was that he wanted us to spend money and buy some property, and that it was the fellows in the hierarchy who did not want us to buy property independently. It was my opinion that they wanted the property in their name so they could control it.

So I began trying to find a way to work around the hierarchy and go directly to this atheist, the Minister of Religion.

I had sent another telex to Dr. Miklos asking to meet with him on my next trip. I received no response to this second telex. What did the lack of response mean? Had he received it? Did he have an interpreter to translate the telex, or did he just choose to ignore it? On the previous trip, I had been met with such a cordial response from Miklos, but was he cordial only because word had come down from Secretariat Grosz that he should meet with me? There seemed a great inconsistency between his apparent cordiality and his continued lack of response to my telexed messages.

Upon my return to Budapest I went directly to the State Office of Church and asked to speak to Dr. Miklos. I was purposely breaking all protocol. It was a big gamble. I did not tell the men at Aradi Street (Second Heaven) about my plans or intentions, but I soon learned that Miklos was in direct contact with them and let them know every move I made. He again received me cordially and, as a matter of fact, we exchanged gifts. However, by the time of my next meeting with the boys in Second Heaven, they had learned of my abrupt meeting with Miklos and they were furious. They now knew I had neither requested their permission nor informed them of my actions. The stakes certainly were getting higher.

Some time previous to this, I was in London and went to the office of my Jewish friend, Michael Kovacs. I told him of our activities in Hungary and our desire to find a castle. Wanting to help in some way he suddenly said, "I have an idea. I know of a man who has a castle and wants to sell it. You go over and see this man. Tell him I sent you and he will gladly receive you. He has a beautiful castle that has been renovated and, who knows, maybe he will sell it to you at a good price. This man is very powerful in Hungary. Kadar thinks he is Jesus Christ."

"What do you mean by that statement?" I asked him.

"Well, you know. Kadar thinks he is like an assistant God. He can do anything."

I wanted to know, "What, exactly, does this man do?"

"He is in control of all of the media for Kadar," Michael answered. "He manages the press and the media so well that Kadar thinks he can do anything. He is very close to Kadar and is the chairman of all the Hungarian newspapers. Be sure to tell him I sent you. And, by the way, be sure to talk to him like you talked to me, yes?"

In other words, my friend Michael wanted me to tell Norbert Shiklosi about Jesus Christ, the Messiah.

On that trip to Budapest, I telephoned the number for Norbert Shiklosi given to me by Michael Kovacs. His response was like everyone else to whom Michael referred me.

"Oh, you are a friend of Michael Kovacs? Come, come immediately." Mr. Shiklosi said. He was a man who was very to the point. "I will send my car for you. At which hotel are you staying?"

As promised, Mr. Shiklosi's car picked me up at the hotel and I was driven to the large publishing firm he headed, where more than one Hungarian newspaper was printed. I arrived with a Ryrie Study Bible in hand as a gift for Mr. Shiklosi and I gave my talk that had become standard by now; expressing to Mr. Shiklosi exactly who I was and why I was there. I told him about Jesus Christ and about Word of Life's intentions in Hungary. He seemed very interested.

Mr. Shiklosi then showed me photographs of his castle. It was one of the most beautiful buildings I had seen. However, the asking price amounted to one million US dollars. That was far beyond anything we could consider at Word of Life. I told Mr. Shiklosi the price was just too high for what we had to offer, although certainly the castle was well worth the amount.

Following my appointment with this very powerful and important man, I would be going to Aradi Street to meet with the boys in Second Heaven. By now they would be furious with me for being so very late. Then I did something that was probably done in the flesh. They had no idea I would be meeting with Mr. Shiklosi, or that I even knew anyone with his magnitude of political power.

As I left, I told Dr. Shiklosi's English-speaking secretary that my next appointment was at Free Church headquarters on Aradi Street and that I was running about half an hour late. Would she be so kind as to telephone their office to tell them where I was and that I would arrive there shortly? Frankly, I felt that maybe if they realized I had contact with people so high in power, they might back off just a little. The exact opposite was true.

When I arrived at Aradi Street, Dr. Szakacs, John Viczian, and Emil Kiss were all in one room, pacing in circles. They pounced on me like a hungry dog on a hamburger. I told them where I had been and they replied, "Yes, we know."

John Viczian boomed, "Do you know who this man is? Do you know how powerful he is here in Hungary? Do you know what he can do to you...or what he can do to us?"

Yes, I thought to myself, *you are especially concerned with what he could do to "us."* I had obviously miscalculated. Instead of causing them to back off, I had jacked up the odds. This was not what I had wanted to do. They now perceived me as a totally loose cannon, as one who could cause great damage and who was not marching to their drumbeat, and one that somehow simply had to be controlled. They feared the harm I could do to them because I was definitely out of their "box."

After taking a strong verbal rebuke I left their office. Feeling let down that my plans had not worked out positively, I took a taxi to my hotel and went for a long walk down along the Danube, past the beautiful Vigado Concert Hall. This was one of the loveliest buildings in all of Eastern Europe. It stood right on the bank of the beautiful Danube River in downtown Budapest. Every time I walked by the Vigado Concert Hall I would begin to dream. I dreamed of bringing the Word of Life Collegians from the United States to this beautiful concert hall where they would present the *Passion Play* in English. I even planned how, since the Collegians spoke no Hungarian, they would sing in English and the programs would have the script and all the lyrics translated into Hungarian.

The *Passion Play* is the story of the life of Christ, His humiliation, suffering, crucifixion and resurrection. It first became famous centuries ago in Europe. It is a religious play, but also secular, and a classic, and it would be wonderful if it could be performed in Hungary's Vigado.

I dreamed of renting the Vigado for the five nights leading up to Easter, having a place where Hungarian believers could bring their unsaved friends to hear the gospel in the form of the *Passion Play*. How wonderful it would be for the Christians to be able to enter the Vigado! Most Hungarian Christians I knew never frequented such a place. First of all, they could not afford to do so. Secondly, it was mainly those in high government society who would attend performances there.

So as I walked by the hall, I thought like an American would think in the United States, with all the freedom of opportunity afforded us by a democratic government, and not as one would think in a Communist country, with its many restrictions. I walked into the Vigado and to the office of the general manager. When I found a secretary who knew limited English, I presented my business card and asked to speak to the director of the Vigado. An appointment was made for later that day when I could return with an interpreter.

Knowing my friend, Dr. Akos Bukovsky, worked in a chemical company just around the corner from Vaci Utca, I walked to his office. I needed to be very careful that people in his company not be suspicious of me as an American. Approaching the receptionist I asked to see Dr. Bukovsky and I presented my card.

"I am an old friend of his from America," I told her. "I happen to be in Budapest for a day or two and I would like to see my old friend."

It is true we were old friends. By now we had known each other for all of two years. Old is a relative term, is it not?

When Akos met me in the waiting room he seemed quite tense. I told him what I had just done at the Vigado and asked if he might accompany me to my appointment with the assistant director of the concert hall that afternoon. He agreed, but on the way to the Vigado he gave me a very stern lecture (which, by now, he was very good at delivering) and instructed me to never, ever again contact him at his place of business. It was too risky. He did not want to be identified with Westerners. It could jeopardize his position in the pharmaceutical company.

We walked to the Vigado and up to the assistant director's office. He met us at his office door with a warm and welcoming smile.

I had brought along my Word of Life book of foreign affairs to show this man. It contained many photographs of WOL camps and institutions around the world. The book also listed the staff, both American and national personnel, of which the national staff list was notably longer. In addition, there were facts and figures, including the amount of American dollars invested in that country from the beginning. This always impressed people in Eastern Europe, especially those at the diplomatic level.

We sat down with the assistant director and showed him the book, which we felt would give us credibility and demonstrate that we were not just a small company from America. He looked through it carefully, remarking positively on how beautiful the camps were, and how happy the young people looked.

Through Dr. Bukovsky's interpreting, the assistant director said to me, "We do perform the *Passion Play* here in Hungary, but not in such a place as the Vigado. Instead, it is performed in many of the large churches. That way, the religious people feel comfortable attending. Here at the Vigado we have no religious performances, only cultural productions."

I explained that in America, when we produce and perform the *Passion Play,* we rent large music halls similar to the Vigado. We do this in hopes that the non-religious will come. I agreed that if the play is done in churches, it is the religious who mainly attend, but we were interested in having the non-religious come as well. I then asked him, "Is it not true that the *Passion Play* is highly cultural?"

He had to agree.

"Yes," he said, and Akos translated, "in fact the play does cross over into the cultural area and, therefore, we *would* consider hosting such a performance."

I told the assistant director we intended to secure permission from the State Office of Church and that I merely wanted to learn if the Vigado management would consider such a performance.

"Yes," he said, "we are open to it, and we can agree in principle, as long as you obtain proper clearance."

He then took us on a small tour of the Vigado. We walked through the beautiful music hall and looked at the stage, and all the gorgeous architecture. I was very hopeful, for the assistant director had agreed in principle to my request. Was this too much to dream? Was it too high a goal? Even my good friend Dr. Bukovsky, though I believe he felt I was running too fast, seemed actually excited that we had gotten this far.

As I realized what I was doing I had to ask myself, *Am I, in fact, a loose cannon on the Hungarian scene, or am I directed by God?* Things were moving so rapidly and building momentum. I believed in my heart that what I was doing was exactly what the Lord wanted me to do. Yet, I confess that I felt there was every possibility that at any moment the roof could come crashing in on me.

Zoltan Kovacs and I often talked about the new freedoms we perceived were just ahead in government. Zoltan was a futuristic and positive individual. He either had contacts with people very high up in various government positions, or he was not afraid to contact them and discuss the new possibilities he envisioned for Hungary. This greatly encouraged me and I felt Hungary was on the verge of a new era.

I had begun making statements about the political future of Hungary. Without doubt, I should have been more careful where, and to whom I made these comments. I had heard Michael Kovacs postulate that he felt his friend Mr. Grosz, then the number one Secretariat in the country, would eventually be the one to replace Kadar and that very probably Kadar was grooming Grosz for this position. After all, Grosz was the one who appeared to be encouraging the government to move towards a quasi-capitalistic posture. They were now allowing small privately-owned businesses to exist. The government sought out Western funds and hard currency to be invested in Hungary. They were allowing some freedoms in the area of finance. So I would often comment (to various people) how Grosz was probably being groomed to replace Kadar. Every time I mentioned this it brought a strong response from the Hungarians. They all would say emphatically, "No, no, not Grosz. Who is Grosz? He is nobody. You are mistaken."

Only recently did I learn why Grosz was selected over others to become Prime Minister and eventually replace Kadar as Chairman of the Communist Party. A Communist faithful by the name of Berecz, coming from a peasant background, had become Chairman of the International Department of Hungary's Communist Party. In the Communist mentality, he had a perfect background. However, because of his peasant background, he also offended the intellectual community. Grosz, meanwhile, was an economist, who was quietly being influenced by a very wealthy capitalist, my friend Michael Kovacs. Kadar saw Grosz as acceptable to both the intellectual community and the party. In addition, by using a quasi-capitalistic approach, he was successfully stimulating the economy.

I was very unwise to involve myself in any way in conversation about the political future of Hungary. I knew my comments and words were being tape recorded or repeated, and yet it was very hard to get used to having to mind what I said. This was foolish of me, for the officials in denominational headquarters (Second Heaven) were learning about my comments. In time, Miklos heard reports of my statements. They were surprised to learn that my political predictions were well founded, for at this time Communist Chairman Kadar very abruptly appointed Grosz to be Prime Minister. This came as a great surprise to everyone in Hungary, except for my friend Michael Kovacs. It came as a surprise especially to those working in the government.

About six weeks after this we returned to Budapest, bringing with us people from our Word of Life Board of Directors. Joining us were Dr. Charles Ryrie, Perry Brown, Bob and Mary Steed, and several other business couples as well as George and Marcia Slothower, members of our staff at Schroon Lake.

On this important trip in April 1987, we returned to Oroszlany to re-inspect the beautiful monastery property and meet with members of the city council, including a Member of Parliament. From my diary I quote: "All of us inspected the potential property and met with the city council of Oroszlany. We learned that the cost had escalated beyond belief, too much for us to deal with. What we had believed was a great possibility faded into unreality. In the process of all this, I had sidestepped some proper protocol (I have always had a problem with proper protocol since my high school days) and before the day was over, I went into the lions' den where there was roaring and gnashing of teeth. It wasn't much fun, but then survival is success under some circumstances. The atmosphere became quite tense at times."

I was referring, in my notes, to a very bad scene that occurred after our meeting with the city council. We met with the city council in Oroszlany and had, what I considered, a very good time in telling them again exactly who we were and that we desired to give young Hungarians a proper basis for living a life in Jesus Christ. They listened intently as I explained our whole methodology and approach to working with young people.

After that, we drove from the City Hall at Oroszlany to the Kovacs home for a nice dinner before returning to the Erjabet Hotel in Budapest. Shortly after I entered the hotel lobby, I knew I was in deep trouble. My friend John Viczian, the President of the Baptist Union, stood waiting nervously for us in the lobby. As a matter of fact, he had been waiting for three solid hours. At their approach, John stopped pacing and greeted my American guests. As I was not with them at that moment, he asked them where I was. George Slothower caught me as I passed through the lobby and took me over to John.

John greeted me courteously and then urgently whispered, "I must talk with you, and I must talk with you right now. It is very important."

I could tell he was very distressed, so we went to a far corner of the restaurant at the Erjabet Hotel and sat at a table by ourselves. John began telling me how Miklos had been in contact with him rather abruptly. He recounted how that morning he had been in a meeting in his office with leaders from the American Bible Society, when Miklos telephoned and insisted that he be put right through to John. John realized the call was urgent, so he excused himself and went to the phone. Miklos said something like this:

"Can't you control this man, Bubar? I told you I want him controlled. I want him watched closely, and if you cannot do it, I will get someone else to do it very effectively."

John said to me, "Word of Life is finished in Hungary. You are finished."

When I asked why he would say that, he replied, "Because you have lied to us. You have not kept your word. You have not reported to us and let us know of your moves. You are finished. Word of Life is finished in Hungary." He repeated this several times.

We continued in a verbal combat zone for nearly three hours in that restaurant. I asked him how he felt we had lied to him. He referred to some statements made by Brother Tom Mahairas way back in 1985 when Tom, as our guest, spoke at our first youth camp in Hungary.

Tom had looked around at the limited facilities at Camp Tahi and said, "Oh, what a beautiful place you have here. You should build a building over there, and you ought to have a building over here and this type of a building down there..." In a few words he had, more or less, laid out the potential of things they could do for this Baptist-owned youth camp at Tahi.

To people with a listening ear and who have little or nothing, when a "rich American" arrives on the scene and starts making suggestions as to what *might* be done, they assume you are going to pay to have it done. Though I had told President Viczian several times that Tom Mahairas does *not* speak for Word of Life, and that he was only speaking as an interested brother in Christ who saw the potential of Camp Tahi, the hierarchy took his words as a promise. Therefore, because Word of Life had not spent $25,000 or more in doing these things, they believed Word of Life had lied about their intentions. Also, because we had not reported to them our every move, we were being uncooperative. I must say, of all the times I have verbally sparred, this incident was without question, the worst. Word of Life was at its lowest point in its history in Hungary. On top of it, I was arguing with John, who was a man I cared very much about, and who cared about me and about Word of Life.

It also appeared that, at this time, Dr. Miklos had put out word through the Baptist Union to the Hungarian Baptist pastors that Paul Bubar should not be allowed to preach in any of their churches because, at the least, he worked for the US government and, at worst, he was a member of the US Central Intelligence Agency. Evidently, Miklos based those claims on the fact that I had accurately predicted that Grosz would one day be in a position to replace the Chairman of the Communist Party, Janos Kadar.

When Grosz was appointed as Kadar's Prime Minister, Miklos remembered that I had made those predictions and reasoned, "How would this man, Bubar, have access to such information? How did he know that Grosz would be appointed Prime Minister? Who was his source of information? He must have a contact high up in government. He probably works for the United States government. He probably even works for the CIA."

Somehow, through reasoning like this, Miklos came to that conclusion and put the word out in Hungary. This was not a good feeling. To be in a Communist country and to have a label of working for the United States Central Intelligence Agency is about as bad as having terminal cancer.

CHAPTER 8

DR. ALEX HARASZTI:
RUSSIAN AGENT OR
BRILLIANT SERVANT?

Dr. Alexander Haraszti was a brilliant surgeon and gynecologist. Both he and his wife, Rosalie, were medical doctors with degrees from Hungarian Universities. Dr. Haraszti was, as a young man, a student of theology and a pastor of the Nejipest Baptist Church in Budapest. He also taught at the Baptist Seminary in Buda. Following the Revolution in 1956, he and Rosalie immigrated to the United States and eventually settled near Atlanta, Georgia.

Over the years Dr. Haraszti had, I understand, collected two or three earned doctorates as well as a Masters Degree in Theology. Though deeply involved in the Hungarian Baptist Church movement in North America, he had at the same time actively participated in the Hungarian Baptist movement in Hungary and in Christian efforts in other parts of Eastern Europe. He was a great student of Eastern European diplomacy under Communist domination.

From the very beginning of our dealings in Hungary, I heard the name of Dr. Alex Haraszti, sometimes in a very positive light, but other times in a very negative sense. I soon learned that in Hungary, there were those who admired him and those who wanted nothing to do with him.

One evening, a young man who was a leader of the Hungarian underground church, told me, "Haraszti is a devil. He cannot be trusted. He is an agent of Soviet Russia. Have nothing to do with him."

I thought, *I wonder if that is really true. I would like to find that out for myself.*

By that time I had begun to learn how Hungarian Christians think. For many years, they were under oppression for their Christianity. So much so that if you were the son or daughter of Christian parents, you would not be able to enroll in a State University. This was especially true for the children of a pastor. Pastors would never have any access to the government through political figures, and if they had clout with anyone in government it was automatically assumed they were given political clout because they had played "footsies" with people in the Communist Party.

It didn't matter if you were only bold or had a gutsy personality and simply forged ahead and addressed issues and people outspokenly. If you spoke out and were listened to by any of the Communist figures, Hungarian Christians assumed that you had gotten that political clout by compromising your convictions and by being a party to Communist ideals. I knew all of this, and I wondered if maybe that was why Dr. Haraszti was getting bad press with many Hungarian believers.

On the other hand, if he were not a party to any of the Communist leaders but instead simply a very wise, prudent, studious negotiator, I wanted to have something to do with him. I knew he was a student of Eastern European governments and politics. In fact, the Billy Graham Organization retained him as a consultant on Eastern European affairs. I knew he had been the chief negotiator in influencing Billy Graham's Crusades and meetings in much of Eastern Europe, including the Soviet Union.

I knew he was a very influential man and that because of the circles in which he traveled, he was the only man known to me who had any clout or influence over Dr. Miklos, who held an iron fist over all of the churches in Hungary.

I learned that indeed Dr. Haraszti was very well connected. He had cultivated a relationship with Dr. Berecz, who was the Chairman of the International Department of the Communist Party. Miklos knew this and, as far as I could tell, he either greatly admired or feared Berecz. Therefore, Miklos always gave great deference to Dr. Haraszti.

For many months I pondered and prayed as to whether I should make contact with Haraszti. Some Christians called him a devil; others said he was a good man. Who should I believe? I somehow felt in my heart that Haraszti was key to any further forward movement for us in that country.

This was, for us, the most discouraging time for our efforts in Eastern Europe. It appeared there could be no further progress for Word of Life in Hungary, since we had been instructed by Hungarian officials not to return. I dared not share this information with too many people, and especially not with my superiors. Knowing them and their great love and concern for me, if I were to relay to them the actual situation they might refuse to allow me to return for fear of my being arrested. I knew I needed to share this news with them, but I wanted to wait and see if the situation might change.

I wanted to tell my superiors about Dr. Haraszti, to assure them of this man's brilliance and to obtain their permission to contact him. However, I also felt that with the words of advice we had been given in Hungary about his being an agent of Soviet Russia, my chances of getting permission were next to impossible. I felt they would tell me to leave the issue alone.

Do you knowingly, willfully do something your superiors would not want you to do? I had never done such a thing in my twenty-eight years of ministry with Word of Life. I always practiced the principle that the voice of your superiors is as the voice of God, since God placed them over you. In actuality, they had not told me to avoid Haraszti. As a matter of fact, they didn't know very much about him.

I heard so much bad press on Haraszti in Hungary that I almost feared him, or feared contacting him. I was afraid that people in Hungary would see it as a religious compromise, and that it would reflect badly on Word of Life. I prayed much about this matter and felt compelled to at least get in touch with the man informally, not in any official capacity. Dr. Haraszti lived in the U.S., in the Atlanta area, and I called directory assistance to obtain his office phone number.

I called Dr. Haraszti on a Friday afternoon in August of 1987. I calculated that at 2:00 p.m. eastern time it would be 8:00 p.m. in Budapest on Friday, a weekend night. Few Communist officials in Hungary had home telephones and no one would be at their Budapest offices. It would be impossible for Dr. Haraszti to call anyone in Hungary for information at that time. I felt safe contacting him. I planned to say I would be passing through Atlanta the next day and wanted to see him for a few minutes. I wanted to see what, if anything, Dr. Haraszti knew about Word of Life.

His secretary answered my phone call. The secretary, with a thick Hungarian accent, took the exact spelling of my name, the exact spelling of the organization I represented, the address, and phone number. She then placed me on hold while passing the information to the doctor. Soon he came to the phone.

I introduced myself and told him of my hopes to meet. Dr. Haraszti said he could not see me until the following week. I thought this to be a great disadvantage, but knowing I needed to see him, I agreed.

The day to meet came. Nervous and excited, I met Dr. Haraszti at a Western Sizzler restaurant near the Atlanta airport. There, what was meant to be a few brief minutes of interchange became a five-hour crash course in Eastern European diplomacy.

Talking over dinner, I used the same approach I used so advantageously in Hungary and Eastern Europe. I took a long drink of cold water and began, "I am not a diplomat. I am just a simple preacher and administrator. I am very naive when it comes to diplomacy."

Dr. Haraszti immediately rebuked me. He reached his hand across the table and said, "Excuse me. Do not tell me you are naive. You are not naive. You are very bright. You know what you are doing, so don't act naive. That won't work anymore. You are a very clever person. Now, let's have a good understanding right from the beginning. "

From that point on, I shot completely straight with Dr. Haraszti. I knew there was no need to beat around the bush. I told him everything I had done in Eastern Europe. I told him I knew I was in trouble with Miklos and the government. I said I was aware he had great influence over this atheistic Communist who had a stranglehold on all the churches in Hungary. And I wound up my tale by asking him for his help in getting us through the difficult impasse we were in with Miklos.

This gentlemanly, white-haired man said, "How much money can I tell the Hungarian authorities you are willing to spend? Remember, in Hungary it is dollars for Gospel. They are not the least bit interested in your Gospel. They are interested strictly in the amount you are willing to spend. Now, how much will you spend for permission to preach the Gospel to the youth of Hungary?"

I remember thinking; *I have no authority to spend any dollars. My superiors do not even know I'm here with this man. There is no way I can commit myself to any amount.*

I responded faintly, "Well, sir, I don't know exactly how much we are willing to spend."

He replied straightforwardly, "Nonsense, you are the director of foreign relations for your organization. You have thought about it many times. This is not a new idea to you. You know exactly the amount."

He slapped the table with his flattened hand. I tried not to jump in response. But I was very hesitant to respond with a dollar amount.

He asked again, "How much? Tell me, how much are you willing to spend?"

The truth was I had no authority to advance any amount to him. At this time, my superiors were very much interested in Word of Life's presence in Eastern Europe, but we never discussed how much money we would ultimately part with to minister there.

Dr. Haraszti continued, "Well, how much?"

I had better give him a low figure, I thought to myself, *especially one I can live with, should I have to produce the funds myself. But how much is low?*

I answered rather faintly, yet, trying to appear confident. "I believe that we would probably be willing to spend $200,000 over a ten-year period."

I quickly calculated in my mind, and added, "That is only $20,000 per year. I believe Word of Life would be willing to generate those kinds of funds to have a presence in Eastern Europe."

Dr. Haraszti stared at me silently for what seemed like an eternity, probably all of one minute. Finally, he spoke, "Yes, yes, I think they would be interested in that. I will see what I can do for you.

"Still," he continued, "there is something else you must do. You must separate yourself from Geza Kovacs. Kovacs is so hated by those in authority that you will not be allowed to do anything while maintaining close contact with him. You must break off any relationship with him immediately. I tell you, sever your connection with Kovacs, and you can move ahead."

I had expected this, but I did not want to hear it. I said, "I was told this once before by Dr. Szakacs in Budapest. I will have to tell you what I told him. Geza Kovacs and I are friends of the heart, not mere acquaintances. You do not have the right to determine friends of the heart. I'm afraid I cannot meet that demand."

Rather matter-of-factly, Dr. Haraszti continued, "You simply have a choice to make. It is simple: dollars for Gospel and get rid of Kovacs. There is nothing more I can do for you. That is my advice."

Before we left each other, Dr. Haraszti shook my hand firmly and said, "Now, remember, to contact me before you leave for Budapest the next time. You be certain to let me know your decision."

We parted company and I went on my way back to the Atlanta airport. I knew I had been in the presence of a very brilliant, straightforward man who very well understood Eastern European diplomacy. I knew in my heart that this man was not an agent of Soviet Russia but, indeed, a servant of the Lord who wanted nothing more than to see Hungarians come to know the Savior. I saw that Dr. Haraszti was willing to lend any influence he could to see that I was accepted back in Hungary. I did not feel I could meet his demands, especially relating to Geza Kovacs, but I gained new respect and admiration for the practicality and honesty of Dr. Alex Haraszti.

Weeks went by and I told no one, other than my wife and my assistant, Len Charron, that I had met with Dr. Haraszti. I didn't really know what to do, but I discussed all of this with my dear wife. She was the most supportive person I ever had in the ministry. Shirley knew I had been threatened with arrest and told not to return to Hungary. She also knew that in my heart I felt the Hungarian authorities were bluffing and that I probably could return without incident, but I wasn't quite sure. I said to my wife one day, "What do you think? Should I chance it and return?"

Her response surprised me, but pleased me very much as she looked me right in the eyes and said, "Of course, you have to return. You didn't start this whole thing…God did. You have no choice. Is there any question in your mind?"

Her response inspired me. She was right.

Weeks passed after my meeting with Dr. Haraszti. In the meantime, Jack Wyrtzen and his wife, Joan, had planned on taking a vacation trip to Europe. They wanted to go to Budapest, a great city for vacationing Westerners. The prices were very low since the US dollar was very strong. You could have a really neat vacation quite inexpensively.

Jack approached me one day, wanting me to set up the trip for him, complete with meetings at the Budafok Baptist Church and at other churches. I pleaded with my boss not to go through with the trip, saying, "Jack, you don't need to go to Budapest at this time."

"Why not?" he asked, looking me straight in the eye.

"Because I can tell you exactly what will happen when you arrive there. You will be summoned to come to Second Heaven (denominational headquarters) and there you will be told that Paul Bubar has been a 'bad boy', and that he doesn't obey very well. You will be asked why you cannot control me. Now, I've told you what they are going to tell you, and you don't need to go through that hassle."

I should have known better than to suggest this to Jack because over the years as I have worked for him, whenever he has felt that God wanted him to do something it was impossible to change his mind. Jack Wyrtzen believed the Lord wanted him to go to Hungary, and that was it.

I told Jack, "I don't know if you should preach at the Budafok Baptist Church. The authorities hate this man, Kovacs. They have told me I should not preach in his church or have anything more to do with him. For you to go there as the top representative in this ministry will deliver the wrong message to the authorities. Couldn't you wait a while?"

"Paul," Jack responded confidently, "I know how to handle these fellows. You just leave it to me."

I thought, but did not verbalize, *Jack Wyrtzen, what experience have you had in dealing with these fellows? I know how clever they are. I know how you can be misled.*

So, Jack and Joan, along with their close friends, board member Leander Chute and his wife, Ann, went on to Budapest. Jack preached at the Budafok Baptist Church and was summoned to denominational headquarters at Aradi Street exactly as I predicted. They questioned him and asked, almost to the word, the exact questions I said they would ask him. However, Jack Wyrtzen can also be a silver fox.

The authorities told him, "Paul Bubar may not return to Hungary. If he does, he will be arrested and thrown out of the country."

Jack, without batting an eye, said through his interpreter, "I don't think you want to do that."

"Why not?" they demanded of him.

"Do you know who Paul Bubar really is?" Jack replied.

Almost leaping out of their chairs they said, "No, but we would like to know who he really is. Who is he?"

Then Jack Wyrtzen began to do something I have heard him do to other staff members many times. Jack thought that there was no one in the world who was any better or any more qualified than people who serve with him on his team. He began to paint a picture of Paul Bubar that was beyond reality.

"Why, Paul Bubar is the Executive Director of our Overseas Division. He is responsible for the ministry of Word of Life in twenty-six countries around the world. He is responsible for Word of Life operations everywhere around the world outside the continental United States. He travels to all of these countries, meeting with the Christian leaders. If he is not permitted to return to Hungary, he will be asked why not. Word will get around. When he is asked that question, Paul will have to give an honest answer. When he does, it will sound as though there is no religious freedom in Hungary. Would it not?"

Jack had just reached out and pressed against a very sensitive wound. You see, the hierarchy wanted to show to the world that there was now religious freedom in their country. They wanted to attract the support of any and every church from the West that they could. They wanted to bring hundreds of thousands, even millions of dollars into their coffers. The government had put out the official word that even the churches were to help by bringing hard Western currency into their economy. They were able to do this by showing how much religious freedom truly existed in Hungary.

With these words from Jack, the hierarchy began to back-pedal. "Well," they said, "why not allow Chuck Kosman to come and not Bubar?" Chuck Kosman was then the Director of Word of Life Germany. They knew him quite well. He was more readily accepted by them than I was. Chuck had not been drawn into the conflict and controversy at this point. They did not perceive him as working for the United States government. They knew he was a Canadian citizen.

Jack's response was instant, "I don't think you want that because, you see, that would be like having the Secretary of State instead of the President or Vice President. Bubar needs to have the freedom to come back to your country and do his business here."

Finally, they grudgingly conceded to Jack's demand. It was John Viczian who spoke.

"All right, he may return," John told Jack. He added this warning, "But I want to remind you, Mr. Wyrtzen, that we have a FBI too, in our country. Our FBI will be two steps behind Paul Bubar at all times. He will be followed. They will know every move he makes, should he return."

When Jack and Joan and their friends returned from Budapest, they reported this good news. Shirley and I were thrilled. I clasped Jack's hand in mine at hearing the news.

"Wonderful!" I said, and then had to laugh a little at the warning. "Actually, nothing has changed there. They always knew where I was and every move I made before."

"They've been tracking him for years," Shirley added, "This is no change."

"I guess you folks have gotten used to this spy game," Jack joked.

But I thought only of the good news of going back to do the work God had given us.

"Praise the Lord, this is great," I made thanks, "I can return!"

Weeks had gone by, and I had not been in contact with Dr. Haraszti or the people in Hungary. I was still praying, pondering, and wondering about what should be our next step. Meanwhile, the Lord was making some other arrangements in some very important areas. After all, Dr. Haraszti was to contact Miklos, the Hungarian President of the State Office of Church. Would Haraszti get in touch with me? Would he let me know when things had been cleared up with Dr. Miklos? Unknown to me, God was still at work, arranging my affairs and the affairs of Word of Life. Nothing was happening by chance.

Living at Schroon Lake for many years were dear friends of ours, George and Norma Swanson. George had spent a lifetime as a career Navy chaplain. After retirement from the Navy, he was a pastor at several churches in New England before receiving an invitation to join the Billy Graham Evangelistic Association as a liaison to pastors, meeting with them in advance of the Graham Crusades. In September of that year, George and Norma had gone to Georgia for a retreat of the Billy Graham Evangelistic Association leaders.

At the retreat, George was stricken with a nagging chest cold and needed to have a prescription filled. His doctor in New York had written the prescription. He did not want to go to another doctor, but he did need a local doctor to authorize the prescription. As George scanned the retreat's program he noticed that Dr. Haraszti was to give a report on events taking place in Eastern Europe. Dr. Haraszti was a licensed doctor in the state of Georgia. Approaching Dr. Haraszti to ask him to write a prescription for him, George presented his official card that read "Billy Graham Evangelistic Association" and his home address. George did this to show Dr. Haraszti that he was a member of the Graham Association and could be trusted.

As Dr. Haraszti looked at the card he noticed the address. He smiled at George and asked, "Schroon Lake, New York. Have you ever heard of an organization called Word of Life?"

"Of course," George answered, smiling back. "I have known Jack Wyrtzen for thirty years. He is a great friend of ours. Word of Life is a great ministry. They work with young people all over the world."

Haraszti continued, "Have you ever heard of a man by the name of Paul Bubar?"

"Why, I have known Paul for twenty-five years," George replied, "ever since he has been with Word of Life. He started the Word of Life Bible Club ministry and has seen it grow to tremendous proportions. More recently, he has been involved with the overseas ministry, directing that for Word of Life. By the way, he has become quite active in Eastern Europe...Hungary in particular. Oh, they would do a great work in Hungary. I wish you could meet him."

That was all Dr. Haraszti needed: the seal of approval from someone he knew was on the same team as he was on. George Swanson attached no significance to that brief conversation, but it was key to Word of Life's forward progression in Eastern Europe.

What George didn't know was that within two weeks of that conversation, Dr. Miklos was going to be in Washington, DC as a guest of the United States Information Agency, and Dr. Haraszti was going to meet with him. At this meeting, Haraszti approached Miklos and spoke to him about me. He said, as if it were nothing at all, "Oh, by the way, you are mistaken about Bubar and Word of Life. He does not work for the United States government. He has nothing to do with the US government. The people with Word of Life are good people, and they will do you much good in Hungary. You should welcome them."

Again, Bubar and Word of Life were given the seal of approval to the one man who could keep us from ministering in Hungary. This had all happened without my knowledge, and I was only able to put these pieces together some weeks after they occurred. There truly was Someone else arranging the affairs of my life and arranging for the ministry of Word of Life to have a permanent role in winning the youth of Hungary to Jesus Christ. I could never have arranged those events; I could never have thought them through to that extent. To God be the glory!

On September 29, 1987, a group of ten people left with me to return to Hungary. This was to be my first visit since receiving the warning of my imminent arrest, should I return. I felt the best way to prove to the Hungarian authorities that I was not any kind of a security threat to them was to have my own family and a number of senior citizens along with me.

Certainly, I would not be foolish enough to do anything to incur the wrath of the Communist government while I had these family members and guests along. We could not get rooms at the Vaci Utca, and there were no hotel vacancies in Budapest. The only available rooms were forty-five minutes outside Budapest in the village of Tahi. There was a new motel there, and we were able to secure a sufficient number of rooms. Here, my wife felt we were constantly under suspicion and surveillance. This made her quite nervous, and she did not believe the ever present, English-speaking "uncle" from Detroit, who was also a guest at the Pension, was only an American tourist.

Our flight arrived in Vienna on September 30, and we drove by van to Hungary. Arriving at Tahi very late at night, we had one day to recuperate from the long flight before driving on to the university city of Debrecen to speak at a great youth rally that had just been arranged. More than two hundred young people flooded the beautiful new Debrecen Baptist Church where Pastor Pocsik (who is now with the Lord after a heart attack), and Pastor Bela Patkai hosted the conference.

Both pastors were warned previously by the hierarchy not to permit me to speak in either of their churches. Were I to speak, serious consequences would follow for these godly men. I was aware of this warning, and as I met with these pastors I asked if they were fearful at all in having me preach in their churches. Bela responded, "What can they do to us? Of course we want you here. We want you to preach the Gospel."

This was during the time when some in Hungary believed that I worked for the United States government and possibly for the Central Intelligence Agency. Everyone seemed nervous. Not wanting the wonderful guests in my party to sense any problem, I acted very nonchalant in their presence. Yet, on the inside, I felt rather nervous.

I did not want to meet the demands to break ties with Pastor Kovacs, and I wondered if that decision would have any bearing on the future. According to my notes, our first day back in Budapest brought us immediately into a meeting with officials to discuss the rumors regarding my occupation and lay them to rest. I assured them that in no way did I have anything to do with the United States government other than paying taxes, and that I definitely had no connections with the Central Intelligence Agency. I explained my awareness of these rumors and stressed to them that the rumors simply were not true. I also told them of my contact with Dr. Haraszti and said how I thought he would soon be in touch with them. Through God's grace we were permitted to continue to function in Hungary, at least temporarily. The Hungarian officials even agreed to our planned return in December for the express purpose of meeting with the church hierarchy to discuss the future of Word of Life in Hungary.

Friday night we found ourselves in a wonderful church in Nyiregyhaza near the Russian-Romanian border. This was the church where Bela Patkai was the pastor. He was a youthful man who loved young people. Bela Patkai was not especially in the good graces of the government leaders or the church hierarchy. He did not like to be controlled by the government.

What a sweet time of fellowship and renewing of friendships we had that evening. The church was filled, mostly with young people. I was delighted to have my son, Dan, along on that trip. He shared his testimony and told how God called him to Europe as a missionary. At that time, as far as Dan knew, he was headed to Sweden, to work through Word of Life to bring young people to Christ. Dan was young himself, about twenty-three years of age.

Dan was a man who was very sensitive to God's direction in his life, and because of that he would do whatever he felt God would want him to do. On that trip he fell in love with the Hungarian people, and I knew God could easily redirect him to this great land should the Lord open those doors.

As everything else in this wonderful story, Dan's being on this tourist trip to Hungary was not an accident, or merely by chance. It would clearly be the hand of God's careful direction and would become obvious in several months when he would return as a missionary with Elet Szava (Word of Life) in Hungary.

Saturday I served as the main speaker at a Baptist Youth Conference with some three hundred young people in attendance. The conference was held at the beautiful new Baptist church in Debrecen. Pastor Pocsik, as he so often had before, opened his arms wide to us. I challenged the youth to surrender their lives to the call of God to become pastors and Christian workers in Hungary. More than twenty responded to that invitation and seven others came forward to receive salvation that day. This was just more confirmation of our wonderful, sovereign God's desire for us to continue the ministry in Hungary. On this trip I tried to keep as low a profile as possible. I was careful to avoid any activity that might be interpreted as disrespectful of Hungarian laws and regulations. I stayed very close to my dear wife, my mother-in-law, my son, and our guests who joined me not only in Hungary, but also in Germany and on to Sweden before returning to the United States.

In our brief meeting with the hierarchy, however, we set up an appointment for December 7, 1987, when we would return without our guests for some very straightforward talk with the leaders to discuss the future of our ministry in that country.

This was also the trip in which another promise was fulfilled. Jack Wyrtzen, on his previous trip, was promised that the Hungarian government also has a FBI and should Paul Bubar return, their FBI would be two steps behind his every move. I felt that promise was carried out.

It was obvious "my friends" were with me at every turn. This was so obvious it was almost a joke. Their presence was not a problem since I had nothing to hide. Word of Life is not a clandestine operation.

We left Budapest in the Word of Life van and drove through Vienna to Starnberg, Germany and on to an exploratory trip in Sweden.

It was December when we would return to settle, conclusively, the entire matter of our future in Hungary. My faithful associate, Len Charron, accompanied me on this next trip. Len joined the staff of Word of Life Bible Clubs a few years earlier as our business manager. He came out of the world of business and had been a Bible Club leader and an associate staff member in New England for a number of years. He often traveled with me to large gatherings of our staff, such as we would have at the Castles in Germany that December. As the business manager, Len would be on hand to help our overseas directors work through many of the problems they face in directing a ministry in a foreign country. Len returned with me to Budapest for one of the most difficult and yet most rewarding trips I experienced. At least on this trip

I would be returning with some hope. I had been promised that I would have an opportunity to meet privately with John Viczian and, possibly, we would even have an independent interpreter.

Until this time, the interpreters had always been a member of the hierarchy, and so I never was quite sure whether I was being understood or interpreted accurately. I was told we never had independent interpreters because the hierarchy did not want anyone in the country to know the nature of their conversations with foreigners, so the interpreters were always kept within their inner circle. I felt the quality of their interpreting was poor at best.

Two days before I left for Budapest I decided to keep my promise to Dr. Haraszti and telephoned him before returning to Hungary. It was a Sunday evening when I put through a call to his residence in Atlanta. A young male voice answered. I learned later that this was the doctor's grandson. When I asked to speak to Dr. Haraszti he exclaimed, "Oh, you have just missed him. He just left for the airport. I am sorry."

"Oh," I said, "I so much wanted to talk to him. When will he return?"

The grandson replied, "It will be at least two weeks before he is back in Atlanta. He is leaving now for Moscow."

I told the young man, "Should he call his home, be certain that he knows I called asking for him, and tell him I am leaving in two days for Budapest." As I hung up the phone, my mind was flooded with thoughts, thoughts I did not like to think.

You see, at this point, I still did not know who Haraszti was. Was he friend or foe? I wondered whether he was what the people in Hungary described, or whether he was a brilliant negotiator and servant of Jesus Christ. I muttered to myself, hanging up the phone, "That figures. Of course he is in Moscow. He is probably getting more instructions."

I had no reason to think that, but my mind had been flavored by the comments from underground church leaders in Budapest. I shared the conversation with my wife.

"Are you afraid to return to Budapest?" Shirley asked.

"No, not really," I said. "It's just like you said yourself: I did not start this whole mission. From the beginning, Hungary has not been my idea. It is something I have found myself thrust into and caught up in. It has been of God from the beginning. If there is anything to fear, the Lord is just going to have to take care of things for me."

My dear wife responded, "Yes, you must return. You have no choice. The Lord will take care of everything for us, and the Lord will take care of you."

Her words of encouragement seemed to momentarily dispel all of the tension I felt. What a woman I married! She has always been my greatest encourager. She has always been my cheerleader. She fulfills everything I dreamed of marrying when I was a young man.

I would be feeling a lot of tension as I returned to Budapest the next time. I had told my Shirley and others that I felt the hierarchy's warning was merely a bluff, but I did not know this for certain. Anyway, I felt that if they were not bluffing, any resulting arrest would be only temporary. I owned an American passport and, because of that, in the event of any trouble my government would soon take steps to retrieve me. I had been careful to build a relationship with the American Ambassador to Hungary, Mark Palmer, who I consider to be a great credit to the name of the United States of America.

Ambassador Marcus Hooker Palmer was every inch a

professional diplomat and a man of great poise and grace. By now, I was so nervous that I kept the private phone number of Ambassador Palmer both in my address book and in my pocket calculator under the name "Hooker." There were few, I believed, who knew the man's middle name. Should the officials place me under arrest, people might think the obvious instead of this being the ambassador's name. I then figured a code of the digits in the phone number and entered them. Such were my precautionary measures.

Len Charron and I left Schroon Lake for Munich and the Word of Life Castles where we would conduct our staff conference of European Word of Life directors. What a great time of fellowship we shared with these men, who were all godly, enthusiastic visionaries. Chuck Kosman who, along with Bob Parschauer and others, pioneered the early movement in and out of Eastern Europe, was fast becoming the obvious leader of all of our European directors.

Len and I made the nine hour drive from Starnberg to Budapest, arriving at the Taverna Hotel around 10:00 p.m. At the Hungarian border we crossed as tourists. I had an 8:00 a.m. appointment at hierarchy headquarters the next morning, but I very much wanted to talk with Geza Kovacs before that meeting. I wanted to hear an update on any new developments in Hungary or any rumors that were circulating. I wanted to get every bit of information I could before that important meeting with all of the leaders of the hierarchy.

I had the overwhelming feeling I was under surveillance. We had been promised this would happen. I did not want people, under any circumstances, to know I was meeting with Pastor Kovacs. As a matter of fact, he did not even know I planned to contact him. Since I arrived in a rented car from the Vienna airport, I assumed anyone wanting to know my whereabouts would be looking for a new car with Vienna plates. Assuming that, as promised, I was being followed, I decided to shake off any informers before visiting Pastor Kovacs. I went down the hotel elevator to the basement to go to my car, only to walk up the basement ramp, jump in a Budapest taxi and ask to be delivered to the Elizabeth Hotel. At that hotel I went into the men's room, then back up the stairs, quickly out the front door, and into another waiting cab. I asked to be driven to the Duna Continental Hotel down on the banks of the Danube. Repeating the same pattern there, I took a cab to the Gellert Hotel on the Buda side of the Danube.

Repeating the pattern at the Gellert Hotel, I asked the driver to bring me to Pastor Kovacs' church address in Budafok. My arrival was quite a surprise to him. After our initial greeting, he picked up a telegram from his table and said in his broken English, "Guess what! I have a telegram from John Viczian. He has asked me to come to Aradi Street for a meeting with him and Dr. Szakacs tomorrow at 8:00 am."

My heart did a flip. "Did you say 8:00 am?"

"Yes," my friend replied, "8:00 tomorrow morning. I just received the telegram tonight."

"Pastor Kovacs," I told him, "that is exactly the time at which I am to meet with President Viczian and President Szakacs."

Geza Kovacs continued, "And guess what else. Do you know who is in town? He arrived just today. Haraszti!"

"Haraszti? Haraszti is in town? No, Haraszti is in Moscow."

"He cannot be in Moscow," Geza replied, "because he has arrived in Budapest only this afternoon. He also will be at the meeting tomorrow morning."

I knew I was in deep trouble and I remember thinking, *Dear Lord, help me. Make me wiser than I have ever been in my life.* I knew it was shoot out time at the O.K. Corral, so to speak.

Perhaps this would be the end of Word of Life in Hungary.

After being briefed on many of the rumors circulating around Budapest about Word of Life and our involvement with Pastor Kovacs, I took a taxi directly back to the Taverna Hotel where I found my faithful associate, Len Charron, sound asleep catching the rest he so desperately needed. I crawled into my bed, but could not sleep. My mind would not stop. I tried quoting Scripture and meditating on Scripture to calm down, but I could not quiet my mind. All I could think of was the appointment the next morning at Aradi Street. What would be the outcome? I lay there remembering all the verbal encounters of the past — all of the threats. I remembered the warnings of arrest and reviewed in my mind the possible scenarios. If I were accused of "this," my answer would simply be "that." If I were accused of "that," my answer would be something else. My dear friend, Len, woke up and realized I could not sleep. Together we prayed and committed the events of the next day to the Lord. Somewhere around 3:00 am I must have dropped off to sleep.

My clock's alarm sounded at 6:00 a.m. Though we had slept only about three hours, the anticipation kept our adrenaline flowing hard from the moment Len and I awoke. We did not feel tired, only filled with tension. My quiet time that morning was straight from the Lord. I went to Ephesians 1:18-23. In verses 18-20, Paul is writing to the believers at Ephesus and he is reminding them how special they were to God; how he wants them to be filled with the knowledge of God's will about the future. In verse 19, Paul prays that they will begin to realize how great God's power is to do exactly what He says He would, to help those who believe in Christ. He says the same mighty power that raised Jesus from the dead and seated Him at the right hand of God in Heaven is available to us.

I remember the thrill and peace that settled over me as I sat there pondering that passage. It was as though God was saying to me, "Don't worry about anything. I've planned it all out and everything is under control. You go ahead with your meeting with the authorities. They can't hurt you. I can change their minds very easily. Relax and place your confidence in me."

I remember thinking; *it's going to be okay. God is going to give us the desires of our heart!*

After that special quiet time prepared for me by my Lord, I knew the day would go well. God's perfect will would certainly prevail. I did not know how, but that was the beauty of this quiet assurance. I knew the events that lay ahead were by my God's sovereign plan. So be it!

At about ten minutes before 8:00 am, I entered the offices of the Free Church Council at Aradi Street. Walking in, I looked across the hallway into a large reception room where Dr. Haraszti was seated, already at work on some papers.

Trying to act surprised at finding him there I shouted, "Dr. Haraszti, is that you? What are you doing in Budapest? I thought you were in Moscow."

I wanted him to know I knew he had been in Moscow. The only way I could have known this was by calling his home in Atlanta as he had instructed me to do.

I went on to tell him, "I talked with your son in Atlanta."

He interrupted, "No that would be my grandson."

"Oh yes, your grandson. It was he who told me you were in Moscow."

"Yes," he replied, "I have been there, but I arrived here yesterday afternoon."

"Are you here for my meeting with Dr. Szakacs and John

Viczian?" I asked Dr. Haraszti.

"Yes, yes. They invited me to sit in on this meeting and be the translator."

Praise God! I thought. *At last, I have one of the best English-to-Hungarian translators possible. I have a man who has spent twenty years in America and who understands the ways of American Christian ministries, and this same man understands how the Hungarian church leadership thinks and moves.*

The meeting started on schedule and did not finish until 7:00 p.m., with a two-hour break for lunch. It was a long, hard day. I felt very good, however, about having my words translated by Dr. Haraszti.

As the morning went on, I was again accused of working for the United States government. As a matter of fact, Len Charron, my associate, was also accused of working for the CIA since his manner of dress fit their profile of an American CIA agent. We laughed about this, though it really was not funny.

I soon learned how valuable Dr. Alex Haraszti would be. This man not only is a medical doctor with a Masters Degree in Theology, he is also one of the most brilliant negotiators I have ever met. At no time have I ever heard him mince any words. He reaches right for the jugular.

During those nine hours of negotiation we reviewed everything with which Word of Life had been involved, from the perceived promises of renovating Camp Tahi, to the reasons we had gone to investigate the monastery at Oroszlany without their foreknowledge, to my having contact with Mr. Shiklosi and with many other friends of Michael Kovacs. They had heard the rumor that I had sent a Ryrie Study Bible directly to Communist Party Chairman Grosz. I told them the story of Michael Kovacs in London, always referring to him only as "my dear Jewish friend."

At times the conversation became very confrontational as everything was placed on the table. I reminded the men in the leadership that they had told me Geza Kovacs was a devil, and that if we ever wanted to do anything in Hungary with the churches, we would have to disassociate ourselves from Geza. I told them we would never do that. At one point in time, I agreed to back off from preaching at Budafok, but I could not disassociate with this man and his family because we were more than just Christian brothers — we were, indeed, friends of the heart. I had also shared this with Dr. Haraszti in Atlanta.

I believe Dr. Haraszti recognized this as a sticking point in any of the negotiations. He seemed to know that the church leadership hated Geza Kovacs and yet he recognized that he was one of the few that we in Word of Life really trusted. During these critical negotiations, Dr. Haraszti looked at Dr. Szakacs and President Viczian and asked them, point blank, "Do you want Word of Life in Hungary? It is that simple. Do you think that Word of Life would be good for the youth of Hungary? If your answer is yes, then you must bring Geza Kovacs out from under the table, place him on top of the table, and bring him into the negotiations. It is obvious that Word of Life trusts Geza Kovacs. They are only going to go under the table to him and get his advice anyway. So, unless you want them always to go under the table and filter everything through him, you must, whether you like him or not, bring him right on top of the table and allow him to be a part of this entire negotiation."

That was truly a turning point. Harazsti had put the facts down as they were, and now it was up to the others to make their decision. It was at that point that we took a two-hour break to allow Dr. Szakacs and John Viczian to visit Parliament to conduct some business and Dr. Haraszti, Pastor Kovacs, Len Charron, and I lunched at the Forum Hotel. Dr. Haraszti and Geza Kovacs had not seen each other, to my knowledge, for many, many years. There had been some tension between these two Christian brothers. During this two-hour respite I began to see two old friends reconciling in gentlemanly conversation. They gained a renewed understanding and, perhaps, even an appreciation for each other.

Later in the afternoon, the negotiations continued at Aradi Street. It was agreed that since Word of Life had no staff living in the country that Pastor Geza Kovacs would speak for Word of Life and represent the ministry to the churches and to the government during the months that would follow. Word of Life, indeed, had a brand new beginning in this country. All parties agreed that this was a good move. Dr. Haraszti had been the catalyst to make it all happen. He was the key player at this very precarious time.

In my opinion, had it not been for Dr. Haraszti's wisdom and skill, along with his desire to see the youth of Hungary won for Jesus Christ and his understanding of the system in Hungary, we would have been dead in the water at the time of those negotiations. I grew to recognize that Dr. Haraszti was indeed a brilliant servant and gifted negotiator. He has been a true friend to Word of Life and, because of that; many thousands of Hungarian young people will be won to Jesus Christ in the future.

I sang in my heart over and over, *To God be the glory, great things He hath done.* Thank you, Lord; for allowing us to be just a small part of all this. Thank you for Dr. Haraszti and his help. Thank you for leading in almost miraculous ways, ways too great to comprehend.

After our lengthy meeting at Aradi Street that day, I finally believed that Word of Life would have a bright future in reaching the youth of Hungary for Jesus Christ.

CHAPTER 9

DAYLIGHT AT LAST

After the very long, confrontational meeting at Aradi Street when Dr. Haraszti so ably served as translator and negotiator, all agreed that Pastor Geza Kovacs would represent Word of Life to the government and to the Hungarian churches. He served as spokesman until we had a team in place and a director appointed. This was a great move forward.

Before leaving Budapest, we set a proposed date for our return when we could look at some property and begin to put together some form of organization. This was still rather premature and tenuous.

As we approached the tentative date for our return, April of 1988, we had heard nothing from the officials in Budapest. I had been in contact with them indirectly through our German Director, Chuck Kosman. Chuck was, in the meantime, developing greatly in his leadership and his overall grasp of the ministry on the entire continent of Europe. The decision was made at our International Headquarters to ask Kosman to oversee all of the Word of Life ministries in Europe.

The time came for our trip to Budapest, but we had no conclusive word — no specific appointments. It has always been very difficult to communicate with people in Budapest since most of those with whom we dealt had no home telephone.

Shirley and I flew first to London where we visited my friend, Michael Kovacs, in his beautiful country home. Michael entertains many people in his home in the interest of his homeland, Hungary. For two nights my wife and I stayed at the Heathrow Sheraton before we drove a rented car out into the country to the Kovacs farm. I was able to share with my friend the many difficulties and wrong perceptions the authorities and people held in Hungary. None of this was new to him since he had experienced these attitudes many times over the years.

Michael was a very gracious host. We shared warm conversations reminiscing over the Pan Am flight #301 on which we met. Michael asked my wife, "Do you really go along with all this man is doing? Do you believe like he believes?"

Shirley, with her beautiful smile, replied, "Of course I do. We think exactly alike. We believe exactly alike, and I want to be his greatest encourager in everything Paul does for the Lord."

Pensively, Michael said to me, "You are a very, very fortunate man. You are to be envied."

While we were at Michael Kovacs country home I learned he had just received the highest civilian award from the Communist government of Hungary. It was called the "Gold Leaf Award." There are three special recognition awards the government presents. One is in the political arena, another in the military, and the third is a civilian award. A dinner had been held in Budapest in Michael's honor. At the dinner, Peter Veres who was the Minister for Foreign Trade, in presenting the award, said something like this, "Twice Michael Kovacs was driven from his homeland, and twice he has returned to invest in and help the economy of our country. We want to honor him for that."

Accepting the award, Michael, in his very diplomatic manner, said to the guests, "I did not invite Hitler to my country. I did not invite Joe Stalin to my country. I love my countrymen. I love my country, and I want to do all I can to help my countrymen."

He was very careful not to say he appreciated them as Communists because he despised the whole Communist system and what it does to a country. Yet, the Minister of this Communist government had become his friend. Michael Kovacs could influence men. He knew the Communist Prime Ministers for many years. It is my opinion that, as soon as he had built a relationship with Dr. Grosz, the Prime Minister, he sought to influence him towards the use of the Free Enterprise system. After all, it was Prime Minister Grosz who, even as First Secretariat, had an influence in moving the Communist government of the People's Republic of Hungary towards a quasi free enterprise posture. Behind all of that stood a man doing a lot to influence minds and I am certain it was my friend, Kovacs, the Hungarian Jew.

After a long visit and a delicious meal prepared by our friend, Shirley and I returned to the Heathrow Sheraton, not knowing for certain if we would continue on to Budapest. At the hotel I received a message to call Chuck Kosman. When I placed the call to Chuck in Germany I learned we had, indeed, been invited to return to Budapest and carry out our original plan. That was good news.

Returning to Budapest without a lot of pressure was a new experience for me. We had come to a clear understanding. I did not have to sneak around cautiously for fear of being seen with my friends, the Kovacs. I no longer worried whether or not I was being followed; at least I felt that I didn't need to be concerned. I had asked Pastor Kovacs, who now officially represented Word of Life to the Hungarian government, to look for some camp property along one of Hungary's waterways. I felt it would be very important to have waterfront access for swimming, waterskiing, and other water sports.

When my wife and I arrived in Budapest, I discovered that a very tightly-woven schedule had been prepared for me. Not knowing quite where to begin looking for waterfront property, Pastor Kovacs went to the city offices in Erd on a particular morning and asked the receptionist to direct him to someone who knew about property available for purchase along Hungary's waterways.

Just then a man stopped in the hallway behind him. Entering the room, he said, "Excuse me, sir. I could not help but overhear your question. May I introduce myself? I am Sandor, the new Director of Waterways for the People's Republic of Hungary. This is my first trip to your city hall, and I happened to hear you as I passed by. I think I am the one to help you."

Now what are the chances of this happening? A man only a month in his newly appointed position, coming out from the Central Government offices in Budapest to the City Hall of Erd, and walking by an open door precisely at that moment to hear Pastor Kovacs inquire about waterfront property – the timing was incredible!

Sandor began to tell Pastor Kovacs about several pieces of property, but noted one in particular, located on the outskirts of the village of Kiskore. Not only were there several properties suggested, but arrangements were made for us to use a government airplane. When my wife and I arrived, we were treated like dignitaries. We were driven to a government airfield where a pilot, an engineer, and others waited to fly us around the country. While we were flying over Hungary viewing properties from the air, Dr. Geza Kovacs interpreted for us and described, as best he could, the dimensions and characteristics of the various sites. Finally we arrived near the outskirts of Kiskore where additional government officials met us, until our party grew to include twenty-one people. This area of the country, according to government planners, was to be the new tourist area in Hungary.

Here there was a beautiful piece of property bordering a massive, man-made lake where the Tisza River had been damned up.

After looking over this property, we were taken to a government motor launch that carried us down the Tisza River.

At noonday, we arrived at a lovely old villa used by the local government to promote western investment in tourism. Awaiting us was a marvelous banquet provided by the local government. As we were taken into the villa, we were treated like royalty. I could not help but be amazed at the government's vast change of attitude toward Word of Life in just a matter of two months!

After formal greetings, much bowing and scraping, my wife and I were seated at the head of a long banquet table, next to the local Lord Mayor.

After finishing the delectable fish dinner, I asked to address the entire government delegation. I began with what had become my standard approach to the many different government officials with whom I dealt.

Speaking through an interpreter, I said, "Gentlemen, I must tell you why we are here. You need to understand clearly who we are and exactly what we would like to be permitted to do in your country. I represent an international Christian organization. We are Christians, not in the general sense as distinct from Jews or Muslims, but we are followers of Jesus Christ who accept a literal interpretation of the Bible. Our primary goal and objective is to tell young people about Jesus Christ. We believe when a young person, or anyone, enters into a right relationship with God through Jesus Christ, his thinking is changed. This changed thinking changes his attitudes about life. It is this change in attitude that affects his lifestyle. Anyone who comes to God through Jesus Christ literally undergoes a change in his lifestyle. He becomes a different kind of person."

I continued to tell these men that their country held the distinction of having the highest rate of suicide per capita of any nation in the world. I told them that the youth of Hungary needed the life-changing experience of knowing the Savior, Jesus Christ, in a personal way. I explained our goal of telling the youth of Hungary about Jesus Christ in order to give them a reason for living.

"It is my opinion," I went on, "that the youth of your country have turned away from religion in this last generation not only because of government philosophy, but also because, in my view, the religionists of Hungary have conducted too many 'boring meetings' for too many years. Your religionists have been so ritualistic and formal that the young people think, 'what does this have to do with me and with how I live?'"

At this point in my address, several of the government officials looked at one another with smiles on their faces, and they began nodding their heads.

I said, "If we are allowed to build a youth camp in your country, we will build into it a very high profile in sports. Sports will attract young people from every background and way of life. Young people like fun and lots of good activity. However, I want you to understand that every morning and every evening we will gather the young people together and, for one hour, open the Scriptures and teach them the teachings of Jesus Christ."

"This book," I continued, holding my Bible high in the air, "the Bible, is the most exciting book ever written. The unfortunate fact is that many people who speak about this wonderful book do so in a very dull and boring manner. When we teach the Word of God to Hungary's youth, we will do so with great enthusiasm and excitement. God, the Holy Spirit, will use this to bring the young people of your country to the Word of God and to Jesus Christ."

When I concluded my address, Sandor, the Director of Waterways, asked to speak. He spoke in heavily accented English and was interpreted into Hungarian as I had been. He said, "Gentlemen, many years ago there came a man to this country by the name of John Calvin. He promoted the doctrine of ah, ah, ah..."

I then interjected, "Predestination."

"Yes, yes," Sandor continued, "that is what he promoted. I have to ask a question. Keep in mind, I am one month in my new position as the Director of Waterways. I happened, on a particular morning, to go to the suburb of Erd and enter the city offices precisely at the time that this man," Sandor pointed to Pastor Kovacs, "was asking about property along waterways. I overheard his request. As a result, we are here today. I have to ask, could it be that this is what John Calvin was talking about in his theory of predestination?"

I thought to myself, *You bet...not by chance.* With a smile on my face I said in front of all gathered there, "Sandor, that is exactly what John Calvin was talking about. However, I want to remind you that John Calvin did not discover the doctrine. That is a doctrine that is taken from the very pages of Scripture — from the Word of God. Yes, I believe this meeting today was foreordained and predestined by God."

You would have thought I was at a Baptist revival meeting. These diplomats were looking at each other, shaking their heads and saying, "egan, egan," which translated is, "yes, yes." What a thrilling experience this was!

By now it was late in the day, and we needed to return to Budapest. Arriving back at the airfield we discovered that in falling behind schedule, the pilot had lost his slot for the prearranged flight plan back to Budapest. Our aircraft was parked in a low spot in a valley, and he could not raise Budapest government radio from this low ground. We had to waste another hour while he went back into town and made a phone call requesting the rescheduling of our flight. Returning to the airfield, the pilot announced that we would have to fly back to Budapest at an altitude of less than

100 feet because there were Russian MIG maneuvers going on overhead.

"Your option is to either fly at that altitude, or remain here," he told us.

"Let's go," I said. This was an exciting flight for me, being an old private plane pilot myself and having owned two piper cubs when I was in my early twenties.

I hadn't had such fun since those days in my youth. Everyone else seemed a little nervous, however. We flew so low over the farm fields that the pilot had to gain altitude to climb above the high voltage electric lines.

Sitting in the seat behind me, Shirley leaned forward and whispered in my ear, "Should I be afraid?" "With any other pilot in any other aircraft, yes," I answered, "but not this pilot or this aircraft." This is what this man does for a living. This is a waterways-owned aircraft, and they fly at low altitudes inspecting many of their waterways and tributaries all over the country."

We arrived back in Budapest hardly able to believe what we had experienced all in one day. There was such an incredible attitude change among the government officials that it was hard to believe. We had been so accustomed to fighting for every inch that to suddenly have gained a whole mile was beyond our wildest imagination. The thought kept pounding in my mind, *not by chance, only by the plan of God.*

I had told the Hungarian authorities I could not make any kind of decision regarding property at that point in time. I explained that I was only one member of the Word of Life team and, though I was the Director of the Overseas Division of our organization, I had to answer to my superiors and a Board of Directors. I told them I would return to the United States with all of the information and get back in touch with them to let them know of our interest.

Arriving back in the United States, I shared the good news with our directors and with several members of our Board. It was almost too much for them to accept as fact.

Not Every Road is the Right Road!

Things were moving too fast. Could this all be true? It was obvious to me that we were on to something that had to be pursued. There appeared to be no stopping. Kosman and I seemed to be wheeling and dealing in big stuff. Could it mean that our American organization would be responsible for some huge foreign debt? If so, the timing was very bad because in the United States, Word of Life was entering a program to build a multi-million dollar conference center in Florida. We could in no way commit ourselves to any great Hungarian debt.

In the course of events, the next trip to Hungary was scheduled. We would return with a member of our International Board of Directors, our European director, and several other interested parties. Several weeks passed. Upon our arrival back in Budapest, we went immediately to Kiskore to inspect the beautiful Tisza River property once again. There were some big, unanswered questions in my mind. . . Is this the right property? How much money do they expect? How much is too much? I had a figure in mind of $200,000 in U.S. dollars. I would later learn that the figure they had in mind was much, much different. After inspecting the property on the river, we were taken to a very unique hunting lodge and served the most delicious venison steak I have ever enjoyed.

Having discussed possible terms of purchase for any property with the directors at Schroon Lake before leaving for Hungary, I felt confident that we could make an offer of $200,000 and possibly even as much as $300,000 to establish a camping facility in Hungary. However, that would be the absolute limit.

After the meal, we got down to some hard negotiations. Chuck Kosman was seated to my left, our interpreter to my right, and to his right was Bob Moore, a member of our American Board of Directors. Across from me was the official representative of the government and the Department of Forestry. To his right was Pastor Kovacs. Through my interpreter, I made some opening statements and presented an offer for the Tisza River property.

Hungarians are very gracious people, even in negotiating. The official representing the Hungarian government absolutely startled me when he shared all of the possibilities they had for developing this property and their price was 2.7 million U.S. dollars. It was all I could do just to keep from laughing out loud.

Immediately I responded, saying, "Gentlemen, Word of Life is a non-profit Christian organization. By non-profit I mean we are designed so as not to make a profit. We are not a wealthy American company. We have no funds, only those monies entrusted to us by wonderful Christian people in America who care about the youth of your country. Because of that, there is no way we can come up to your expectations. Therefore, I want to thank you for this gracious meal. I want to thank you for all the time you have taken in meeting with us. We are serious in our negotiation and our offer, but we are miles and miles apart in what we can do."

I had started to terminate the conversation when Bob Moore, our American board member, scribbled a note on a napkin and passed it up the table to me. "Ask for a recess," it read. "Ask for a fifteen minute break. Then we can return."

I took his suggestion wondering what he had in mind. I turned to the Hungarian officials and begged their pardon, asking for a fifteen or twenty-minute recess to give us opportunity to discuss matters as a delegation. Our hosts graciously agreed.

During the recess, Chuck Kosman, Bob Moore, and I went for a stroll down one of the many weeded paths. Bob said, "I think what we need to do is find a way to give them what they want while still getting what we want."

"My friend," I said, "there's no way we could ever come up with $2.7 million dollars for this property. It has no buildings, infrastructure, utilities, nothing. There is no way we can meet that kind of price."

Bob Moore asked, "Can you come up with $200,000?"

"Yes," I said, "I think I can."

He then said, "Then I have a plan. I don't think they have learned about compounded interest here yet. Let's go back in there and offer them the price they are asking for, but see if you can spread the payments out over thirty years without interest. We can offer them $200,000 down and then $50,000 per year for the next ten years, $60,000 per year for the second ten years, and $65,000 per year for the third ten years. I believe that I can put $400,000 in an interest-bearing account in a bank in America and it will yield enough interest each year to make those payments for you."

"I cannot believe your generosity," I told him, "but if my superiors in Schroon Lake hear that I have actually made them an offer in the name of Word of Life for $2.7 million dollars, I am in big trouble. I will be dead meat, but on *that* side of the Atlantic this time."

"It is a sound principle," Bob said, "I am willing to put $400,000 in an interest-bearing account if they will accept this as payment for this beautiful property."

"I still have to reckon with my directors back in America," I replied. "An offer like that will absolutely terrify them. I have no authority whatsoever to make that kind of commitment."

Bob said, "You go ahead and do it. I will take it upon myself to explain everything to your directors. It is my risk. It is my money, and I am willing to stand behind this offer."

With a considerable amount of uncertainty and nervousness, we resumed the negotiation session and followed through with the new plan. The offer was accepted in principle, and we felt we had just about closed the deal on potentially one of the most beautiful pieces of land in all of Hungary. The Hungarian officials advised us they would inform us within three weeks whether or not they could accept our offer.

The offer we presented was passed up the government chain of command until it reached the Minister of Finance. Unfortunately, or fortunately, depending on how you look at the situation, the Minister of Finance *did* understand compound interest and the offer was rejected.

Soon after that I contacted my wonderful friend in London, Michael Kovacs. I told him of the offer we had made on the property and suggested he should get in touch with Dr. Grosz, who had by this time, moved up from Prime Minister to replace Janos Kadar as the Chairman of the Communist Party. I suggested he tell Chairman Grosz of the offer we had presented for $2.7 million dollars over thirty years; and that Grosz might wish to talk with his Minister of Finance to tell him this was a good deal, and that he should accept our offer. Michael agreed to speak with Grosz, but I was beginning to experience fear over this whole deal. I told Michael, "No, on second thought, do nothing about this until I get in touch with you again." The longer time went on, the more I realized that the Tisza River property was probably not in the plan of God for Word of Life.

We did make one more trip to the Tisza River property and presented an offer of $80,000 with payments spread over twenty years for one-half of the original property. The officials really wanted to negotiate a deal on those terms, but we told them that because the government had such a high price on the original property, we had lost the interest and backing of some of the contributors in the United States. Therefore, we were no longer interested in the property. We believed the Lord had something else for us.

By now we could see that the government under Grosz was undergoing significant change, and the People's Republic of Hungary was moving closer and closer to a free-enterprise approach to conducting business within its borders.

I had been advised by Dr. Haraszti to maintain contact with Dr. Miklos, who was still the President of the State Office of Church. However, as a result of the tremendous change foreseen in the future of the Hungarian Government, he would soon be forced into retirement. We would no longer have to fear Miklos. I was advised that his Deputy, Barnabas Sarkadi Nagy, would replace Miklos, and eventually the government would do away with governmental control of religion. Or Nagy would serve as a transitional figure from one form of government to another. He had spent many of his years marching to the whistle of Miklos and the Communist party, but he knew that the days of Communism were coming to an end. He was a slender man with thinning blond hair and blue eyes. He was also highly educated and intelligent.

I learned that Sarkadi Nagy would be making a trip to the United States at the invitation of the United States Information Agency. He would be in the U.S. to do a month-long study on separation of church and state and how the churches in America operate. He would investigate the relationship between religion and government and the freedom of religion enjoyed in America. Dr. Haraszti urged me to discreetly contact Sarkadi Nagy, without

Miklos' knowledge. Through intermediaries, I sent a message to Sarkadi Nagy requesting him to allow at least two days in his American itinerary to visit Word of Life in Schroon Lake, New York, to inspect our program. The man agreed; soon I was in touch with the U.S. Information Agency in Washington, D.C. ensuring that Sarkadi Nagy's schedule included Word of Life.

In the meantime, the president of the Baptist Union in Hungary, John Viczian, called me from the Bahamas where he was on official business with some church leaders. I invited him to come to Schroon Lake and spend a few days with us. I had invited John many times before, but until now, he had never been able to accept the offer.

John Viczian joined us for several days at Schroon Lake. I was so glad to have the chance to show him our camps! We had known each other for several years by now and had been through many disputes; most notably the one when he informed me that Word of Life would no longer be welcome in Hungary. Now, this was a new opportunity to show Word of Life in a very positive light to my friend. I wanted to expose John to as much of our camping ministry as possible. I wanted him to *see* the tremendous difference in approach we used at our camps at Word of Life Island, Ranch, Inn, and Campground. It was vastly different from the very primitive camping program they had in Hungary.

During his visit, John was very cordial and told me directly, "I want to be your friend. I want to help you. There are other properties available to you in my country. I want to help in any way I can. We do want Word of Life in Hungary."

John Viczian's attitude confirmed what I had felt all along — that he was a man who desired nothing but the best for his countrymen and for the churches in Hungary. He wanted the freedom we all wanted, but he was a man tightly controlled by the State Office of Church and, in particular, Miklos. He was on a five-foot long leash and had to jump at Miklos' every demand. To not jump to attention at the snap of Miklos' finger meant the loss of his position and prestige. I believe that John felt that by holding onto his position, he could better serve the evangelical cause in Hungary.

I always had mixed feelings about John. He was an obstacle in the way of our being allowed to reach the youth of Hungary, and I did not like that. I disliked the things he believed he needed to do —the roadblocks he put in our way. On the other hand, I pitied the man because I knew how Miklos controlled him. And I also knew that he was a good man who wanted to help his countrymen.

The time came for Sarkadi Nagy's visit to Word of Life. His visit came at the wrong time of the year for us to show him our camping ministry in action, so I needed to be creative in showing him our Bible Institute operation. He was to arrive at Schroon Lake on a Saturday when all of our Bible Institute students were out on weekend ministries. I wanted to give him as broad a picture of Word of Life operations and ministries as possible, so this was going to be a whirlwind two days!

I met him on Saturday at the Montreal airport. From Montreal, we boarded a plane and flew to Philadelphia where we picked up a rental car and drove to a Word of Life tour concert in Allentown, Pennsylvania. I found this scenario quiet laughable in one sense. Here I was bringing a Communist leader and professed atheist to see a musical dramatization of the Book of Genesis and the story of Creation!

We arrived just a few minutes late to the production. I had tried to prepare Sarkadi Nagy for what he would see that night, right from ground zero. He was very impressed by what he saw, and very impressed with the enthusiasm of the students and the sincerity of their acting and singing. Whether he believed their message at the time was immaterial. At least he was impressed with their sincerity. He was able to see how clean, fresh, and sharp these wonderful Christian students were. .

From Allentown my plan was to travel back to the airport in Philadelphia, fly to Albany and arrive at the Word of Life Inn at Schroon Lake for lunch. The flights that day, as usual, were running very late. By the time we landed in Albany it was apparent that we would not make it to the Inn for lunch, so I phoned my wife, asking her to prepare lunch at our home. After lunch Sarkadi Nagy and I could tour the facilities.

I also suggested to Shirley that she contact Ildiko Barbarics, a Hungarian attorney who was enrolled in the Bible Institute that year. This way my guest could enjoy lunch with another Hungarian and, perhaps feel more at ease.

Along with Ildiko, Shirley invited our son, Jonathan, also a Bible Institute student; and our daughter Sarah. Of course, my wife joined us as well. As we sat around the table, after asking the blessing on the delicious food, we all enjoyed each other's company in a very informal, friendly time.

Through the Word of Life Bible Institute, we carry out an extensive ministry in the prisons of upstate New York. Some of our students are converted ex-convicts. That evening at the Word of Life Inn, I invited two ex-convict students to meet Sarkadi Nagy and share their testimony of faith in Jesus Christ with him.

José Lugo had spent more of his life inside prison than out of prison. He had been marvelously saved and was a truly transformed person. José shared his testimony very humbly with this Communist official. Sarkadi Nagy, however, appeared unimpressed. I finally allowed him to retire to his room for a good night's sleep since we had only a few hours to rest the night before.

Sunday morning arrived and I met with Sarkadi Nagy for

an hour before driving him to the Albany Airport for his trip to Washington, D.C. During what turned into a two-hour meeting, I sought his help in opening official channels for the establishment of the Word of Life ministry in Hungary.

As we spoke, this slender, gracious man shared with me, "Mr. Bubar, I know you are an honest man. I know this because I made certain observations in your home yesterday. An old proverb says that 'a hypocrite's home is filled with much tension.' I saw nothing at your home yesterday but goodness, kindness, and a lot of love. Your children and wife were excited about your being there with them."

When I told Shirley of this comment she replied, "I didn't realize that I was making a statement by preparing lunch and having our children there with us."

I thought, *to the watching world, how important it is for them to see our love for the Lord Jesus, and for one another.*

Sarkadi Nagy continued, "I want you to know that I was very impressed with the young man we met with last night. We have nothing like that in our country. We need something like that, and in the future there is the great possibility that the prisons of our country will be open to you to carry on a ministry such as you have here. After talking with you about the possibilities of securing some property in Hungary, are you convinced that the Tisza River property is where you want to locate?"

"It is very beautiful," I told him. "It has great potential, but it is very expensive."

"Yes," he replied. "It is very expensive. I want to suggest that you not be in a hurry. Do not hurry. There are properties that will soon become available in our country — properties owned by some of the trade unions. The trade unions will soon be selling some of the hotels and vacation spots they currently manage. Do not be in a hurry."

I felt I had been given not only good advice, but also that Sarkadi Nagy was telling me something that perhaps later he would be forced to deny. Yet, he was letting me in on some of the trends of the future. Dr. Haraszti advised me to send a letter to Dr. Miklos letting him know when I would be in Hungary next; thereby making myself available to him should he want to discuss any matters with me. The idea was to do everything in the open so that there could be no thought of my doing anything behind Miklos' back or under the table. Though I did not relish the thought of ever meeting with Miklos, I sent the letter as Dr. Haraszti suggested.

Sure enough, Dr. Miklos responded positively and established a meeting time at his office. I will never forget that meeting! It was my last meeting with Miklos, for which I thank God. Miklos and I were seated on opposite sides of a long, narrow, tapestry-covered table. His mouth was set in a straight line, and his brows were down. His interpreter was to his left and his Deputy, Sarkadi Nagy, to his immediate right. To my left sat John Viczian and I directly faced Dr. Miklos and his frowning countenance.

Looking like a Mafia godfather, he slapped the table with his hand and said, through his interpreter, "Well, what is the matter? Why haven't you bought any property? Is it because you have no money? Is that why you have done nothing?"

How did he know? I thought to myself.

Sarkadi Nagy sat with a very passive expression on his face, looking down at the table in front of him. I felt like saying to Miklos, *Look, you atheistic idiot, you're telling* me *to hurry, but your Deputy is telling me to go slow. I want to hurry, but it is more prudent if I take it slow.*

In order to keep from being intimidated by Miklos, while he was speaking in Hungarian, I thought, *you old man. Your goose is already cooked. You're nothing but a toothless old man,* so *don't sit there and make threats to try to intimidate me.*

Of course, I only thought those things. I explained to Miklos that we wanted to be very careful to select the right property so we could create the greatest impact on the youth of his society. Very frankly, at this time we were playing a quiet waiting game; waiting for Miklos to be turned out of office. I could not even tell John Viczian of my conversation with Sarkadi Nagy, who had been so kind to me and so helpful in urging us to go slow and not spend money needlessly.

I met John Viczian for dinner that night at a Budapest Hotel. We thoroughly enjoyed our meal and our visit, but during the conversation, John told me, "Well, you must hurry." Later on in the talk he said, "Do not be in a hurry."

In essence he was saying out of one side of his mouth, "Hurry, hurry!" Then ten minutes later, out of the other side of his mouth he was telling me, "slow, slow," and I wondered why. Could it be that he wanted to honestly tell Miklos, if he were called upon to give a report of our conversation, "Oh, yes, I told Bubar to hurry and make a deal." Or, if Deputy Nagy called him in, John could truthfully say, "Yes, I told Bubar to take it slow." I honestly do not know what motivated John's double-talk that night.

This particular trip to Hungary was extremely brief. I was meeting with our newly formed Board of Directors in Warsaw, Poland and had very little time to spend in Hungary. However, I did stay in Budapest about thirty-six hours.

Someone had told Pastor Kovacs about a potentially available property owned by one of the trade unions in the little town of Toalmas, just an hour drive from Budapest. It was an historic castle and an interesting prospect. I remembered Sarkadi Nagy's words. I had no time to spare, but I managed to squeeze seeing the castle into my schedule.

I discovered the castle at Toalmas to be the loveliest castle property I have ever seen, with the exception of our exquisite castles in Starnberg, Germany. The castle was tall and gothic, with German influence. It was made from stucco and stone. There were seventy-eight acres of fields and forest and, right in the middle, there was the spacious, fifty-four-room castle building surrounded by ten outbuildings. The property included fishing ponds, soccer fields, and just about everything we possibly could want, except a lake for waterskiing.

Events were moving rapidly in other areas. The Communist government was coming down to its final death rattle on a fast track headed for change. As mentioned earlier, Zoltan Kovacs had purchased an old villa in southern Hungary with his own funds. He had been allowed to incorporate as a Hungarian Christian corporation under the Department of Health and Human Services. Zoltan had succeeded in breaking out of the tightly controlled "religion box," and now Word of Life was about to break free and become the first western, Christian organization to incorporate as a non-profit entity under the Communist government of Hungary.

Ildiko Barbarics, a brilliant young lawyer who had earned her doctorate in a State University, had come to the Word of Life Bible Institute for a quarter and now was back in Hungary. She, along with one of her legal instructors at the State University, was working on pulling everything together to help Word of Life structure its organization.

There were still attempts being made by the church authorities to control us. They wanted the make-up of our board of directors to include several people from the Baptist Union. We, of course, replied that we did not want to be an organization made up solely of Baptists. Though we wanted to serve the Baptist churches of Hungary, we also wanted to serve all the Gospel-preaching churches, including the Plymouth Brethren Assemblies, and others. Because of this, we refused their request.

We went through much posturing since the Christian community in Hungary had not lived for more than forty years under any kind of a democracy. They knew little of the structuring of Christian organizations. Finally, everything was ready and in April of 1989, Dr. Harry Bollback, Chuck Kosman, and I returned to finalize our corporation and host the first meeting of our Hungarian Board of Directors.

Harry Bollback Comes to Hungary

Harry Bollback is the Senior Director of Word of Life who stood shoulder to shoulder with Jack Wyrtzen for nearly fifty years. He was the first Word of Life missionary to start the first Word of Life ministry in a foreign country — Brazil. Later he was appointed to start the official overseas ministries of Word of Life in 1969. He is a very effective evangelist. He is a very determined man with true dedication to God and his ministry. As a young man, he survived every South Pacific battle in World War II, including Pellalou. Out of about two hundred men in his battle group at Pellalou, only six survived, and Harry was one of them.

We had been unable to get him to visit Hungary because of his very pressured schedule. But finally, Harry was actually coming to Hungary and at a very crucial time: the night we were to conduct the first meeting with the new Board of Directors! Harry Bollback was preaching at the Budafok Baptist Church. Attorney Barbarics had urged her legal professor from the university, who had assisted us in the formation of this new corporation, to come to the evangelistic church meeting since our Board meeting would immediately follow.

What a thrill, when Harry gave the Gospel invitation, to see among the many others coming down the aisle to confess Christ as Savior, this legal instructor from the State University! We believed this was another token for good. The woman who had helped form this new Christian organization had found Jesus Christ for herself! Here, I believed, was a clear indication of God's blessing on the future of this ministry.

My superior, Harry Bollback, however, was experiencing different thoughts. The next morning over breakfast at our hotel he began to share with me his misgivings.

"Paul, things here are not being done as they should," Harry began. "Everything is wrong here. It is not going at all by our pattern of opening a country. By your own word, Paul Bubar, you do not have a root system. You do not have a director. You do not have our Bible Clubs. All of these things need to precede the establishment of a camping ministry. Everything is premature. We should not be here yet."

These words by my superior nearly blew me out of the water. What he was saying was actually correct. In any other country around the world, we would not have established a ministry as we did in Hungary. Under normal procedure we first go in with a man who has been called of God to open the ministry in that country. Next, he would very quietly begin to establish our Bible Clubs.

After establishing a number of Clubs and setting up a root system, he would see many young people come to know Jesus Christ as Savior. From those young people, this man would begin to disciple future leaders. He would develop the Club ministry in many of the Gospel-preaching churches. These churches would stand behind the ministry of Word of Life. Eventually a Board of Directors would be established after long relationships had been developed.

In Hungary, however, we did have a root system of sorts, because Word of Life evangelistic teams had been crisscrossing the country for five years now. They had conducted evangelistic meetings in more than thirty-five churches with more than 1,500 young people publicly trusting Jesus Christ as Savior. Yet, what Harry Bollback was laying on me that morning was really true. What had happened in Hungary was completely out of step with the way we had established ministries in more than twenty-five other nations around the world.

I remember feeling I had done something wrong; something my superiors would not approve. The last thing I would ever have wanted was to go against the wishes of these godly men. Somehow, from the very beginning, everything had been different while trying to establish a ministry in this Eastern European country. The events had been completely out of order when compared with all the other countries Word of Life has entered. I considered, however, that this was our first experience in a Communist controlled country. God seemed to be working in a very different and special way.

Following breakfast at the hotel in Budapest that morning, we drove out to inspect the castle property at Toalmas. I will never forget seeing the twinkle in Harry Bollback's eyes as we walked the beautiful Toalmas property. Everything we needed was already in place. It was already built. In how many countries had Harry seen directors struggle through a costly building program? How many times had he been through the process himself? Here everything was laid out for us. I knew that Harry could picture in his mind young people swarming the property, involved in all kinds of sports. He could picture, too, these youth hearing the Word of God preached in their native tongue. He could envision hundreds coming to know Christ as their Savior. That excited him. God was doing a work in Harry Bollback's heart.

It was true that, by all our previous standards, we were doing things in a very different way. We were incorporated and had a Board of Directors in place that was selected by someone other than the director. This normally does not work well. Board members are usually loyal to the one forming the work or inviting them to serve. We, at that point, did not even have a director for Hungary, though Eric Murphy showed great interest.

Since when does God have to be submissive to our plans and do things in the chronological order that we have decided? I have observed that when God plans something, the details work out perfectly, according to the precise chronological order He has predetermined. Obviously, all that was happening in Hungary for Word of Life was in God's plan.

It was absolutely essential to have the approval of Word of Life's Senior Director, Harry Bollback. As Harry walked around the beautiful land and through the historic castle, I could see his attitude changing. I saw how excited he was becoming as he talked with the Trade Union engineers and leaders about possibly acquiring this magnificent site to be used to reach thousands of Eastern European young people for Christ. He could envision hundreds of people trained in a Bible Institute here who would go across Europe preaching the gospel. This prospect touched Harry's heart.

From the Toalmas Castle we drove to the headquarters of the SZOT Trade Union at Hero's Square in Budapest to meet with the director of the Trade Union and some of his aides. There was much bowing and scraping as usual during the proceedings, as the Hungarians are a very gracious and hospitable people. Pastor Kovacs and his son, Zoltan, had arranged this meeting, and Ildiko Barbarics accompanied us and served as our attorney and interpreter.

Harry opened the conversation by briefly describing the work of Word of Life around the world. He told how young people in over twenty-five countries are turned from a life of decadence to a life of victory because of Jesus Christ.

When Harry finished, I explained Word of Life's philosophy of camping and ministry as I had told so many other officials in Hungary. I spoke about the high profile we give to sports and how the teachings of Jesus Christ are taught and preached every morning and every night.

The director of the SZOT Union appeared to be increasingly interested in the content of our program. We were seeking to lease the castle property, using as our top figure $3,000 per month.

The trade union director asked, "If such a proposal were accepted, would Word of Life allow children of the Trade Union members to attend the camp?"

"Of course," I replied, "as long as they submit to the community rules of the camp along with everyone else."

The union director went on to explain how the Union was responsible to provide vacations for the children of its members. If we would allow a predetermined number of their children to attend our camp, then they might be willing to lease us the entire property for a period of ten years with *no monthly charge required!* We would simply need to accept in the vicinity of fifty union children each week of camp at no cost to the families.

We could hardly believe what we were hearing. What this man was actually saying was, "If you will accept fifty unconverted Hungarian young people into your program each week, with Word of Life funding their stay, we will drop all lease costs."

The union director looked at Harry and said, "If we could agree on a proposition such as this, when would Word of Life be interested in beginning such an undertaking?"

Harry, nearly jumping out of his shoes, tried not to appear overzealous and said in a very controlled voice, "How about *right now?* If you and the Union will agree to that, I want to sign a preagreement before I leave this room! Is this possible?"

The trade union director gulped, looked at his secretary, and then said, "Yes, I think it is possible for us to make up an agreement today. We can do that."

We all looked at each other in disbelief. Everything was coming together so fast! I was so happy that the director of our international organization was there to be a part of it. This was almost unbelievable. It was as though all the details had been worked out in advance and we were simply watching the plan unfold. This was, indeed, a historic occasion. It was a first for the trade union, for up until that time, no such joint agreement with Americans had been made in Hungary under a Communist government. It was a first for Word of Life, and it was rather scary.

Within forty-five minutes, a pre-contractual agreement had been drawn up and signed by Harry Bollback, Chuck Kosman, and me. This was a miracle and it had all been prearranged by a sovereign, loving God who wanted to send an evangelistic, discipling ministry such as Word of Life to reach the youth of a country where officially God had been declared dead for forty years.

Another First

One month earlier, Pastor Kovacs and our attorneys had drawn up papers seeking non-profit, religious recognition for Word of Life from the Communist government. Kosman and I had been praying, hoping, and planning for these arrangements for more than four years. At first it was only a dream. Later it turned into heavy conflict and confrontation. Now, with obvious changes about to take place in the government, things were moving rapidly.

The day after the historic SZOT Trade Union meeting and

pre-contractual agreement, Harry, Chuck Kosman, the Kovacs, Ildiko Barbarics, and I went to the offices of the Deputy Minister of Health and Human Services. There we were to sign final papers legalizing Word of Life as the very first Christian organization from the West to receive government approval to exist under the Department of Health and Human Services. The significance of this was that we were being recognized under a department other than the Department of Religion. For more than forty years everything of a religious nature operated solely under the Department of Religion and its president, the atheistic Dr. Miklos. This is how the Communist government controlled all religious activity.

Up to this time, no one had ever been able to get out of that "religion box" of control. But things were changing rapidly in the Grosz government. Word of Life had pushed the limits of change. A year earlier, this brought conflict, confrontation, and the threat of arrest. However, on May 23, 1989, when we went to the office of the Deputy Director of Health and Human Services, we broke out of the religion box and became a free, legal entity. We were told this was a historic day by virtue of our being granted this privilege in Hungary.

When Harry, Chuck, Pastor Kovacs, and I put our signatures on that document, history was made. From that day on, the repressive Department of Religion would have absolutely no control over the ministry of Word of Life. What a day for rejoicing and praising our Lord!

A Slippery Tight Rope and the Joint Agreement

During the month of June, the trade union was to put together a final contract on the Toalmas Castle property for us to sign. I was to return with Chuck Kosman to finalize this historic agreement at the end of June 1989.

Upon meeting with the union director, we learned that though the plan would probably still come together, there were some very slippery obstacles to overcome. It seemed the problems stemmed around the Castle Committee Chairman who was just a bit unhappy with the entire arrangement. The entire deal had been put together by the director of the union, but no one had remembered to inform the Castle Committee Chairman that Word of Life would be the new tenants.

First of all, the chairman and his family were away on a vacation. They had to send for him and ask him to return to SZOT headquarters in Budapest so they could tell him what was going on with "his" castle. Secondly, there are fishing ponds on the castle property that he had personally stocked with fish. Fishing was his favorite pastime. If this deal went through, he would lose his fishing rights. The man was more than a little upset when we met with him at SZOT headquarters that 29th of June.

Seated along one side of the negotiation table were Pastor Kovacs, Kosman, and myself. On each end of the table sat the attorneys.

The chairman began making his demands, "You must totally provide scholarships for fifty trade union children each week. You are responsible for all renovations. You must be responsible for all inventory."

We agreed to all of his demands since we were agreeable to them before he ever knew what was happening. Then the chairman said, "How do we know you are financially responsible?"

I replied, "You don't, so we are prepared to produce a credit line to you."

"Yes, yes," he continued, "you must place $250,000 in United States currency in a Hungarian bank as security."

I was stunned by this demand. We were not buying the Castle

property, only leasing it.

I believe I stuttered a little as I said, "Sir, I'm not sure you understand that we are a non-profit Christian organization. That means we do not operate for a financial profit. The only funds we have are those entrusted to us by our many friends in Europe and America. We are not prepared to place $250,000 in a non-interest bearing account here. That is too much money!"

Even as I spoke I prayed silently, *Lord, you haven't brought us this far only to fail now. Please work this out for us, Lord. Please, Lord, give us victory!*

The chairman insisted, "No, $25,000 is not too much money to ask."

I began to think that I was the one confused now. Did he not just now say "$25,000?" I reminded the chairman that he had just asked for $250,000.

He replied again, "Yes, yes, $25,000."

Chuck Kosman leaned over and whispered, "Take it, take it."

My mind was spinning. Who was confused here? I turned to the attorneys, both of whom spoke English, and said, "Please make a note of this. This man has asked us to place $25,000 in United States currency in a Hungarian bank account as a security." The attorneys both nodded in agreement.

I did not want to push the incident any farther. We all agreed that a final contract would be drawn up the next morning and that we would meet at the SZOT Hotel the next evening for a celebration dinner and an official contract-signing ceremony.

I immediately cornered Kosman after the meeting and asked, "Who is confused, me or the chairman?"

"I'm not sure myself," Kosman replied, "but the attorneys have a note of our agreeing to $25,000."

"Will the chairman discover the radical difference between the demand of $250,000 and $25,000?" I asked.

"We will know tomorrow at noon when the contract will be complete at the SZOT office," Kosman advised.

I prayed, *Lord, keep them confused and keep the demand at only $25,000.* I prayed that same request to the Lord twenty-five times before the next day.

At 2:00 p.m. on June 30, we asked Pastor Kovacs to phone the SZOT office and have them read the contract to him. The answer came…$25,000 dollars!

"Praise God!" Kosman and I shouted. "Thank you, Lord!"

Toalmas Castle would be leased to Word of Life for the next ten years for no monthly rent. We would agree to receive for a week of camp, four hundred children of trade union members each year at no cost to the Trade Union or the families. We would make all necessary renovations and upgrading of facilities. We would also place $25,000 in our own bank account in Budapest. What a deal!

Now that the hand of God had so clearly moved in opening the minds of government leaders to our ministry, would he do the same for our staff leadership? The most vital part of any ministry is not buildings and properties, but the people who lead it. In Hungary, God had miraculously given us an unusually beautiful property. But, who would establish and lead the ministry? The ministry of Word of Life was already moving at a very rapid pace. Yet, I could not possibly leave the care of all of our other ministries around the world to lead the ministry in Hungary. There were several godly Hungarian men already involved, yet they understood very little of how we operated as a ministry to youth. Would God, in His Grace, go before us and prepare the way with a staff as well?

CHAPTER 10

A TEAM COMES
TOGETHER

Until this time, it had been impossible for Westerners to establish residency in Hungary. It was still very much a Communist-controlled nation, though many saw obvious change on the horizon.

In all our planning, we assumed it would be impossible to import experienced Word of Life staff members to Hungary. Yet, there was no question in our minds that bringing aboard experienced Word of Life personnel to train the nationals would be the most effective way to begin our formal ministry in Hungary. Using men who had succeeded elsewhere and knew the workings of every aspect of Word of Life's ministry would save years of training Hungarians by proxy.

Initially, we had planned to bring potentially capable Hungarians to other Word of Life operations where they would be indoctrinated in our style of effective ministry. However, almost overnight, new governmental direction made it possible for us to import as many experienced personnel as necessary to establish Word of Life Hungary.

The Problem of Finding Trained Hungarians

Bible-trained young men are extremely scarce in all Eastern European countries. In Hungary, the Communist government officials looked upon most pastors and Christian workers with contempt. The government made obtaining a Bible education very complicated for young men. In fact, for the 1986-87 school year, the Baptist Seminary (Bible College) in Buda had fewer than thirty students. All graduates, consequently, were drawn immediately into waiting, pastor-less or under-pastored churches. This made finding qualified, Bible-educated young men to staff a missionary organization such as Word of Life extremely difficult.

It became obvious to us that an entire generation of young people would need to be won to Christ, formally educated, and discipled in the ministry before we could fully staff our Hungarian outreach with nationals.

Consequently, when the report reached us saying it would be possible to bring thoroughly trained, experienced Westerners into Hungary, it was very welcomed news. In fact, this news changed our entire strategy.

Word of Life would not only be allowed to occupy a beautiful, well-equipped castle property for a camping facility, but we could also start Bible Clubs to win young people to Christ all over Hungary. In addition to all this, we planned, by God's grace, to start the sixteenth Word of Life Bible Institute where hundreds of Hungarian young people would receive a Bible-education and hundreds of young men would learn to pastor.

Now that we were allowed to bring trained men to staff our Hungarian operations, the question arose as to where we would find the leaders for this very special team. We had people in mind, but would they feel led by God to join in our efforts in Hungary? As with every other detail in this wonderful Hungarian adventure, God already had a plan.

Chuck Kosman

Chuck Kosman was born of Ukrainian parents who sold everything they owned to immigrate to Western Canada. During their first Canadian winter they survived in a cave dug into the side of a hill on property given as a land grant. As Chuck's father began to eke out a living on a scrub farm, children were born to the young couple.

A circuit-riding preacher came through the Canadian farmlands monthly. On one of those visits, Kosman's family embraced Jesus Christ. Chuck's father experienced a dramatic change in his life. By God's grace, he was transformed from a drunkard to a caring, hardworking, godly man who loved his wife and children and wanted them to serve the Lord.

Young Chuck, saved as a boy, resisted God's call on his life and entered the banking field in pursuit of material gain and power. However, God had other plans. One day a swimming accident brought Chuck to death's door. After only narrowly being revived, Chuck's priorities immediately changed. He knew who controlled all of life. Chuck enrolled at the Briarcrest Bible Institute, and a few years later he joined a singing quartet. They went to Germany as singers and evangelists to Germany, after traveling with Jack Wyrtzen across North America for two years.

For twenty-five years the quartet crisscrossed Germany and Western and Eastern Europe. Chuck became thoroughly schooled in European thinking and society, without losing his evangelistic zeal. In 1988 Word of Life invited Chuck to become the Director of Word of Life Europe. Chuck, along with Bob Parschauer and their ministry team were the first to enter Hungary. It was on their second trip that Chuck invited me to come. Chuck Kosman and Bob Parschauer were deeply involved with and loved the Hungarian people. It seemed to me that our wonderful, sovereign Lord had his hand on Kosman and Parschauer, preparing them for such a time as this.

Eric Murphy

Eric, upon graduation from Bob Jones University, married his college sweetheart, Lynne Stanley. He was the pastor of a small church in Alabama before moving to take the position of youth pastor at a much larger church. It was there that Eric met our Word of Life Bible Club area missionary, Mike Calhoun. Loving the effectiveness of Word of Life Clubs in establishing sound youth ministries in local churches, Eric soon joined the Word of Life Clubs staff where he served for eleven years.

Eric, with his dynamic platform presence, was invited to become the director of the new Word of Life Conference Center in Florida, but unbeknownst to anyone else, Eric was not at peace in making that decision. The Murphys had not taken a vacation for several years but they had frugally saved their money. In December of 1988, they ventured on a European vacation.

I had rarely seen Eric and Lynne since I moved from directing the Club ministry to directing the Overseas Division in 1987. In December of 1988, I was at our castles in Starnberg, Germany meeting with our European directors. Leaving the conference room for a break, I literally bumped into my friend Eric in the castle hallway.

"Murphy," I exclaimed, "What are you doing in Germany?"

We invited Eric to join our conference. As we talked about the great opportunities in Hungary, God began to stir the heart of this veteran Word of Life leader. The next day Eric and Lynne continued on their vacation, but God continued to burden Eric's heart and Lynne's as well.

Two days before Harry Bollback and I left for Hungary in 1989, just before signing the documents that would legalize Word of Life and the pre-contractual agreement on the Toalmas Castle, I received a phone call from Lynne Murphy in Florida. Her mother and father were taking a trip through Europe and had asked Lynne to accompany them as their guide, since she had been to Europe just a few months before. Lynne wanted to know the address of the Budafok Baptist Church so she and her parents could visit there the following Sunday. Little did she know that Harry and I would be there and that Harry would be preaching.

While she and her parents were in Hungary, God so moved in Lynne's heart that she phoned Eric at home and pleaded with him to return to Europe so they could pray together about this burden God was impressing upon them both. Meanwhile, in Florida, all Eric could think about was Hungary. When he received his wife's call, he told her, "I'll be there right away!"

Eric is now the director of this growing, exciting ministry in Hungary. As one looks back on the events that moved his heart toward Hungary, one realizes it was simply another work of our sovereign God's marvelous plan to raise up a ministry that would present Christ to the youth of that nation. It certainly was not by coincidence or by chance.

Dan Bubar

Dan is the second son born to my wife, Shirley, and me. Before he was born, we surrendered him to the Lord. As Dan was growing up, I was the program director for the teen camp on Word of Life Island. This allowed Dan to spend all of his summers on the Island. For more than twenty years Dan watched and observed the Word of Life camp program and dreamed of one day being able to run a Word of Life Camp.

No one had more experience in seeing how to run a Christian youth camp than Dan. On the Island, he worked on operations staff, as a senior counselor, a unit leader, and then as the assistant dean of the Summer Institute of Camping. One summer he worked for Chuck Kosman at our castles in Germany. That was where God burdened Dan's heart for Europe.

After graduating from the Word of Life Bible Institute and the School of Youth Ministries, Dan enrolled at Tennessee Temple University. There his burden for the people of Europe grew. Believing God wanted him to open a new field for Word of Life in Sweden, Dan pursued that goal.

When Harry and I were at the contract signing in Budapest, Harry suddenly said, "Your son, Dan, must come to Hungary and minister. This is the field for him. Call Dan today!"

I was not only Dan's father, but also the director of all Word of Life overseas ministries. I needed to be very careful not to *tell* Dan to come to Hungary. God had to tell him that. Upon my return to the United States, my wife and I met Dan in New Jersey where he was teaching school while on deputation for Sweden. I carefully shared with him the words of my boss, Harry Bollback, but God had already been at work.

Some of the original team planning to go to Sweden had withdrawn and doubts had emerged in Dan's mind. He had been to Hungary and he loved the Hungarian people. He also knew of my love for these people. Dan asked for a few days to seek the Lord's face in the matter. An excitement about Hungary began to stir within his heart. By the next week, Dan knew God wanted him to go to Hungary to minister through camping and Bible Clubs.

To Dan, and to me, it was very evident that the intricate working of our Lord brought this experienced young man into the team to create a dynamic camping and Bible Club ministry for the youth of Hungary.

Rich and Alissa Hood

After graduating from Appalachian State University in Boone, North Carolina, with a degree in Business Administration, Rich Hood went on to receive a Master's Degree in Counseling from Liberty University. Soon afterward, Rich was accepted by Word of Life to join a team going to Singapore. However, within months, the man heading the Singapore team felt led to enter the pastorate. Rich was to be the business administrator and not the team leader. Now that the team was without a leader, Rich often prayed, "God, what do you want me to do now?"

Working each summer at the Word of Life camps in Schroon Lake, Rich heard of the miraculous working of God in opening Hungary to Word of Life. He often thought how he would love to be a part of that team! Many times he heard me talk of the need for a business manager for our operations in Hungary. Thoughts of ministering in Hungary began to dominate Rich's mind. His wife, Alissa, was also very interested in going to Hungary to help teach young women and bring them to Christ.

What would the leaders think if I asked to change fields? Rich wondered. Finally, he could no longer suppress his feelings. With Alissa's encouragement, he had to speak out.

Many times I had thought how well Rich and Alissa would complement the Hungary team, but I wanted God to be the one to move them toward such a decision. Rich made an appointment one day to tell me of this burden God seemed to be creating within his heart. He and Alissa could now think of nothing but Hungary. When we talked, I knew this was no coincidence. God was adding to our team another experienced professional.

Dave and Karen James

Dave James was an unconverted student at the Rose-Hulman Institute of Technology majoring in Mechanical Engineering when he and his wife, Karen, realized they had no answers to the questions and issues of life.

When this couple invited Christ into their lives, they were completely changed. They used to laugh at churchgoing people who needed a "crutch" to hobble through life. Now, they *loved* being in God's house every time the doors were open. They couldn't get enough of studying God's Word.

A godly pastor suggested the couple enroll in the Word of Life Bible Institute at Schroon Lake. Upon graduation, Dave enrolled at Dallas Theological Seminary, working towards a Master of Divinity degree. He could not shake Word of Life from his thoughts, so when Dallas Seminary required an internship, Dave and Karen returned to Schroon Lake for Dave to be the Dean of Men at the Bible Institute. In that position, Dave studied and memorized every intricate facet and method of a specialized Bible Institute such as Word of Life. Together, he and Karen were also raising a family.

For two years Dave and Karen heard the miraculous reports on the developments in Hungary. When we announced our incorporation in Hungary, we also announced that we would be permitted to start a Bible Institute at Toalmas Castle. Dave and Karen began praying about their desire to be in on the ground floor of starting a new Bible Institute. How exciting it would be to be part of a team that would help train future pastors and Christian workers–even future missionaries–in Hungary! Making a trip to Hungary for the dedication of the Toalmas Castle only confirmed in the couple's heart and mind what God was doing.

Dave was a man uniquely equipped to establish and manage a Bible Institute and was available precisely when we needed someone to fill this role in Hungary. Only one more year of study at Dallas would earn Dave his Master's degree. He would then become the Executive Dean of the Hungarian Bible Institute starting in September of 1994. His wife, Karen, was also a woman of God who wanted to support her husband and see the ministry of Word of Life grow in a country sorely lacking in the truth of God's Word. She wanted to do all she could to assist. Only God knew how significant would be their call to serve with Word of Life in Hungary. Word of Life has a great debt of gratitude to Dave and Karen James.

God had a special purpose for this young couple when he saved them. God gave Dave James all the years of education and administrative level experience at the Word of Life Bible Institute in Schroon Lake for a distinct purpose.

Alex and Pam Konya

Alex and Pam Konya lived in South Bend, Indiana, where Alex was the pastor of the Mayflower Baptist Church. He had been a student at Grace Theological Seminary in Winona Lake, Indiana, before becoming a pastor. As the church grew in size, he and his wife, Pam, adopted Word of Life Clubs as his church's outreach to teenagers. They saw how the ministry functioned, how the clubs evangelize youth and were able to coach their youth leaders. They liked everything about this ministry. The club ministry was helping Alex's church to grow!

Then along came Hungary. Alex and Pam watched and listened with great interest. Alex told Doug Armbrecht, the Indiana Word of Life Club missionary, that he and Pam were interested in what Word of Life was doing in Hungary and that they would love to go on a trip to that country with Word of Life.

Alex is Hungarian. As a matter of fact, his great-grandfather immigrated to the United States in the early part of the 1900's and helped start the first Hungarian Baptist Church in America. Though his great-grandfather died years before Alex was born, he learned from his Aunt Rose that the man prayed often that God would one day raise up someone from his family who would return to Hungary as a missionary. His prayers were answered through Alex.

Alex had been a pastor for fourteen years as well as a solid student of theology. When he heard of the Hungarian pastors having to shepherd as many as five churches at a time, his heart was moved to do something to help them. But how? The answer was simple. Young men in Hungary *must* be trained in good theology and pastoring. When he learned of the plan to start a Word of Life Bible Institute in Hungary, his heart was moved even more. He and Pam both felt they had to do something. They decided to go to Hungary and see things for themselves. Alex was there for the dedication of the Toalmas Castle property. He was overwhelmed by the spiritual hunger he saw there.

Soon after this, Alex, his wife, Pam, and their children arrived in Hungary to help train and disciple future Hungarian pastors at the Word of Life Bible Institute. Little did he know how significant their decision to go to Hungary would be to the future of the ministry there. Little did he know his decision was not by chance, but by special design by a loving God.

Alex and Katie Katona

The story of Alex and Katie Katona's life would fill volumes. As a matter of fact, a book titled, *Forever Together*, has been published. It chronicles their early life in Hungary, the 1965 Revolution and how they fled, finally arriving in America. There, Alex became a successful business owner of an auto repair shop in Laconia, New Hampshire, while Katie stayed home with their children.

The children were raised to love the Lord Jesus Christ. Their son enrolled at the New Brunswick Bible Institute (NBBI) in Andover, New Brunswick, a wonderful school.

I had been invited to be the keynote speaker at the annual Missions Conference at NBBI. The Katonas decided to attend. They had heard what Word of Life was doing in their beloved Hungary, but at this conference they heard the stories and miracles God was doing in their country first hand. Like God breaking the heart of Nehemiah when he heard of the plight of the city of his father's (Nehemiah 1:3), God broke Alex and Katie's hearts for Hungary.

But the couple was past middle age. They were no longer in their twenties or thirties. At the Missions Conference, they wanted to talk. Between meetings, we went to a little rest-stop restaurant on the Trans Canada Highway near the school and had lunch together. They were full of questions. How would they do this at their age? It would mean selling all their earthly goods; everything they owned. It would mean the rigors of travel, and visiting churches and generating support, at their age.

But Alex and Katie were exactly what Eric would need in Toalmas. They were Hungarian, and naturally spoke the language fluently. There was an opportunity that Alex could manage the construction, maintenance and refurbishing of the castle, but also he and Katie would be a perfect liaison to the people of Toalmas village.

That is exactly what they decided to do. Alex and Katie have since worked very hard, long hours to minister to the Hungarian people, literally day and night. They have given everything they have to serve Word of Life. They have very little for retirement. But do they worry? Has it been worth it? I asked them that question one day. And they responded that they would do it all over again in a heartbeat.

God's marvelous plan became so obvious. God wanted a ministry to the younger generation of Hungary to happen, so when He was ready, He began to move in people's hearts. He began to direct their footsteps like a symphony director leading an orchestra. He moved in the heart of Kosman and Parschauer. He clearly moved in my heart and rearranged my steps at the Munich airport so I could be placed on Pan Am #301 out of London where I met Michael Kovacs. He brought us in contact with the Pastor Kovacs family and so many more people who would become key to our ministry in Hungary.

Yet, not always does everything that happens to us appear to be good. For example, I often think of my Jewish friend Michael Kovacs on the Pan Am flight to New York asking me, "Why? Why did my family, all more brilliant than I, why did they perish and I survived? Can you answer that question? Why?"

CHAPTER 11

WHY, GOD?

W hy, God?" Have you ever asked that question of God? When seemingly unjust circumstances come upon good people, when difficult things come your way — a loved one dies, a tragic accident occurs, you've missed an airplane flight or an important appointment — have you ever asked, "Why, God?"

Do things happen simply by chance as in the lottery, or does God truly know what is happening in the world, or more importantly, in my life? Does God have a divine plan? If so, then why do war, repression, suffering, and even martyrdom exist? Does a loving God cause such atrocities to happen, or are they something beyond His control? If God does not want these events to happen, then is His power limited and are some things beyond His control? If so, then what things?

The year 1917 will live in infamy in world history. Though life in Russia under the Czars was far from wonderful, all hell broke loose during the Bolshevik Revolution under Lenin's communism. Life was considered cheap and everything was sacrificed for the cause of the revolution. Historians estimate that over twenty million people were murdered during Stalin's regime, and among them, many wonderful Christians.

On April 27, 1992, George Theis, the Executive Director of Word of Life Fellowship Inc., Bob Parschauer, and I held meetings at the Baptist Church in Zittomar, Ukraine. A few years earlier, the pastor of that church had refused to register his church with the government and thereby submit the church to Communist authority. As a result, the pastor had endured two prison terms, one being in Siberia. He told us how in 1962, under Joseph Stalin, all of the Baptists in the region (more than ten thousand) were gathered by force into a large field where bulldozers had dug huge holes in the earth. The believers were herded into these massive holes and machine gunned. The pastor recounted that perhaps half of the people were not dead when the earth was bulldozed over them, burying them alive. Why? Was this a horrible miscarriage of justice in God's plan for this world? Where was God? How could good ever come out of something as horrible as this?

In 1945, I lived in a remote part of Maine, in the town of Allagash. I was twelve years old, and very much aware that World War II was coming to its conclusion. My father was an avid reader and student of world events. One incident I vividly recall is the Peace Conference at Yalta, off the southern coast of the Ukraine on the Caspian Sea. Present at the peace conference was a world statesman, Winston Churchill; a murderer, Joseph Stalin; and, it is reported, a sick and drunken American president, Franklin Delano Roosevelt. It was said that Stalin intimidated Roosevelt.

Together, these men decided, at the conference, how the spoils of Europe would be apportioned. Europe was geographically divided between east and west. The Russian Block was established and the Iron Curtain was drawn.

I have a mental picture of my dad, with his ear glued to a battery-powered radio, listening to the newscast and shouting, "Why, why? Why would You allow this to happen, God?" I was shocked, because I thought my godly preacher father was questioning God. He was not. He was exercised by events he believed would happen in the years to come as a result of those terrible decisions at Yalta: the Christians who would be imprisoned and murdered, the church that would suffer, and the ruin that would follow. He was crying out for the people of Eastern Europe. What purpose could God have in all of this? Why, God?

In 1949, Mao Tse Tung drove Chiang Kai Shek out of mainland China. Communism was established and the Communist Revolution completed. All of the American "White Devil" missionaries were driven out of the country, many with just the clothes on their backs. Once the missionaries were ousted, the killing and persecution began. The book, *Come Wind: Come Weather* documents the Communist takeover of China. It tells how the death trucks would rattle through the streets at night, going to the homes of known Christians, taking couples by force. Their hands and feet were tied behind their backs, and then they were thrown onto the death trucks and driven to the nearest river or lake where the trucks would dump their human loads into the water. Reportedly 1.5 million followers of Jesus Christ were murdered. Missionary leaders believed it was the end of the organized church in China, and so it seemed to be.

In 1951, Communist hordes crossed the 38th parallel from North Korea. They came plundering and killing. I am told that North Korean Communist soldiers would even enter a worship service, stand the pastor and church leaders against a wall before a terrified congregation, and they would demand that they renounce Christ. When they would not, the pastors and leaders were shot or bayoneted before the eyes of the praying congregation. I am told that in a three-month period during that era, more than three thousand gospel preachers went into eternity that way. Why?

Suppose you were one of those missionaries whose congregation was disseminated or whose church leaders were murdered. Imagine that you were a child whose Christian parents were taken away on a death truck, or that you were a faithful member of a persecuted congregation in Korea. Don't you think you might have thought, *Why, God? Why would you* do *this? They loved you. They only wanted* to *serve you. Why would you allow this to happen?* Could there be any plan by God in *this*?

God Had a Perfect Plan – Before the Beginning

Yes, God has a plan for each life. Not only that, but it is a *perfect* plan because God is perfect. (Psalm 18:30 tells us, "As for God, His way is perfect.") Paul, in Romans 12:2, refers to the good and acceptable and *perfect* will of God. Because God is perfect, He cannot do anything with flaws in it. He cannot sin because He is God. Therefore, any plan God has for my life is *perfect.*

Psalm 139:15-16 says, "My frame was not hidden from you, when I was made in secret, and skillfully wrought in the lowest parts of the earth. Your eyes saw my substance, being yet unformed. And in your book they were written, the days fashioned for me, when as yet there were none of them." (The New King James Version) The Psalmist, under the guiding hand of the Holy Spirit, is saying, "Before the world was formed God scheduled the days of your life." That means that my God, in eternity past, scheduled all my days!

In Jeremiah 29:11, the prophet, under the influence of the Holy Spirit, says, "'I know the thoughts I think toward you,' says the Lord, 'thoughts of peace and not of evil, to give you a future and a hope.'" In other words, God has a plan for your life and mine, and they are plans for good *and not evil,* to give us a future and a hope.

The wonderful plans God has for man are also expressed by the apostle Paul in Ephesians 1:4-5, "According as He hath chosen us in Him before the foundation of the world, that we should be holy and without blame before Him in love: Having predestined us unto the adoption of children by Jesus Christ to Himself, according to the good pleasure of His will."

To think that the God of the universe did this for every one of His children before the universe was put into space is almost incomprehensible to me. The fact is that God has an intricate plan for each of our lives. But, what *is* that plan?

God's plan is that all would receive His Son as their personal Savior from sin. II Peter 3:9 says, "[God is] . . . not willing that any should perish, but that *all* should come to repentance." In John 3:17, Jesus said, "For God did not send His Son into the world to condemn the world, but that the world through Him might be saved." God's perfect plan is for everyone to be able to spend eternity in a prepared place called heaven. God did not plan anyone's eternity in hell, only heaven. Though He knew some men would reject His offer of salvation and, in so doing, become hell-bound, this was not God's perfect plan for mankind.

Paul speaks of the plan of God in Galatians 4:4-5, "But when the fullness of time had come, God sent forth His Son, born of a woman, born under the law, that we might receive the adoption as sons."

In other words, God's revealed plan for man, who had become sinful through Adam's breaking of God's law in the Garden (Gen. 3:17), was that when God was ready, at the time He appointed in eternity past, He would initiate His plan to save man's soul.

It was God's plan to send His very own Son, Jesus Christ, into this world to be offered up as a sacrifice as full payment for our sins. Those who accepted this fact and God's gift would have their sins washed away and be declared righteous by God. In this way all who believed would receive full forgiveness of their sin, receive the position of adopted sons, and be acceptable to God in heaven.

One problem exists. Genesis 1:26-27 says that God created man in His image and likeness. While God is infinite and man is finite, it means that man was created with elements of personality such as God possesses: thinking (Gen. 2:19, 20), feeling (Gen. 3:8), and will (Gen. 3:6, 7). When God created man He gave him the ability to make choices. He did not create him as a robot that could have his every thought and action controlled. God did not create man as a puppet who had to respond exactly as God willed. God wanted man to love Him because man *wanted* to, not *had* to.

Because of this, God gave man a free will: the ability to choose, to accept or reject, to do or not do, to say or not say. Man could even choose to reject God's favor, turn against his Creator and live a life of rebellion, and that is exactly what man did.

Genesis chapter three chronicles the sad story of Satan's deceit and Eve's belief of the big lie. In verse one; Satan drives the wedge of doubt into Eve's mind. He says, "Has God indeed said. . .? Oh, is that what God *really* said?" At that point, Eve began to doubt her loving Creator. Then, Satan followed with the big lie. "You will *not* surely die. For God knows that in the day you eat of it, you will be like God, knowing good and evil" (Genesis 3:4-5). Satan injected doubt, followed with a lie, and then appealed to man's pride: "You will be like God. . ." Adam and Eve, the first of the human race, believed the lie, sinned, and broke God's law. From that point on, they became law-breakers (sinners) and because of this, every man in history has had the inner nature of a law-breaker, a sinner. Sin separated man from God and made him unfit for heaven. As a matter of fact, man became so sinful that of the estimated five billion people on the earth (according to Dr. Henry Morris of the Institute for Creation Research) man's every intent and thought was only evil (Genesis 6:5-6). Because of this, God was sorry He had ever made man.

This is where all the Hitlers and Stalins originated. Their hearts were naturally evil. Men deceive themselves and rationalize their evil deeds. Hitler even called himself a Christian!

From the first sin committed by the first man, men have been trying to make their own way to heaven through good works, education, popularity, recognition, and even through being religious; but all to no avail. All of these things may be satisfying to man, but not to God. There is only one thing that can satisfy God, and that is for man to follow God's plan.

One writer's commentary on Galatians 4:4-7 puts it this way, "But when the right time came, the time God decided on, He sent His Son, born of a woman, born as a Jew, to buy freedom for us who were slaves to the law so that He could adopt us as His very own sons. And because we are His sons, God has sent the Spirit of His Son into our hearts, so now we can rightly speak of God as our dear Father. Now we are no longer slaves, but God's own sons. And since we are His sons, everything He has belongs to us, for that is the way God planned" (The Living Bible).

God's plan was that He would provide, through the willing sacrifice of His Son, Jesus Christ, a way in which all men could have their sins blotted out (Isa.1:18) and become children of God. But men have to choose this way. Any man can have salvation, but he must choose to receive the Lord Jesus. Salvation will not just happen. It is not inherited or earned. Salvation is by choice. It is God's choice to offer you this wonderful salvation and yours to choose to receive it by receiving Christ.

But. . . Were Yalta, China, and Korea a Part of

God's Plan? If so, Why?

If you were to go to China today, you would find a people still enslaved by Communism and a church still plagued by persecution. As a result of the crushing heel of Communism in the 1950s, the evangelical church in China went underground and small groups began meeting secretly in homes. Because the church was persecuted, Christians grew strong in their faith and the church grew until today it is estimated not only to be vibrantly alive, but to number roughly six million believers. Did God have a purpose in allowing evil men to bring persecution and even death to the church in China?

What about Korea and the brutal murders of those godly pastors? Church history reveals that "the blood of the martyrs is the seed of the Church." In Korea today one will find a very dynamic and living church that is fast becoming one of the great missionary sending churches in the world. Did God know what He was doing in Korea? Were the millions who have been won to Jesus Christ worth the sacrifice of those godly pastors? Was this evil thing used by God to further His plan to redeem this world?

What about Yalta and Eastern Europe? How could the human suffering, torture, imprisonment, and death of so many, though not caused by God, be used for good?

The Eastern European scene is far from over yet, and one cannot accurately predict what God has in mind. One thing is for certain, the Church of Jesus Christ is very much alive today in Eastern and Central Europe. In Hungary, Romania, the Czech Republic, the Republic of Slovakia, the Ukraine, Bulgaria, Poland, and Russia, millions are finding Jesus Christ. In Word of Life related ministries alone, since 1987, thousands, perhaps tens of thousands, have publicly turned to Christ as Savior and Lord.

I remember preaching in the great O Street Plymouth Brethren Assembly in Budapest, Hungary in 1989. Freedom had just come to the nation. With the Communist government thrown out, excitement filled the air. I could now speak openly about Communism in a negative way without fear. I told the people, a crowd of about two hundred gathered for a prayer meeting, about my mental picture of my dad crying, "Why, why," over the conference at Yalta. I told them, "I am not a prophet, but I *am* a dreamer, and when I dream of Europe I ask the question (and I mean no sacrilege) 'If I were God, how would I ever penetrate the heart of a continent such as Europe? Europe, the seed-bed of humanism, higher criticism, and atheism?' If I were God, I possibly might allow Europe to be divided down the middle and then place one half of the continent under great pressure and persecution.

The result of the persecution would be a purified and thriving church. Then, when I was ready, I would pull down the walls and barriers that divide the continent. I would turn the purified, alive, dynamic church loose on the rest of the continent to preach the Word of God with zeal, Holy Ghost fire, and conviction."

The audience sat with a look of disbelief that God would do something like this. Many elderly believers wiped tears from their eyes.

I continued, "That is why Word of Life is so interested in Europe, and Eastern Europe in particular. It is our goal to not only see our Bible Club ministry flourish through gospel-preaching churches, but also to start youth camps where young people can get saved and choose to dedicate their lives to serving the Lord. It is our goal to start Bible Institutes where these young people can study the Word of God and learn to be pastors, teachers, and evangelists. It is our goal to turn these young men and women, with knowledge of the Word of God and a holy enthusiasm, loose on the rest of Europe."

By now, old heads were nodding. The people were smiling, and not a few of these old saints who had lived through the hard years were wiping their tear-stained cheeks.

Can God Bring Good Out of Evil?

Is it right that God would exact such a costly price of suffering, torture, imprisonment, and even death on so many? We must remember that our God is an awesome God whose plans for us are good and not evil (Jer. 29: 11). I do not believe that God planned the suffering, torture, and deaths of so many good people. These plans were made by the evil one. Man was created perfect, but by his free will he chose to disobey God. As a result, man inflicted upon himself a sinful nature which, left to its own natural instincts, chooses evil over good. The Stalins, the Mao Tse-Tungs, the Hitlers were all men whose basic nature was unchecked. With no accountability, man does horrendous things. God has told us of man's evil nature in Romans chapter three.

But God...

But God brings good out of evil. In Genesis 37, Joseph's evil brothers wanted to kill him. As the story continues, we read that God spared Joseph as he endured attempted murder, false accusations, betrayal, and imprisonment. God brought Joseph up from prisoner to prime minister. God turned what was meant for evil into good. God blessed Israel and brought glory to Himself through Joseph's bad times.

In Acts 16, we read the account of Paul and Silas at Philippi. They were simply doing what God wanted them to do, and yet they got into trouble – big-time! After standing before the kangaroo court (vv. 20-24), they were beaten and put in prison with their feet in stocks. At midnight (vs. 25), instead of cursing the darkness and their terrible plight, they decided to sing and pray aloud!

God took this evil circumstance and turned it into victory. At midnight, God shook that prison so that everyone was set free. The jailer and his family got saved, and out of that "jail break" at Philippi was born one of the great New Testament churches. Did God know what He was doing? Did He control and use for the good of so many, the evil that came to Paul and Silas?

What about the brutal treatment and death of Christians in Eastern Europe, Korea, and China, and the Baptist Christians at Zittomar, Ukraine? What about their shortened lives?

By dying as martyrs, these wonderful saints reached the same heaven where all true believers will someday dwell. Each martyr was permitted to go there early, and to receive the special recognition of a martyr's crown.

Yes, it is true. Many who have tasted the martyr's death have been elderly, but many were young, even children. In Psalms 90:4, the psalmist claims that a thousand years is like yesterday to our Lord. II Peter 3:8 says, "But beloved, do not forget this one thing, that with the Lord, one day is as a thousand years, and a thousand years as one day." In other words, God is not locked into time zones, years, months, days, or hours as we are. He sees from eternity to eternity. Psalm 90:2 tells us that our God is without beginning or end. He sees the broad picture, not a narrow focus of a few short years as we see.

Evidently, when a person dies and goes into eternity, he, too, knows no time limits. When we die, we will be released from calendars and clocks. If this is true, and I believe it is, then those martyred saints in Russia, China, and Korea have preceded us to heaven by just a brief moment in God's scheme of time. Fifty years compared to a thousand years is just a few minutes.

I remember being at the funeral of Dr. Pierre DuBose, founder of Hamden DuBose Academy. Leon Sullivan, a great Christian leader and businessman who was on our Word of Life Executive Board, was speaking. He had been a close personal friend to Dr. DuBose. Mr. Sullivan looked at the closed casket and said, "If I could talk to my friend, Pierre, I would say, 'It won't be long, Bo. Look over your shoulder. . . I'm coming right behind you!'"

It is so true, though Leon lived another twenty-eight years, on eternity's timetable he *was* right behind his friend "Bo."

Was the martyrdom of so many *good?* I'm not saying it was. I am saying that evil men, with corrupted minds, meant evil toward God and His program. They tortured and murdered the innocent, but God used their evil for His good. As a result of the martyrs, the saints left behind were energized and determined to further the cause of Jesus Christ.

The Church of Jesus Christ was purified. If you weren't a committed Christian, you were fearful and hid your Christianity or removed yourself from identification with it. If you were only "religious" and not truly a born-again child of God, you distanced yourself from the true followers of Christ. It was the "healthy" thing to do. Consequently, the true church of blood-bought believers was purified as the insincere were weeded out and only those willing to die for their faith remained. With this type of conviction, the number of believers multiplied! The Church, though greatly oppressed and persecuted, grew rapidly in these tormented countries. This is how millions were brought to Christ in China, Korea, and Eastern Europe.

Does God really know what He is doing? Does God have a plan for your life and mine? You bet He does! Do things in life happen just by chance? Not in my life they haven't, and they won't in your life either if you will trust the Lord Jesus Christ as Savior.

Heaven is a very real place. It was planned and prepared by our Lord for all who seek Him. In John 13:21-34, Jesus has just told His followers of His imminent betrayal by Judas. He tells them He wants them to truly love one another so everyone would know they were His disciples. In John 14:1-6, Jesus goes on to comfort His followers with these words, "Let not your heart be troubled; you believe in God, believe also in Me. In My Father's house are many mansions; if it were not so, I would have told you. I go to prepare a place for you. And if I go to prepare a place for you, I will come again and receive you to Myself; that where I am, there you may be also. And where I go you know, and the way you know. Thomas said to Him, 'Lord, we do not know where You are going, and how can we know the way?' Jesus said to Him, 'I am the way, the truth, and the life. No one comes to the Father except through Me.'"

If this concept is true, then Eastern Europe would certainly be a proving ground for it. Probably no part of the world has endured such devastation under the heel of such tyrants as Hitler and Stalin.

In view of this, how can anyone explain the events (horrendous events by man's standard) of Eastern Europe in this century? How is it possible that a holy and gracious God could allow these events to take place? Does it mean anything to me now? What does it mean to you?

CHAPTER 12

UP CLOSE & PERSONAL
WHY, GOD?
PART II

The previous chapter has been penned from personal knowledge of Scripture and observations of how God works in people's lives. Putting things in writing, however, helps write them not only on paper, but in one's heart as well. Little did I realize how gracious my sovereign God was being to me and my wife in allowing me to verbalize some answers to the question, "Why, God?"

I had finished writing the manuscript in 1995. It is now the year 2004. Why could I not seem to bring this story of God's work to a conclusion? There were several delays in making final adjustments, double-checking on stories, dates and facts, etc. Somehow, I could not get the manuscript ready for publication. Now, I can understand why God chose to test me in the Biblical rationale I had penned in Chapter 11. Not only that, but God was not finished teaching me all He wanted me to learn yet. He had more instruction for my family and me, only this time it was to be up close and personal — very up close and very, very personal. It was as though God was about to say to me, "Paul Bubar, though I know you've ministered to many who were asking the question, 'why' over the years, put your seat belt on, son; because I now want you to apply all you've been saying. I want to know if you really believe it and can practice it before a watching world."

Sunday Morning, March 17, 1996

It was Sunday morning of our Founder's Week Bible Conference, and I was leading the singing for some seven hundred worshippers, (mostly students and staff) in the Word of Life Bible Institute Field House. Everyone's friend and Word of Life's Founder, Jack Wyrtzen, and his wife, Joan, were seated in the front row of the auditorium.

To honor Jack's ministry, I asked the student body, "How many of you made a consecration of your life to serve the Lord at a Word of Life campfire service somewhere in the world? Would you please stand to your feet?"

I would judge that more than fifty students stood.

"Jack, look at those who follow in your train," I urged.

Jack turned and gazed at them. Harry Bollback was at the keyboard and began to play as I led the students in a song. Part way through the chorus, Jack suddenly slumped forward as his wife, Joan, caught him and kept him from falling. In seconds, Joe Jordan, Christy Page and others had Jack on the floor, loosening his shirt collar and Christy was checking his vital signs. The students could see the commotion at the front and I urged calmness with the words, "Students, Jack appears to have fainted, he is being cared for, and let's continue singing."

Harry stayed at the keyboard as I searched for songs to keep the students singing. It seemed that every song I looked at in the conference songbook was about Heaven and eternity. I didn't want to alarm the students, but Jack looked so pale and lifeless lying there on the floor as they prepared to put him on a stretcher board and carry him into the dining room next to the auditorium.

As a result of what was playing out in front of me, my throat had such a knot in it I could barely keep my voice from breaking. That was Jack Wyrtzen lying there; the one God had so mightily used in so many people's lives for more than sixty years. He was the one God had used so mightily in *my* life; the one who was one of my heroes in the faith; the one who had been my friend. I remember thinking, *Lord, is this how You're going to take Jack Home?* We continued singing until they removed Jack to the adjoining room while they waited for the ambulance and paramedics.

They discovered Jack had an aneurysm of the spleen and had suffered internal bleeding. Days later, some of the last people to visit Jack while still fully conscious, were George Theis and Dr. Jerry Falwell. Jerry had flown in to be with Jack. Jack's last conscious words were spoken to George and Jerry. Feebly pointing a finger toward his attending doctor, Jack said, "...I don't think he's saved!" He was concerned for the soul of his doctor. Shortly after, he slipped into semi-consciousness, never to recover.

On Wednesday morning, April 17, at 9:00 a.m. at the Glens Falls Hospital, Jack Wyrtzen—our associate, our "boss," the role model to all of us in the Word of Life ministry, and my hero of thirty-seven years—slipped out of his tired body into the presence of the Lord he loved and served.

The following Saturday, April 20, 1996, a great Memorial Service was held at the Word of Life Inn Auditorium. Friends came from all over the world. The Memorial Service was conducted by Jack's sons and what a service it was. It certainly glorified the Lord! The following Wednesday morning, April 24, found me speaking to the student body at our Bible Institute. There had been so many tears recently. Word of Life had experienced the Homegoing of so many close friends and associates, Dr. Jack Murray, Joan Theis' father, and now dear Jack, as well as others. Yes, there had been many tears. That Wednesday morning I spoke to the students on *The Ministry of Tears* and what the Bible says about tears. The Scripture has much to say on the subject. I shared with the students how that tears mean brokenness and surrender. I told them, "A Christian leader's ministry won't amount to much, unless he has a few tear-stained pillows." Little did I know what God was about to introduce into *our* lives. Little did we know!

Three days later, I was at a Missions Conference in a great church in Oshawa, Ontario, Canada. For a year, Pastor Lawson and his people at the Calvary Baptist Church had been preparing for the week-long World Missions Conference. I was the keynote speaker, preaching each night.

That night of May 1, 1996, I preached on I John 5:14-15, "And this is the confidence that we have in Him, if we ask anything according to His will, He heareth us, and if He hears us, then we know we have the petitions we ask of Him."

I challenged these dear people to dare to launch out and believe God to do great things through them for the cause of world evangelism. It is the will of God that men are saved. When God would lead them, they should believe the promises of God to meet all of their needs. God delights in giving them the desires of their hearts, if they ask in the will of God. Little did I know that within minutes of preaching that message, my wife and I would be brought to our knees crying out to God and claiming these verses personally.

The service had ended in a great spirit, and I went to Pastor Lawson's study preparing to counsel with a young policeman and his wife. They were young and learning Christians, eager to serve the Lord. The pastor's secretary entered the room telling me I had an emergency phone call from my wife, and I could take the call in the office provided for me during the conference.

As I excused myself and went to the phone, my mind raced in every direction. *Is someone on one of our fields in trouble? Is there some tragedy? Has my wife been involved in an accident — probably not, or she wouldn't be calling me, someone else would be doing it.*

I picked up the phone and heard my dear wife's voice. I could tell by Shirley's voice she was trying to be calm and in control of her emotions. She said, "Paul, it's Dan. He has been in a terrible accident in Budapest, and it looks very bad...Not good at all...He is in surgery right now."

I was stunned by the news. As she continued relating the details of which she had access, I felt numb, as though this was all a bad dream, but I knew it wasn't.

Dan, our second born was a missionary to the youth of Hungary for six years. He had helped start the Word of Life camping and Bible Club ministry in that country. He was one who always tried to do things "the right way." God was mightily using him. And now he was severely injured in an auto accident.

I have dealt with many tragedies during my years of ministry. I have told many people news they were unprepared to receive. But this was different. This was about *our Dan*, one of our four wonderful children. It was very, very personal and untimely and it hurt, oh my, did it hurt!

I wanted to rush to Shirley's side. I wanted to hold her in my arms and assure her we'd get through this tragedy. I was so grateful for the wonderful Word of Life family that we have. Our Pastor, Roger Ellison and his wife, Judy, were by my wife's side, along with our friends of many years, Wayne and Ruthie Lewis, Don and Carol Lough, Bob and Sue Brown, Mike Calhoun, and so many more. They all converged on the Bubar family home in Pottersville, NY to be by Shirley's side.

My wonderful secretary, Deirdre DiPeri, stayed at her office desk, arranging our plane tickets, phoning Budapest, trying to get more details for us and for Dan's supporting churches, individuals, family, friends and others. She stayed on the phone past 2:00 a.m., calling an army of friends and associates, urging them to pray that God would spare Dan's life. One church, with a midweek service of more than 1,000 people, was literally on their knees praying for God to spare this bright, young and effective missionary's life. More than 12,000 people that we knew of were crying out to God on Dan's behalf. My associate, Wayne Lewis, was on his way from Schroon Lake the next morning to continue my meetings at Calvary Baptist's Missions Conference.

The next afternoon, Shirley and I met at JFK airport and were on our way to Budapest to be by Dan's side. My dear friend, Donald Johnson, a brilliant international attorney, left his clients in a Mexico City hotel conference room and was on his way to Budapest to join us and help us through the days ahead.

Many Hungarians considered Dan to be one of the most effective American missionaries in Hungary, not only because of his passion for the souls of young people, but because Dan had learned to speak the very difficult Hungarian language with near perfection. He had led the Word of Life camping program, started the Bible Clubs in 15 centers across Hungary and was loved and respected by youth and adults alike.

He had fallen in love with a beautiful Hungarian young lady, the daughter of one of our Board members, "the young capitalist," Zoltan Kovacs. I had known Kinga since the time she was only eight years old. Dan loved her and wanted to make her his wife — he just had to be patient for her love for him to develop more fully. He had taken her to the Budapest airport to meet some inbound missionaries and was driving her home to Erd, Hungary. It was 11:00 p.m. Budapest time (5:00 pm U.S. time) on Wednesday night, May 1, 1996. They were on a beautiful new highway that circles Budapest. He was holding her hand and singing a lullaby he had heard Shirley and me sing to our daughter, Sarah, when she was a baby, *"Tiny turned up nose, lips just like a rose, only God in Heaven knows how I love this girl of mine..."*

Suddenly, out of the blackness of night came a heavily loaded tandem trailer that had broken free from the truck pulling it. There were no lights, nothing, only a loud crash. Dan did not see or hear anything. Kinga grabbed for the wheel of the car and brought it under control. In the horrible crash of these vehicles, she was spared from even receiving as much as a scratch or a bruise.

The Police and Fire Department Rescue were summoned. Dan was immediately placed on a breathing ventilator and rushed to the Saint Janos Hospital for head trauma in Budapest.

Shirley and I flew direct from JFK to Budapest and were met the next morning by Eric Murphy, Dan's supervisor and the director of Word of Life Hungary. With him was Dan's close associate and friend, Laci Kadar. They updated us on Dan's condition. He had survived brain surgery but was in a deep coma. Arriving at the hospital, we gathered around his comatose body and prayed. Two nights earlier, in Canada, I had preached on 1 John 5:14-15. Did I believe that text? Yes, I did! But the key to those verses is the phrase that says, "... if we ask anything according to His will, he heareth us..." That's easy, I reasoned. Dan Bubar was in the will of God when he became a missionary in Hungary. He brought young people to Christ through his ministry and God needed him to do just that. No one else did what Dan did, and no one else was better suited or more effective than Dan.

Surely, God did not want Dan home in heaven, yet. He was only twenty-nine years old, and he had not really impacted Hungary yet, as God wanted. Therefore, as Shirley and I and now Don Johnson, stood around Dan's bed, we prayed and claimed that verse. We prayed that God, in His grace, would raise Dan up to continue to serve Him. We talked to Dan as we stood around his bed. We had been encouraged to do this by American doctors. I told Dan, "If it were possible, I would gladly exchange places with you. I'm sixty-three years old; you're only twenty-nine. You have so many years in which to serve the Lord; I have only a few, at best."

Many of our friends came to our hotel room each night to pray with us, including Dr. Wendell Kempton, Michael Loftis, and another ABWE (Association of Baptists for World Evangelism) missionary. At night, Shirley and I would hold onto each other and cry and pray. Our hearts were broken, indeed. What would we do without Dan, should God take him? Would God not spare him? *Why, God? We don't understand! Please, Lord, help us to understand your plan in all of this!*

We came to terms with I John 5:14-15 and the key to that passage is, *"...if we ask anything according to His will, He hears us..."* What we were asking God to do may not be in God's perfect plan for our Dan. Maybe his race here on earth was finished. Maybe God wanted him home in heaven. God certainly had that right, should He choose.

In the following days in that hotel room, we came to terms with the possibility that God may take Dan to Heaven and not restore him to us. During this period, we made a decision and a choice. The choice was that we would humbly accept whatever God had determined, and that we would *rejoice* in it. We decided that our sovereign God was much wiser than we were. After all, our sovereign God was into this thing far more than we were. Was He not aware of every little detail that was happening, before it happened? In Matthew 10:29-31, Jesus asks, "Are not two sparrows sold for a farthing? And one of them shall not fall to the ground without your Father. But the very hairs of your head are all numbered. Fear ye not, therefore, ye are of more value than many sparrows." In other words, not one sparrow can fall to the ground without your heavenly Father knowing about it. And besides, the very hairs of your head are numbered. So don't worry, you are of more value to Him than many sparrows.

If our God is aware of even the one sparrow that drops to the ground, if my Heavenly Father is so interested in every little detail of my life (and Dan's) that He has numbered every insignificant hair on our heads, then He was very much aware of our Dan as he traveled that road en route to Erd, Hungary, on the night of May 1.

Over the previous ten years, I had seen so many instances of God's sovereignty in our lives and others, that Psalm 139 had become very meaningful. My wife and I cling to that passage.

Psalm 139:16, tells us that before we were born, God scheduled our days. Verse 17 tells us that God's thoughts are about us as the sand. In other words, God's thoughts about us are beyond counting. But those verses applied not only to two hurting parents, but to our son as well. In other words, if God's thoughts about us are perpetual, that means that at the very moment that loaded trailer broke loose in the middle of the night and struck our son's auto, *God was thinking about him, too!*

Furthermore, not only is *life* in God's plan, but so is death! Before Dan was born, his mother and I freely gave him to the Lord, even as Hannah had done to Samuel in I Sam. 1:28. Dan was the Lord's possession, not ours. We gave that up before he came into this world. Who were we, then, to hold onto him? Those were some of the conclusions we arrived at during the long nights of waiting.

Our prayers over Dan began to change from, *God, will you spare him?* to, *Lord, please spare him, if he would have the physical and mental ability to serve you fully.* We knew that if Dan should survive, but not have the ability to serve the Lord fully, he would die on the inside.

It was as though God had been preparing Dan for his Heavenly Home. Since Dan was still single, Christmas was lonely for him in Hungary. As a result, he would save his money and every Christmas he would take two weeks of his vacation time and fly home to Schroon Lake to be with family and enjoy his mother's good cooking during the wonderful holidays.

On his last trip home, he was a groomsman in his brother, Jonathan's, wedding ceremony. Jonathan married a beautiful girl, Jennifer Greiner, from Dover-Foxcroft, Maine. A few days after Dan arrived home from Hungary, we started driving to Maine in the middle of a heavy snowstorm.

So we could all be together as family and close friends, we had rented an entire Bed and Breakfast House in Dover-Foxcroft. We had a wonderful time as a family. What special memories we have of those days. Daniel was one of Jonathan's heroes, and he and Jennifer were making plans to go to the Czech Republic as missionaries to start the ministry of Word of Life. Jonathan was especially excited because he would be located only a four-hour drive from his older brother, Dan. We eventually made our way back to Schroon Lake and Pottersville for the special Christmas holidays.

I remember Dan seemed restless. Both of his brothers were now married to wonderful young ladies, and they were making plans to serve the Lord while Dan was still serving the Lord alone. One evening, relaxing and lying across his temporary bed, he told his mother, "You know, mom, this isn't home to me anymore. I love coming here, but it's no longer my home. Most of the time I feel that Hungary is my home. Other times, I'm not sure where home is anymore."

God was preparing Dan — and us — for his real Home. He finally went there on May 10, 1996.

Our God knows so much more than we do. He sees from eternity to eternity. God sent so many people into our lives to encourage us. A young girl from India urged us to read Isa. 57:1-2, "The righteous perisheth, and no man layeth it to heart: and merciful men are taken away, none considering that the righteous is taken away from the evil to come. He shall enter into peace: they shall rest in their beds, each one walking in His uprightness."

Could it be that there might have been "evil days" ahead for Dan? Is that why God took him? We'll not know the answer to these questions here. Some day we will. But, for certain, our sovereign God is in control and things were not out of His control on the night of May 1, 1996.

Psalm 139 was written by the great King David. Why did God choose to give the message of that Psalm through King David? Because David knew adversity. David knew what it was to send a son on to Heaven ahead of him. He knew the heartache of being betrayed by another son, Absalom, plus much more adversity in his life. Though David brought much of his adversity on himself, his faith never failed. David knew about and wrote about the wonderful, sovereign plan of God in our lives. So did the Apostle Paul. In Romans 8:28, he said, "And we know that all things work together for good to those who love God, to those who are called according to His purpose." Paul did not say that all *good* things work together for good. He just said *all things.* That means good *and* bad! Somehow, in some way, someday, Dan's Home-going would result in good, right here on earth. Someday, we will understand the answer to, *"Why, God?"*

But, within me, had I really dealt with this question fully? In the weeks that followed, I would again.

Most of the time, Shirley and I were okay. We trusted totally in God's sovereign plan. Yet, I confess there were times, especially when I would be driving in my car alone, when, as my thoughts would turn to Dan, there would come that tightening in the throat, that heaviness in the chest, and the tears would freely flow. I remember one day, in particular. I was driving home from my office alone. My thoughts went to what I viewed as Dan's uncompleted ministry in Hungary. My thoughts went to his unfinished goals and dreams.

I was talking to the Lord and I began to sob, "Lord, help me to understand. Why, God, why? Why would you allow him to be taken before he even reached the prime of his ministry?" The tears nearly blinded me as I drove the six miles home that afternoon. I soon found myself crying, "Why, God? Help me to understand!" I suddenly realized I was questioning God's wisdom. That shocked me and it was very scary. When I realized what I was saying, I felt humbled and rebuked by the Holy Spirit and through the tears I said, "O, God, I'm so sorry for questioning your love and your wisdom. O, Lord, I love you, as I know you loved our Dan. Lord, I love you so much that I will never again question your wisdom and sovereignty." What happened on the night of May 1st was allowed to happen while my sovereign God was thinking about our Dan as well as those of us who would continue with our lives here on earth.

By this time, I was nearly home and I pulled my car over to the side of the road by the cemetery where Dan's earthly body lies, just 500 feet up the street from our home. Looking over to the gravesite from the car, I continued praying, "Lord, I will patiently wait to understand your loving plan for our son's short life. You are such a God of love that you had only good thoughts in taking Dan to his Heavenly Home. I will never again question your wisdom. Forgive me, Lord. "

Since the time of Dan's Home-going and as a result of his leaving us, scores of Hungarian young people have trusted Christ, scores have consecrated their lives to follow the Lord. Some have said, "I want to take Dan's place." Atilla Bahn, the young Hungarian being discipled and trained by Dan to lead the Club ministry, made a full commitment to step into Dan's position. He is now being coached and discipled by Eric Murphy to do just that. God is blessing Atilla, and now an all-Hungarian staff leads the club ministry, as Dan had proposed. Atilla is resolute to take the role left vacant by his friend and mentor.

Two nights following Dan's accident, word began to spread

through the little village of Toalmas. But the reports of Dan's condition conflicted. Was he only badly hurt and in a coma? Was he already dead and being kept alive with life support equipment?

Dan had led a Word of Life Bible Club for the teenagers of Toalmas the previous year. He cared deeply about them and they knew it. Dan had turned the leadership of the Club over to Peter, a very caring, bright Hungarian who is the Dean of Men at the Bible Institute.

A group of twenty-six of the village teenagers came as a group to the castle. They wanted to know what was happening with Dan. They really wanted to understand why something like this could happen to this American who had come to their village, who learned their language so well, cared about their souls, who taught them about Christ and who cared about them.

Peter, sensing their tender, confused and hurting spirit, invited them into the castle, where he began to open the Word of God to them. They listened to every word. Knowing that only about six of them knew Christ as Savior, Peter told them again of God's love and about Heaven. He then gave them an opportunity to receive this Jesus Christ that Dan had told them about. Sixteen of those young people received Jesus as Savior that night.

Pastors of Dan's supporting churches, as they received updates on Dan's condition, informed their youth and congregations. Many of them had teenagers commit their lives to go to Bible School and become a missionary like Dan Bubar.

It's too early yet to know the true impact of the life of our son on this earth. But this I know: in God's program, He makes no errors or miscalculations because God is perfect and, therefore, His ways are perfect (Psalm 18:30). His actions are always for our good. That means for Dan's good as well as the good of those Dan left here on earth.

Dying is not a terrible tragedy for those who know Christ. It's hardest on those who remain behind. God did not make us for separation. Adam's sin in the garden caused death and separation. We often do not deal with this area well. I remember saying aloud to our son's comatose body (hoping he might be able to hear), "Son, it won't be long. I am sixty-three years old. What will it be? Maybe twenty years and we will be together again. Twenty years will go by very fast." For the child of God, it is simply a transition from earthly existence to a heavenly existence (2 Cor. 5:6-8) where we will continue to worship and work for our Lord. The passing of the child of God from earth to Heaven is not by chance. It is by God's wonderful and sovereign plan, though it may not be the plans we would choose.

In Eternity Past, God Chose Us...

In Ephesians 1:3-7, we read "Blessed be the God and Father of our Lord Jesus Christ, who has blessed us with every spiritual blessing in the heavenly places in Christ. Just as He chose us in Him before the foundation of the world, that we should be holy and without blame before Him in love, having predestined us to adoption as sons by Jesus Christ to Himself, according to the good pleasure of His will, to the praise of the glory of His grace, by which He made us accepted in the beloved."

In other words, Paul is telling us that before this world was put together, God knew all about us. He selected us to one day inherit His wonderful salvation, so that we would be with Him in Heaven for all eternity. And in verse 6, Paul says that He has given us a position that is like that of an adopted son. He further tells us in the same verse that God did this just because He wanted to, because it would make Him happy to do so: "... to the good pleasure of His will."

The tragedy is that so many people go against the will and plan of God and reject God's special salvation given through His Son Jesus; they don't have to.

My salvation, our son Dan's salvation, your salvation, is all part of God's wonderful sovereign plan. So was our son's death and Home-going. So will be your death and Home-going. It will not be by chance. It will be a part of God's marvelous plan, especially if you have one day seized the opportunity to invite Jesus Christ to become your Lord and Savior.

The most real part of life is death. Many people avoid thinking about it. That does not remove the reality of it. Paul says in Hebrews 9:27, "And as it is appointed unto men once to die, but after this, the judgment." Death, however, does not end everything. It ends the life of our mortal bodies, but it is only the *beginning* of our eternity. Dan is more alive today than he was ten years ago. His body is in a casket buried in the cemetery up the street from our home in Pottersville, New York. But the real Dan is very much alive in heaven. Now that he has experienced the wonders of heaven, I couldn't coax him back if I wanted to. Because he received the Lord Jesus Christ as a boy, we know he is in heaven.

This is what takes the sting out of death. This is what robs the grave of any victory. Death and dying need not be such an awful thing when you know it is just a new beginning. When you *know* your loved one is in heaven with Christ. It is not by chance. It is all a part of God's marvelous plan.

CHAPTER 13

SIGNED, SEALED, AND DELIVERED

Can anyone seriously question the precise plan of a sovereign and grace-filled God for this world, or even for our individual lives? If you had been able to view God's obvious plan with regard to the ministry of Word of Life in Hungary and the merging of people's lives in carrying out this special plan, you would believe in a sovereign, gracious God by observing these happenings alone.

The story does not end with the leasing of the beautiful Toalmas Castle for ten years, or what would appear to us as the untimely Home-going of Dan Bubar. The Hungary story continues.

Toalmas Castle

For eight years, Word of Life Foundation, known as Elet Szava Alapitvany, leased the beautiful Toalmas Castle from a department of the Hungarian government. Rumors around the village of Toalmas surfaced periodically that a resort hotel chain from Germany was seeking to purchase the Castle. Another rumor was that a corporation from Italy was interested in turning it into a gambling casino. Eight years of the ten-year lease passed. Literally, thousands of young people had passed through the camping program and thousands had found Christ as Savior. A wonderful Bible Institute was implemented under the watchful eye and teaching of Dave James, Al Konya and scores of the world's best Bible teachers who would come on a visiting lectureship basis. The Bible Club ministry, under the leadership of Bahn Attila, is successfully helping churches all across Hungary. Hundreds of youth rallies, special evangelistic events and students have been implemented.

Eric Murphy has been very successfully attracting scores of work teams and hundreds of thousands of dollars to rebuild student dormitories and renovate the main Castle building. But, the clock was ticking on our ten-year lease. Only two more years to go.

Occasionally, when in Hungary, I would visit my Jewish friend, Michael Kovacs. I was always concerned about his soul. Michael would always listen to what I would say about Jesus Christ, but there was little movement towards receiving Christ as Messiah. Michael has become very successful in his business ventures in Hungary but that was about to end. At the time, he had more than two hundred business outlets and more than eighty banking outlets.

One morning at 6:00 a.m., the police arrived at his estate, and placed him under arrest for "banking irregularities." All the irregularities were in areas where he had tried to get clarification from the Banking Central Committee and could get none. During this time, all two hundred of his businesses and all eighty of his banks were taken over by the government, but Michael was still far from ruined or broke financially.

It was during this period that Michael advised me that Word of Life should buy the Castle property. "It is worth at least five million dollars. Buy it, if you can!"

I would reply, "Michael, you know we don't have that kind of money; we are a financially poor organization."

"Then why not ask one of your rich Jewish friends to help you?" he replied.

My heart skipped a beat. Was he offering to purchase the Castle for Word of Life?

He continued "what you must do is establish a Hungarian Limited Liability Company (known as a Kft.) and when that is achieved, buy the Castle and lease it to Elet Szava (Word of Life) for twenty more years for $1.00 per year." This all sounded too amazing to be true, but, in my opinion, we had nothing to lose.

I had carefully maintained a good relationship with Dr. Gayer, the attorney. Since the fall of communism, Dr. Gayer has established a most reputable law firm, called Gayer & Partners. Dr. Gayer had been elevated by his peers to be the Deputy President of the Central European Bar Association. After conferring with our Word of Life leadership at Schroon Lake, I contacted Dr. Gayer to establish a Hungarian Kft. that could become a holding company for the beautiful Toalmas Castle property.

After many months, when the Kft. had been completed, I returned to see Michael and ask him if he was referring to himself when he suggested I get one of my rich Jewish friends to buy the Castle for us. He replied, "six months ago I might have wanted to do just that, but not now. I have become discouraged with any more investments in Eastern Europe." And well he should have been discouraged.

I remember praying, "Lord, what do you have in mind? Have I spent $5,000 of Word of Life's money to form a Hungarian Kft. only to have the entire adventure fail? Lord, show me; lead me in a way that it will be very clear. Sometimes I'm a little thick and slow in understanding. Lord, time is running out on our lease and there are all these rumors of other ungodly organizations wanting to purchase the Castle. Certainly, You would not have done all of these things for us, all of these miracles, only to see us, and the young people of Hungary, lose this Castle. Lord, help me to be very sensitive to what You're saying and how You're leading us."

So, it appeared all of the effort in putting a legal framework in place to purchase the Castle property had come to a dead end. I returned to New York somewhat disappointed, confused and a little discouraged.

September 1997

Four months later found me back in Budapest again. We were holding the annual Board meeting of our Word of Life Europe Corporation at Toalmas Castle. All of our European country directors and a few friends and guests were there. One of those present was a board member from a Western European country. Early the next morning, before any of our meetings began; we went for a walk around the property at Toalmas.

As we walked, he wanted to know about the ministry in Hungary and other countries. As we talked about Hungary and Toalmas, knowing our lease was nearing its time limit, he suggested we should buy the Castle. I reminded him that everyone thinks we should buy it, but we just didn't have the money. I knew our friend had a great heart for the youth of Europe, especially those of Eastern Europe, because he had graciously provided camp scholarships that brought teenagers to our camps all over Eastern Europe for many years. I had no clue as to this brother's financial status. I assumed that his giving was at maximum through his generous scholarship funding.

In our conversations, I had explained as best I could, the political situation in Hungary. I told him of my conversations with Michael and his suggestion we establish a Hungarian Kft. that would be a holding company. I also told him of Michael's decision not to purchase the property for us and my great disappointment. Having spent $5,000 US dollars to form the company, I wondered aloud why we had done all of this only to be back to where we had started.

He said, "Well, it appears you have done the correct thing. Yes, you have done the right thing. I believe God wants Word of Life to have this beautiful place. I have $800,000 that I can invest. Go to the Hungarian government and negotiate for the very best deal you can make. If you can negotiate for under $800,000, you may use the remainder to begin renovation."

I stopped walking and stared intently at this dear brother. I was stunned at his words. Though his English was excellent, he did have a relatively thick accent to my ears, and I wanted to be certain he said what I thought I had heard. I found myself stuttering.

"Brother, did I hear you correctly? Did you just tell me I should go to the government, negotiate the best purchase deal I could and if the purchase price is less than $800,000, we could use the remainder to commence renovation?"

He responded, "Yes, that's exactly what I said."

I said, "Excuse me for stuttering, but I have never had anyone ever make such an offer to me. Thank you, I will do exactly as you have said."

In the past, I have heard many stories of God's gracious hand of provision; many incidents could be called miraculous. Yet, I had never been made privy to such a benevolent offer before. I barely knew how to respond to such benevolence–such an answer to prayer. I wanted to skip, jump and shout as loud as I could, "Thank you, Lord Jesus!" But I dared tell no one at that point.

After this eventful walk and talk, we went in the conference room where the Board of Word of Life Europe went into session. We conducted our ministry business filled with wonderful reports of God's gracious working in the lives of young people all over Europe — hundreds of kids finding Christ through evangelistic meetings, activities and camps. When the three days of Euro

Directors' meetings were finished, we all returned to our ministries, some across Europe and the rest of us to Schroon Lake.

To this day, I still do not fully understand my subconsciously doubting spirit about all that had just happened only a few days earlier. Why would I, who had so often witnessed the mighty hand of God at work, still doubt what this gracious and benevolent brother was doing?

Wanting to tell everyone from the directors of Word of Life International down to anyone who would listen, I had to make absolutely certain that this wonderful thing was really going to happen.

I remember thinking; I must get this in writing before I tell everyone. I composed a typewritten fax to our benefactor. In the fax I said, "I want to be certain I handle this exactly as you would want, so please allow me to recite for you what I understood you to say." I ended the fax with the words, "Did I understand it all correctly?"

Within a day, a fax returned, with only the words, "You understood it correctly. Do it!" With this brief fax, in my mind there was no longer any doubt. Sitting at my desk, I let out a shout at the top of my lungs saying, "Yes! Hallelujah. Thank you, Lord Jesus! Thank you! Thank you, for this dear man!"

The next step was to contact my good friend and attorney, Don Johnson and ask him to return to Budapest with me. I desperately needed Don, who had abilities beyond mine. I had nerve, aggressiveness and trust in God's sovereign plan, but Don had insights into financial and legal matters and procedures that I lacked. Within a couple of weeks we had made appointments with the Hungarian government's agency that handled the Castle, Hunguest. Hunguest was a department of government set up to manage all hospitality properties. In the meanwhile, I had the joy of giving the good news to Joe Jordan, Don Lough, and Eric

Murphy.

However, there were many hoops to jump through yet. Not only would Don Johnson be a key player, but also so would Ildiko Barbarics, Dr. Gayer and our Hungarian Director of Word of Life, Eric Murphy. It would be a team effort. For the immediate and initial negotiation, it would be Don Johnson, with Ildiko as our interpreter, and me.

The bottom line was that the government wanted to divest themselves of these properties. Word of Life (Elet Szava) had gained a good reputation with the Hunguest organization; and we wanted to be able to own this beautiful property for God's glory.

Finally a deal was made: they would sell for only $550,000, plus we would have to pay the Value Added tax of 25% of purchase price. There had been many hours of offers and counter offers. There had to be an agreeable conclusion about camp scholarships for the children of Hunguest members, etc. But, when it all shook down, there was a company (known as Word of Life Europe Friends WOLEF) and there was even a little money left over. What a great day it was when the representatives of Hunguest, Don Johnson, Ildiko Barbarics, Eric Murphy and I gathered at the Hunguest offices to sign documents that would finalize the long process. Thank you, Lord! It was finally over, complete. Well, not quite. There would still be a few bumps in the road ahead; bumps we had never planned on!

In the meanwhile, the Bible Institute was growing under the wise direction of Dave James and the excellent teaching of Alex Konya. Alex Katona was managing the Hungarian operational staff, the renovation of buildings and grounds while building relationships with the local people and with the business community. His wife, Katie, made the castle facilities look beautiful and the director, Eric Murphy, had done a superb job of generating funds and work teams to renovate the dormitories, meeting hall, and many other buildings.

When the Kft. (Limited Liability Company, known as WOLEF) was formed, it was decided that with all my history with the Hungarian organization, plus the International organization, I should be the manager of the Kft., in spite of my New York residence. This would later create some issues since the Kft. was to be a taxable revenue-producing company that would generate tax forints (money) for the Hungarian government. The government watched all Kft.'s very carefully to be certain they were putting tax money into the government account. Several times Ildiko would warn me that the government was watching to see if we were generating enough tax revenue. If we weren't, they could declare us as a phantom corporation, which is punishable by law. A phantom company is one that is established purposely to avoid taxation. That made this American feel very uncomfortable at times. Something would need to be done and soon.

A New Foundation

The Elet Szava Foundation was established in 1989 when the Hungarian government was still under communist rule. The dynamics today are totally different. Since Word of Life was the first Western religious non-profit youth ministry to be established in Hungary, especially since we were Western and religious, we believed we needed four founding groups of our organization. They were the Baptists, the Plymouth Brethren, Menedek (the first Hungarian religious non-profit led by Zoltan Kovacs, a Board member) and Word of Life International. Key organizational decisions can be made only by a unanimous decision of the founders. This was making managing it more and more unwieldy. In addition, the benevolent donor wanted guarantees that twenty years down the road when we were all in heaven, his investment would still be operating on a solid Biblical focus of bringing young people to Christ.

The government regulations governing business and investment entities had changed, and sufficiently made foreign investment easier. The time was now ripe to form a new nonprofit Foundation with only one Founder: Word of Life Fellowship in New York. This decision was made to ease operations. It would be Hungarian and it would be a simplified Foundation with the same Board members. After months of negotiating and legal maneuvering, it became a reality. Again, thank you, Lord!

A New Bump in the Road

The Hungarian government, concerned about all of the corporations being formed and properties being bought, began to protect itself against too much foreign ownership. Unknown to us, at about the same time as our new Foundation was completed, a new Hungarian law was enacted that in districts where local properties were purchased with foreign funds, the local municipality would have the legal right to preemptive ownership. In other words, the village of Toalmas suddenly had the option to buy the Toalmas Castle out from under us at the original purchase price, and the mayor of Toalmas village made it known that they intended to do just that. We could lose Toalmas.

I remember clearly how devastated I felt. I remember praying, *Lord, would you bring us through all the miracles of your grace, all the precise steps, all the joys, excitement and gratitude, only to have the village of Toalmas purchase this property from under us?*

Our attorney, Dr. Gayer, seemed undisturbed. "Don't worry, they cannot even afford paper for the children in the local school. How could they come up with the necessary money?"

Eric Murphy kept a cool head, though he had heard local rumors of the mayor seeking foreign funds, even trying to attract a gambling casino corporation to put up the money for them. Outwardly, he seemed at ease as he reminded me, "We will lose this property only if God wants us to lose it and that would mean He has an even better place for us." Of course, Eric was right and his words were a comfort to me, for a few days, at least.

In my forty-year history with Word of Life, there have been few nights when I could not sleep. With this development, however, there were many nights when I would lie in my bed praying and finally sleep would come through prayer. To complicate matters and heighten tension, a deadline date would come and the Toalmas Village government would ask for an extension — and get it! Finally, all of their appeals were exhausted, and so were we! The new Hungarian Foundation was finally formed, and the Toalmas Castle property was at last deeded to the Foundation. That was a great day for rejoicing.

The Bible Institute was growing under the leadership of Eric Murphy, Dave James and Alex Konya. They sent teams out in churches and villages each weekend and their numbers grew steadily. The Bible Club ministry grew under the leadership of Attila Bahn; camps full to overflowing and many special conferences were developing. My dear wife, Shirley, spoke on two occasions at their Women's Conference.

My mind goes back to those Sunday dinners in Olga's kitchen (the home of Pastor Kovacs and his beloved Olga, now in Heaven) in 1985-88 and the expression of dreams for the youth of Hungary. It is now 2004 and by the grace of a gracious and loving God, all those dreams have come true. *Thank you, Lord Jesus. These things were all a part of your sovereign plan; they did not happen by chance, but as a part of Your sovereign plan. Thank you, Lord, for allowing my family and me (my dear wife and fellow laborer, Shirley, and our son, Dan, who went to Heaven from Hungary), to be a part of this wonderful thing You have done.*

Dear friend, may I remind you that our wonderful God, according to Psalms 139:1-18, knows everything there is to know about you, and He still loves you. His plan for you is that you would be reconciled to God through simple trust and faith in what Jesus Christ accomplished for you in His death, burial and resurrection (Rom. 5:12-21; II Cor.5:17-21).

Another part of His sovereign plan for you is that you would offer yourself to be available to Him. If you are willing to lay aside personal plans and say, "Lord, here I am. I'm available to You. Please work out Your marvelous plan in my life! Open doors of opportunity for me and help me to recognize an opportunity when it comes. I will walk through that door and please You."

Make yourself available to your pastor, your church, missionaries, or those happily going about God's work, and you will see the opportunities God will give you. Taste of and enjoy the wonderful, marvelous plans of a gracious, loving and merciful God and experience His sovereign plan. I have and I marvel at it every day! Every day becomes a new and exciting adventure through life. You can experience this in your life, too (2Timothy 1:9).

CHAPTER 14

THE BEAT GOES ON

On September 21, 2008, I found myself driving across the flat Hungarian countryside, as I had so many times before. I was on my way to our beautiful castle property in Toalmas, having flown from New York to Vienna, Austria. This was my 85th trip to Hungary, covering a time span of more than twenty-six years. Democracy officially came to Hungary in 1989, the same year that God brought Word of Life Hungary into official existence. The differences between today's Hungary and the Hungary of those early days could hardly be overstated. I still can well remember those early trips into then-Communist Hungary. There was such tension on the Hungarian-Austrian border, for this marked the entrance through the "Iron Curtain." As we approached the border, we would see the barbed wire, the guard towers, and the military border guards, fully armed and carrying machine guns. Then we endured the lines of vehicles, the document checks, and vehicle inspections. Crossing into Hungary, we traveled mainly on narrow two-lane highways eastward towards Budapest, and then continued for another hour's drive to Toalmas. We would get behind little sub-standard cars with tiny engines. And there were the old, creaky trucks that belched great billows of smoke out of their blackened exhaust pipes as they groaned along. Gasoline stations were few and far between, and we could not pay cash for gas—we had to purchase gas coupons.

Now, twenty-five years later, as I approached the Hungarian border from Austria, I did not even have to stop, because Hungary is now a member of the European Union. I drove across the border much as one would drive from New York into Pennsylvania. Not even a passport check! I continued along a ribbon of beautiful expressway, clipping along at the allowed speed of about 80 mph.

Pricey BMW and Mercedes autos whizzed by—with Hungarian license plates on them. Brightly lit gas stations dotted the route—clean and modern. The city of Budapest sparkled. The decades of soot that covered its elegant, stately old buildings has been sandblasted away, the trolley and commuter trains had been replaced with crisp new models, and well over a dozen new malls now stand in easy access from virtually every part of the city.

Arriving at the castle in Toalmas, I parked the car and went inside to say hello to Alex Konya. Alex assumed the directorship at Word of Life Hungary in 2004, and he greeted me warmly. The main reason for this trip was to minister to and encourage the Word of Life Hungary team and to be the main speaker for the annual Bible Clubs and Youth Leaders Conference held at the end of September each year.

During the few days before the conference, Alex and I once again had time to visit my dear Jewish friend, Michael Kovacs, who was used by God to pave the way for Word of Life's acceptance on a governmental level in Hungary more than twenty years ago. We also visited Dr. Gayer, the brilliant Hungarian lawyer who helped us so much with legal issues in those early days. Both of these men cordially received us. They are now well-advanced in years, but remain in good health and still offer their help to the Word of Life Hungary Foundation.

On Wednesday of that week I spoke to the Word of Life Hungary staff: thirty-two missionaries and fifteen interns. Oh, how this ministry has grown! In the beginning there were just two couples, along with our son Dan, and Ildiko Barbarics, our legal counsel. A special time of sharing with the staff came on Friday, numbering eighteen members including chefs, maintenance workers, gardeners, accounts and administrative staff. All are needed to keep up the ten buildings and seventy-eight acres of beautiful property, and to carry on the administrative work.

The youth workers conference began on Friday evening and

was held in the main auditorium, a meeting room with adjoining offices where summer camp rallies, Bible School classes, and various conferences are held. This auditorium is beautifully renovated, and is now officially known as "Dan Bubar Auditorium," named after our precious son Dan. It is amazing to realize that, since the days when Harry Bollback and I first strolled on these grounds two decades ago, more than 18,000 Hungarian young people have attended camps here, and more than 7,000 of them have made recorded decisions for Christ. In addition, thousands of others have come for conferences and special days. Many of them have had their lives changed forever. More than a hundred soccer teams have taken part in soccer marathons; these teams have come primarily from Hungarian public schools. The Gospel is presented, invitations are given, and many of these young people have found new life in Christ. On one occasion an entire team came forward to trust Christ as Savior!

In addition to a number of Hungarian guests at the conference that evening, there were fifty-two students from the Bible Institute and a dozen interns. Since the Word of Life Hungary Bible Institute opened in 2004, more than 300 students have come to study God's Word, coming from nearly twenty countries—mainly from Hungary and Central Europe. Also arriving for the conference were literally vanloads and busloads of people from Poland, Slovakia, and Serbia. God in His sovereign plan has obviously chosen to use Word of Life Hungary as a regional center for Central Europe and beyond. Every year many people from these countries come to Toalmas for the annual Christian youth workers conference and the missions conference.

Guest teachers from the Bible Institute also travel to these countries to hold intensive Bible teaching and discipleship conferences. The story of how God opened the door to Serbia is a particularly exciting story—and one that happened "not by chance."

A Quiet Time Diary and an Open Door

Serbia is a country that borders Hungary on the southeast. Smaller than the state of Indiana, there are about eight million people living in Serbia, and another two million or so living in the disputed land of Kosovo. Serbia is composed of thirty-six different nationalities and ethnic groups, some of whom have chosen to retain their own cultural traditions and language.

Serbia was involved in a horrific war from 1998-2000 under the rule of Slobodan Milosevic. This war included savage fighting and atrocities on both sides, as well as the slaughter of many innocent people under the guise of "ethnic cleansing." Word of Life Hungary staff members can still remember watching American military aircraft flying over their homes in Hungary on their way to Serbia. (The Serbian border is only a couple of hours' drive away from Toalmas.) The war devastated Serbia, and the effects of it can still be seen a decade later. With a drained treasury, the Serbian government has been unable to complete the development of new highways and infrastructure. Many homes and public buildings are still pockmarked by bullet holes or lie in ruins. The economy has been painfully slow to recover, and some towns and villages still have an unofficial unemployment rate of up to 75%.

Spiritually, Serbia could be aptly called the forgotten country of Europe. Only a handful of evangelical churches dot the country. And to make matters worse, Serbia has proportionately the fewest number of missionaries of any country in Europe. The vast majority of Serbians belong to the Serbian Orthodox church, which blends formal religion with Serbian ethnic identity. This means that for many Serbians, to leave the Serbian church is to deny their national heritage, a most sensitive issue given Serbia's recent history.

The year 2005 had not been an easy one for a Serbian couple named Darko and Erzebet Vika. Darko was a Serbian pastor, serving in a small church in the town of Sid. God was blessing

Darko's ministry, especially with youth. He had an active youth fellowship in the church and felt a great burden for them. But things were not going well. Doctrinal and local church issues were developing within the denominational leadership, and a there was a growing resistance to the youth program. Darko and Erzsi sought the Lord in earnest prayer, crying out to Him for direction.

About that time, a member of Darko's church was traveling in Austria. While there, he stumbled across a Word of Life Quiet Time Diary. This is a simple journal published yearly that contains Bible passages to read each day, with a place to write what that passage meant, as well as prayer requests and answers to prayer. Word of Life has been publishing Quiet Time Diaries for some fifty years. They are translated into many languages and are used by Christians on virtually every continent of the world. When Darko's friend found a ten-year-old Quiet Time Diary in Austria and leafed through it, he was excited. Immediately upon his return to Serbia, he showed it to Pastor Darko. Darko was thrilled, and wrote to Word of Life headquarters in Schroon Lake, New York. What is this "Word of Life?" he thought. "And could I get permission from them to publish this in Serbia?" On May 30, 2005 Darko sent the following e-mail:

Dear Brothers and Sisters in Christ,

My name is Darko Vika. I am a pastor of a lively Methodist Church in Sid, Serbia, Europe. I am 36 and have a four children family with my wife Elisabeth. I also work with youth in my local congregation but in the whole denomination in Serbia too. I received a Quiet Time Diary that you printed in USA in 95/96 (I am not sure). This Diary is something wonderful! There is no possibility to buy something like that in Serbia. Because of that, I translated it into Serbian language. Now, I would like to ask you for permission to print it and share with all the churches are interested. Also, I am interested about all materials you have for work with youth. Please contact me for more information and let me know your answer. May the Lord Jesus bless you and keep you in your ministry to give the Gospel of Jesus Christ to youth.

Yours in His service,

Darko Vika

Darko's e-mail arrived at our headquarters in Schroon Lake and found its way to Don Lough Jr., who was serving as our Director of International Ministries. Don contacted Alex Konya, who along with a couple of other members of the Word of life Hungary team, traveled to Serbia to spend a few days with Darko and his family. It seemed obvious to everyone who met him that he was a "Word of Life" kind of guy! Darko enrolled in the Word of Life Bible School that fall, and in 2007 he completed his two years of study. In October 2008, Darko and Erzebet attended Word of Life's missionary candidate school held at the castle property and were accepted as full-time missionaries. They now are key members of the new Word of Life Serbia team.

At the time that Alex and his team went to visit Darko and his family in Serbia, there was a student at the Word of Life Hungary Bible School named Pascal Parraghy. Pascal is a Swiss citizen, but his grandfather was a well-known Baptist preacher in Serbia—a fact almost nobody on the staff realized at the time. In fact, Pascal spent about eight years of his childhood living in the Serbian town of Pacser, where his mother still owns a home. During his time as a Bible school student, Pascal would bring some of his fellow students to Serbia for a week in the summer to help the local Baptist church in Pacser. They would hold something similar to a vacation Bible school for the children each morning for a week.

Pascal invited Alex to come to Pacser to see what was going on. Sensing God could be opening a door to something significant in Serbia, Alex agreed. What he saw there was truly wonderful—this tiny church building was overflowing with children!

When Pascal returned to school in September, he and Alex began to dream. What would it be like to give kids like this a week at a Word of Life camp, right there in Serbia? But there was a problem. Camp facilities suitable for a Word of Life camp program were nearly impossible to find in Serbia. A plan began to emerge. Why not have a Word of Life camp in the neighboring town of Moravica, on the property of the Baptist Church there? They could perhaps put up a tent and have a fully developed camp program but send the kids home to sleep at night. These plans were carried out, and a tent and chairs were found that would handle up to a hundred people. The tent would be erected in the church yard. The kids would have their lunch and sports at the local school, a five-minute walk from the tent. And perhaps they could even swim in the huge, privately owned pool located about a ten-minute walk from the tent.

Pascal begin contacting people in order to organize a first ever week of Word of Life camp in Serbia, to be held July 10-14, 2006 in Moravica. The local response was overwhelmingly positive. The school offered its facilities, and the local bus driver offered to bring kids from the town of Pacser at no charge. The baker donated bread, and the owner of the swimming pool offered the kids not one but two free trips to swim in the pool. And none of these people were believers!

The day finally came for the camp to begin. The Word of Life team had no idea what to expect, since nothing like this had ever been done in Serbia. The staff committed the week to the Lord, and anxiously waited to see what would happen. The kids came, crowding the entryway and spilling out onto the sidewalk. About ninety-five kids, ages ten to fifteen, came daily to camp. On the first day, the team really saw how little these precious kids knew about spiritual things. When the first Bible hour was held, nobody knew who Jonah was, and virtually nobody had a Bible. Thankfully, the Gideons had donated enough Bibles so that each camper could have a Bible of his own. The invitation was given on Thursday afternoon for the kids to publicly meet with their counselors if they wanted to trust Christ as their Savior. The result was one of the most memorable our team had ever experienced. Around seventy kids went to their counselors, deciding to trust Christ as Savior! Many kids had tears in their eyes, and the counseling showed that the vast majority clearly understood what they were doing.

The effects of that first week of camp are still being felt in Serbia. Virtually the whole town was watching what went on – and most liked what they saw. We found out that the father of one of our team members had been born in that area, another incredible thing that was "not by chance." This team member was interviewed on the radio and had the opportunity to give his testimony which then resulted in a TV station airing a program about the camp, and two newspaper articles were written. In fact, the daughter of one of the reporters accepted Christ at camp and shared her testimony with her unbelieving mother.

There are now four weeks of summer camp held in Serbia in two locations, and plans call for at least doubling this in the years to come. Since that first camp in 2006, 530 campers have attended Word of Life Serbian camps, and about 300 of these have trusted Christ as their Savior. In addition to this, children and teen Word of Life clubs have started in Serbian local churches. Word of Life Serbia also sponsors an annual prophecy conference. Jimmy DeYoung is the speaker, and this conference is the largest evangelical gathering in the country. And Pascal has joined Darko and his family as a full-time member of the new Word of Life Serbia team. The beat goes on!

Born Again to a Living Hope

For several years some key leaders on the Word of Life

Hungary team had a deep desire to see the Word of Life drama *"Born Again to a Living Hope"* adapted into Hungarian and used to reach Hungarian young people, especially those who would never set foot on the camp property or in a local church. Sadly, in the years since democracy and a free-market economy have come to Hungary, Hungarian youth have become increasingly more difficult to reach for Christ. A recent survey showed that a stunning 56% of Hungarians polled claimed that they did not believe in any sort of supreme being. And among Hungarian youth, the statistics are even higher. A consequence of this is that Hungarian young people are turning in ever greater numbers to partying, alcohol, drugs, pornography, and sexual experimentation.

Born Again to a Living Hope is a gripping musical-drama presentation that portrays the life and world of Pablo and Adriana Riolo, two young people living in Buenos Aires, Argentina. Escaping from difficult situations at home, they ended up turning to alcohol and drugs, and began living on the streets. Although not married, they began living together. They loved each other, but their lives became filled with emptiness and disorder as they descended into the nightmare world of heroin addiction. As a result of the Word of Life Argentina outreach to street people in Buenos Aires, Pablo and Adriana ended up attending a week of summer camp at Word of Life Argentina in 1990. That week changed their lives forever. They heard the Gospel message and were "born again to a living hope." They chose to turn from their destructive lifestyle to Jesus Christ.

Since Pablo and Adriana now had new life through Christ, they determined to live differently. They stopped living together and were provided with much-needed medical help and counseling. Their future seemed bright. But then a medical test showed that both were stricken with AIDS. They married and even began to attend Bible school, but both died before their twenty-fourth birthdays. Pablo never finished his first year of Bible school, and Adriana outlived him by less than two years. But before she died, she carefully wrote down her story. This became the basis for the drama *Born Again to a Living Hope.* It is Pablo and Adriana's story – their adventures, their hurts, their feelings, and their faith – in their own words.

Born Again to a Living Hope became a reality in Hungary in January 2007. Music has been reworked and lyrics have been adapted from the original Spanish into Hungarian. A multi-media portion features a Hungarian medical specialist, and at one point a giant Hungarian flag is stretched across the entire stage. The drama team goes out at least weekly during the Bible school year. *Born Again* is presented in public schools, universities, community civic centers, orphanages, juvenile detention centers, and the toughest prisons. God has blessed this unique outreach in a very special way. Thousands of Hungarians have heard the Gospel at *Born Again* presentations. In fact, more people hear the Gospel in just a few weeks' time through *Born Again* than in an entire year though the camping program.

After a typical *Born Again* presentation, the cast members immediately go out to meet the audience and share the Gospel personally with as many people as are willing to listen. At this time many young people and adults open their hearts, sharing their struggles with peer pressure, alcohol, and drugs. And some of them decide to trust Christ as their Savior.

Cast members still remember the time when a young woman in her early twenties wandered into a *Born Again* presentation at the civic center in a small Hungarian city. She was married, with a young husband and little baby waiting for her at home. But she was despondent and weary from battling alcohol abuse. In her desperation, she decided that she would leave her little family that night. She felt worthless, and believed that she was putting her family through a living hell. She reasoned that she would not return home. Instead, she would wander the streets until she found another place to live.

As she walked down the street, she saw a sign advertizing a presentation of *Born Again* at the civic center, and she decided to go. As she watched and listened to the story of how Adriana descended into a life of alcohol and drugs, she saw the future that awaited her too if she continued on this path. What should she do? Fortunately the young man who played Pablo came to talk with her immediately after the presentation. He could identify with her desperation, because he himself had been raised in a home with a violent, alcoholic father. He came to Christ as a teenager at a Hungarian evangelical church that had a Word of Life teen club, then graduated from our Bible school in Hungary and became a missionary for Word of Life. After about a half-hour of earnest conversation, this young lady trusted Christ as her Savior, ditched her plans to abandon her family, and returned to them "born again to a living hope."

On another occasion, the team was doing a *Born Again* presentation on a Saturday afternoon in an orphanage located in northeast Hungary. A fifteen-year-old girl quietly strolled into the auditorium and sat down. Nobody knew it at the time, but this girl was possibly just hours away from slipping into eternity. Her life had been difficult and filled with abandonment, rejection, and disappointment. She had been thinking, and decided that life was not worth living. That morning she sat down and wrote a suicide note. She wrote a final goodbye to her few friends, and carefully planned where and how she would kill herself later that evening. She had heard about the *Born Again* presentation and did not want to go, but decided to wander in anyway. She was moved by what she saw. Even more surprising to her, the young lady who played the lead role of "Adriana" personally came up to her afterwards to talk to her. The cast member spent a long time in conversation with her and gave the girl her cell phone number. She also gave her a pamphlet explaining the Gospel in detail. But the girl would not pray to trust Christ. When the team heard about this girl, they prayed specifically for her. What would happen to her? Saturday night passed — no news. Then on Sunday evening, the cast member's cell phone rang. It was the young girl from the home. She excitedly told her she decided not to kill herself, and that she had trusted Christ as her Savior. She even memorized every Bible verse in the pamphlet! The follow-up with this girl continues, and her life is not without its challenges, but she now has hope in Christ. The beat goes on!

A Grand Old Lady Gets a Facelift

Anyone who drives onto the Word of Life property in Toalmas is immediately drawn to the stately, ornate mansion of four stories and fifty rooms known as The Castle. The Castle was built in the late nineteenth century and was once owned by the Andrassy family, one of Hungary's most famous aristocratic families. It is an official historical landmark and a tourist attraction. Several films have been shot on location there (before Word of Life acquired the property) and both tour groups and individuals come to see this grand reminder of a bygone age of counts and noblemen in Hungary. The Andrassy family was deeply involved in horticulture and environmental concerns, and they collected plants and trees from all over the world in their extensive travels. As a result, the seventy-eight acres of property are dotted with rare and beautiful trees. In fact, the property is the only fully intact park left in Hungary that was once owned by a count, and it is accordingly an environmentally protected preserve.

The Castle and its property, as beautiful as they are, have always been regarded as a tool, albeit an incredibly beautiful and unique tool. And as the years have gone by, it has become an ever more expensive tool. A creaking, troublesome heating system, a leaking roof, and the gradually crumbling castle exterior had been taking its toll on both building and pocketbook. As prices for natural gas and electricity soared, the heat bills had begun to strain the Word of Life Hungary budget nearly to the breaking point. After all, nineteenth-century counts were not too worried about energy costs!

The ministry leadership set up a special fund to begin repairing the heating system and $40,000 was given to get this started. But as things progressed, the question began to be asked: "Is it perhaps time to consider selling the castle property and investing the money in a down-sized, smaller facility that can be built with modern energy and upkeep costs in mind? Should we consider relocating?" Serious prayer, research, and information-gathering followed in early 2008. After all the factors were taken into consideration and the numbers were crunched, it was discovered that relocation was not as financially attractive as it initially seemed. The Hungary leadership team, the Word of Life International leadership in New York, and the Word of Life Hungary Board of Directors all concluded that The Castle should not be sold. But where could the funding for a massive renovation project come from?

A renovation expert was contacted, and in July 2008, he made an initial visit to The Castle to examine it and to make preliminary recommendations. He was eminently qualified and had earned special international recognition for his work, having renovated some of Hungary's most well-known historical buildings. As he spent the afternoon looking over The Castle, he marveled at how sound it was structurally. But once again the nagging question came up: where would the funding for a massive renovation project come from? The renovation expert suggested that significant grant money could be obtained through the European Union, and indeed it was true. But as it turned out, the cost of the detailed plans, permits, and paperwork that would be needed just to have a chance to get grants like this was beyond Word of Life's ability to pay.

The first week of October was destined to change everything. The excitement began the day after I said goodbye to Alex and the Word of Life Hungary team, heading home after speaking at the conference I wrote about at the beginning of this chapter. On that Tuesday around noontime, Alex was meeting in his office with another staff member when the receptionist called. "Alex," she said, "there is a gentleman who came by wanting to talk to you personally, and he will be waiting in the hall outside your office." Since the man had not called ahead, and Alex was having an important conversation with the staff member, the man had to wait quietly outside for about ten minutes. Finally Alex invited him in.

"You probably do not know me," the man said, "but have you ever heard of the following businesses?" As he rattled off the list, Alex recognized them as some of the most well-known enterprises in Hungary. It turned out that this man either owned or directed them, and he was very wealthy. The conversation continued. "Mr. Konya, I need your help," he said. "I have had my eye on this property for some time and I would like to buy it. I can assure you I have the money to do so, and will even give you time to relocate."

Alex cautiously explained to him that The Castle was not for sale, but the man persisted, inviting him to lunch at the five-star restaurant that he owned. Alex accepted, figuring it would be a great chance to share the Gospel. Then, just two days later, two realtors representing another client came into Alex's office and sat down to meet with Alex, some key team members, and a Board member. As they listened, the realtors began their pitch. "We represent a very wealthy foreign client who is looking for a mansion like yours for a personal country estate. Do you have hunting here? Is there a place to build a helicopter pad? How far from the airport are you located?" The list went on, but the more the conversation continued, the more uneasy the entire team got about the situation. The realtors were courteously thanked and escorted to their cars. But what was going on?

The time for the restaurant appointment with the Hungarian businessman had almost arrived when Alex got another phone call in his office. It was from Word of Life headquarters in New York. Alex was informed that Word of Life Hungary would be getting an extremely generous gift, and the anonymous source stated the gift was being given to renovate The Castle. Now what?

On the appointed day, Alex had lunch with the businessman

at the man's restaurant. He had a wonderful chance to share the Gospel, and the man courteously explained that he wanted to buy The Castle in order to turn it into a wellness center. Alex drove back to Toalmas. Sitting at his desk, he began to pray, "Lord, I don't know what to think of all of this. I do not know this man or his heart. We have no intention to sell this castle, but *you* are the owner. Guide this process, protect us from unseen danger, and show us clearly what to do about this offer, because we are at a loss." About ninety minutes later the phone rang. It was a call from, literally the other side of the world, a friend who had been to Word of Life Hungary and loved the ministry there.

"Alex, is The Castle for sale?" he asked.

"No, it is not," Alex answered. "That issue was settled by the Board of Directors six months ago. But what in the world made you call today and ask a question like this?"

"Well, do you know a man named John Doe?" (The friend referred to the businessman by name.)

"Why, yes, I know him. I just had lunch with him today!" Alex answered.

The friend went on to explain to Alex how a person in the large city where he lived knew this Hungarian businessman and his intentions. This mysterious person then proceeded to share some important advice with the friend now calling Alex, knowing that this friend had been to a castle in Toalmas. After hearing the information, it was all too apparent to Alex that God had miraculously protected Word of Life Hungary from making what may have been a tragic and costly mistake. The Castle would not be sold!

With new funding available, the detailed renovation planning began. Experts began to examine the castle beam by beam, and what they found only confirmed that God had provided for Word of Life in a timely way that only He could have planned. It turned out that the castle roof was in much worse condition than anyone had suspected. The leaks were slowly destroying the beams, the delicate exterior walls and other areas. In addition, the heating system was a disaster area. In fact, at one point the inspector said, "I know this is a religious institution, and God must be on your side, because only God is keeping this heat system working through this winter!" Once again, God had known the need all along, and at just the critical moment, provided for the castle to be renovated.

And still another surprise awaited the team. As the planner began to pore over the drawings, original castle plans, old pictures, and inspection results, his attention was drawn more and more to the castle attic. Walking into the castle attic is a bit like going through an obstacle course at a carnival. There are chimneys, beams and roof joists everywhere, with a thick dirt-and-brick floor. Nobody had ever given this huge, congested space any attention – except the planner. As he worked, a creative idea began to take shape, and when he was finished, he presented it to the Word of Life Hungary renovation committee. Due to the redesign and repair of the roof, this old, dark space could be transformed into a 110-seat auditorium, two thirty-seat classrooms, the school library and another multi-purpose room. Virtually the entire Bible school program could eventually be moved into the castle. The renovation continues, and in the future this wonderful transformation of the castle attic will become a reality. The Castle is getting a facelift, the heat system is being completely replaced with an energy efficient one, and God will get the glory. The beat goes on!

A Final Word

My mind goes back to those Sunday dinners years ago with Pastor Geza Kovacs and his precious wife Olga, when from 1985 to 1988 we sat in their home and dreamed together of great things for the youth of Hungary. Olga was called home to Heaven several years ago, but Pastor Kovacs continues to preach the Word and remains closely involved with Word of Life Hungary.

He serves on the Board of Directors and continues to teach at the Bible Institute. In December 2008 Word of Life Hungary honored him by naming a men's dormitory after him. It is now 2010, and by the goodness of a gracious and loving God, all those dreams have come true and more. *Thank You, Lord Jesus. These things were all a part of your sovereign plan. They did not happen by chance, but as a part of Your sovereign plan. Thank you, Lord, for allowing my family and me (my dear wife and fellow-laborer, Shirley, and our son Dan, who went to Heaven from Hungary) to be a part of this wonderful thing You have done.*

Dear friend, may I remind you that our wonderful God, according to Psalm 139:1-18, knows everything there is to know about you, and He still loves you. His plan for you is that you would be reconciled to God through simple trust and faith in what Jesus Christ has accomplished for you in His death, burial and resurrection (Romans 5:12-21, 2 Corinthians 5:17-21).

Another part of His sovereign plan for you is that you would offer yourself to be available to Him, if you are willing to lay aside personal plans and say, "Lord, here I am. I'm available to you. Please work out Your marvelous plan in my life! Open doors of opportunity for me and help me to recognize an opportunity when it comes. I will walk through that door and please You."

Make yourself available to your pastor, your church, missionaries, or those happily going about God's work, and you will see the opportunities God will give you. Taste of and enjoy the wonderful, marvelous plans of a gracious, loving, and merciful God, and experience His sovereign plan. I have and I marvel at it every day. Every day becomes a new and exciting adventure through life. You can experience this in your life, too (2 Timothy 1:9).

1. Inside the Budafok Baptist Church, the Church that was so supportive during those beginning days.

2. Pastor Geza Kovacs, Paul Bubar and Harry Bollback at the signing of the preliminary ten-year lease agreement between Word of Life (Elet Szava) and The Szott Trade Union, dated May 3, 1989.

3. Michael Kovacs, businessman, entrepreneur and friend who opened doors at a political level under the then still communist government. Pictured with Paul Bubar and Jack Wyrtzen at the Toalmas Castle dedication. 1992

4. Shirley Bubar, my dear wife and constant encourager through the sometimes rough waters in Hungary. 1992

5. Jack Wyrtzen with Pastor Geza Kovacs and his wife Olga in front of the famous Budafok Baptist in Hungary.

6. Pastor Geza Kovacs, Budafok Baptist Church – loved by Hungarians, hated by the Communist government. The man who with his son Zoltan opened many doors of opportunity to Word of Life.

7. A meeting with Church leaders arranged by the Leaders of the Baptist Union. Our attempt to introduce Word of Life Bible Clubs to the Churches of Hungary. 1986.

8. Jack Wyrtzen, Dr. Alex Haraszti, Paul Bubar. Dr Haraszti was used of God to make final acceptance of Word of Life by the Baptist Union Leadership.

9. Beautiful Toalmas Castle now owned by Word of Life Hungary Foundation. Location of Word of Life administration offices, camps, and Bible Institute.

10. Dan Bubar giving out decision slips to the scores of youth who received Christ or dedicated their life to serve Christ at the castle dedication and Euro youth conference. 1992.

11. Jack Wyrtzen, Harry Bollback, Paul Bubar and translator giving Michael Kovacs an award for his influence in introducing Word of Life at a political level. Picture taken at Euro youth / castle dedication. 1992.

12. Joe Steiner, translator and 1956 escapee from the Hungarian Revolution, pictured With Jack Wyrtzen, Bob Parschauer and Pastor Geza Kovacs. Picture taken at Camp TAHI – a 3 acre piece of "Holy Ground." For many years, the only Christian Youth Camp in 3 Eastern European Countries. Owned since 1928 by the Hungarian Baptist Union, where our first two Word of Life Camps were held.

13. Pastor Geza Kovacs with a deputy minister of the Peoples Republic of Hungary – still a communist style government – at the signing of documents declaring Word of Life as the first, western, religious, non-profit foundation in Hungary. May 1989.

14. Two exceptional attorneys, Dr. Ildiko Barbarics Dobos and Dr. Don Johnson. Ildiko helped guide us in very sensitive legal matters since before our legal existance. Don, a friend and legal counsel helped in several Eastern Europe countries and was a great friend during the time of Dan Bubar's death.

15. Paul Bubar and Dr. Gayer, Deputy Director of the Central European Bar Association and a great legal advisor to Word of Life Hungary. Deceased in April 2010.

16. Students of the Word of Life Bible Institute, dining room in beautiful Toalmas castle. 1995

17. Paul lecturing to a class at the Bible Institute with Dan translating. 1995

POSTSCRIPT

The seemingly 'premature' home-going of an effective young missionary who was just beginning to make an impact in his field of service is difficult for everyone—parents, siblings, staff, friends, supporters and supporting churches, and to all those to whom he was ministering!

While Shirley and I, the Word of Life Hungary staff, along with attorney Don Johnson were at the trauma hospital in Budapest daily and hourly, there were so many others, praying, pleading with God for Dan's healing. Did our God not hear these heart-wringing prayers? Of course He did! But, an all-knowing, all-wise and allowing God would not, in my opinion, leave Dan alive, but severely handicapped, broken or limited in ministry. Dan's earthly body was broken and God in His mercy and grace said, "It's time, Dan, come on home." For all of us, our days are numbered: only a sovereign, gracious God knows when that time is in His marvelous plan. Dan's days here on earth were about to end; he would be ushered by angels into the presence of his Lord.

We were in daily communication with my (then) assistant Don Lough and my wonderful secretary, Deirdre Schrader. The two of them spent many long hours communicating to family, staff, friends and supporters. In 2011, Don becomes the International Executive Director of Word of Life.

Following are copies of faxes I sent to our home office and through them to literally hundreds of family, friends and pastors. Shirley and I were also very much aware of our other three wonderful children who were walking down this path with us. Though we were not there to counsel and comfort them, many of our friends, along with our pastor Dr. Roger Ellison, were with them. I want to share some of those faxes and communications with you. Included in this postscript also, is a very tender poem written by Dan's younger brother, Jonathan. I have also included a letter written by Sarah, Dan's younger sister; knowing it would never be sent anywhere, it was her way of dealing with her indescribable grief. David, Dan's older brother was too sensitive to be able to even express his grief in words: it was just too painful for him to speak of Dan without being reduced to tears.

In April of 1998, Shirley and I were back at Toalmas Castle for a meeting of our Hungarian Board of Directors. It was Shirley's first return since being at the castle for Dan's hastily arranged memorial service on May 14, 1996. Without considering the emotions my wife would be experiencing, and without thinking, I left her to settle into our room on the top floor of the castle. She was still grieving. While she waited in my absence, she penned the following words as she sat alone. I have included this because I want you to understand the heart of this great woman I married, one of the major factors in Dan's greatness. (See page 287)

Nearly fourteen years have passed and time does help heal the hurts and trauma. I will never forget the words of my friend and superior, Joe Jordan when upon our return from Hungary to prepare for Dan's memorial service in 1996. Joe told Shirley and me, "You will never be the same. Your life will forever be impacted by your loss…but God will sustain you, I promise!" He was right. Rarely a day goes by, but what we think of our wonderful son, Dan. I can honestly say there has never been a day of anger or bitterness: only gratitude to the Lord for allowing us to raise him for the glory of God. We both think about heaven much more than we ever did before. We have a greater interest in it than ever before. Shirley has read every book she can find about heaven. Our love for this world is much, much less than ever before, and we both look forward to that great day when we will see Dan again. We are filled with questions: What will he look like? Will he look like he did when he left us? Will he look older? What will be our first words?

How thankful we are for our three other wonderful children. Dan's home-going has also impacted their lives, but God has also sustained them and given them joy. There truly is joy in serving Jesus.

Most importantly, it is our personal relationship with Jesus Christ that takes the awful sting out of death. When you know without question from God's Word how very real heaven is and how easy it is to gain access to heaven when you leave this life, there is a great difference in how you view death and dying. Of course, there will be tears, but the tears are because we will miss that loved one. We need to remember that tears are OK. Men DO cry, or they should be able to cry, because tears truly are the language of the soul. So, don't be embarrassed by tears and grieving at the passing of a loved one or friend. Just **make sure** of heaven, is as simple as ABC:

- **A**dmit to God in simple prayer that you are a sinner (spiritual law breaker).

- **B**elieve that Jesus Christ went to the cross, and by dying there, He paid for your sinning. (**John** 3:16-17)

- **C**onfess (admit) your need and simply invite the Lord Jesus into your life. (**Romans** 10:9-10)

Believe that God means what He says (**John** 1:12) and begin looking for a good local church where there is a pastor who uses the Bible as his pulpit and can tell you clearly what the Bible says. Don't be ashamed to receive Christ; He is not ashamed of you. Read I **John** 5:11-13 and believe it. God wants you to KNOW that you have eternal life–a know-so salvation.

This is what made Dan Bubar such a neat and confident young man and why Shirley, myself and Dan's siblings do not grieve like many people grieve. When you meet people who have lost children or siblings in death, don't avoid them, but talk to them about the one they lost. Often people would avoid talking to us because they thought it would be hard for us and they wouldn't know what to say. In reality, Shirley and I love to talk about Dan. We love to tell "Dan Bubar stories." The one thing parents fear the most, I believe, is that their son or daughter will be forgotten. So talk to them without fear of hurting them or embarrassing them.

It is for this reason that Shirley and I want to share these faxes and special words with you.

FAX #1

TO: Dan Bubar Friends and Prayer Warriors

FROM: Paul & Shirley Bubar

DATE: May 3, 1996

RE: Dan's Condition Update

Dear Friends:

Shirley and I arrived in Budapest Thursday morning, May 3. We were met at the airport by Eric Murphy and Laci Kadar. We went immediately to the Saint Janos Hospital Intensive Care Unit to see our Daniel. He was struck by an out of control Coca Cola truck trailer. He was in the right lane of a four lane highway with no median barrier. The trailer was in a skid and come out of the night with no warning. The point of impact was in Dan's door. He had only time to turn his head. His girl friend, Kinga Kovacs, was uninjured, and grabbed the wheel, steering the car and keeping it from crashing again. Dan took a direct hit in the head by the careening trailer. He has massive head trauma to the brain. Rescue workers had to cut him from the auto.

He is stabilizing—kidney function, blood pressure, heartbeat, etc. He cannot breathe on his own and is on a life support ventilator. The local doctors are not optimistic because of the swelling of the brain. American neurologist specialists, however, have encouraged us by saying what is happening is normal under the circumstances.

He must remain on the ventilator for a week or more until the swelling of the brain subsides. We are optimistic. Little did I know a week ago when I spoke in our Bible Institute Chapel on "The

Ministry of Tears" that Shirley and I would be given that ministry so quickly.

Pray for Dan. Pray that God will shrink the swelling of his brain. If that happens, he has chance of returning to normalcy.

In a wonderful Missions Conference at the Calvary Baptist Church in Oshawa, Ontario, Canada, the night of Dan's accident, I had preached on I John 5:14-15. The idea is praying in the will of God. Dan is in the will of God here. He is successfully doing the will of God. He was wonderfully happy in his ministry. John said, if we pray in the will of God, we will have the petitions we ask of Him. Will you "spread the word" to raise up an army of prayer warriors? If God should decide to take Dan home, we are prepared to accept that, but we truly believe God will spare him. Will you believe and pray with supplication and thanksgiving with us? God is sovereign. He truly is. He makes no mistakes. We need your prayers now!

We will keep you posted. The Word of Life Hungary fax #'s are 011-36-1-251-4575 (Budapest office; #011-36-29-426-003 (Toalmas Castle).

We are, as Jack used to say, "living on the victory side!"

FAX #2

TO: Dan Bubar Friends and Prayer Warriors

FROM: Paul & Shirley Bubar

DATE: May 4, 1996

RE: Dan's Condition Update

Dear Ones:

Daniel's condition remains very critical. To quote one of the Hungarian doctors last night, *"We are trained to not be optimistic!"*

And then he added, *"Yes, there is some brain activity."*

Today, my friend Donald Johnson arrived, flying from a Mexico City business trip. Through his friend, Dr. Ed Law, President of International Neurological Association, the top Neurosurgeons in Hungary will examine Daniel tomorrow (Sunday) morning. They will determine if he can or should be flown to Munich, Germany.

The accident occurred at 11:00 p.m. Wednesday night. Eight teens from Toalmas came to the Castle inquiring of Dan. His accident was on Budapest TV the next morning. Dan's associate met with the teens and led 6 of them to Christ. On Friday, the Toalmas club leader visited all of the local teens who had ever visited the club when Dan led it. Forty-three (43) came to the club meeting. The club leader challenged the teens to give their lives to serve Christ as Dan had. He said, *"If Dan comes back, it will be wonderful. If he doesn't, who will take his place?"* Twenty-five (25) of the youth determined to give their lives over to serve the Lord!

The good news on Dan's condition is that his pulse rate has dropped from 126 yesterday to 80 beats per minute. His temperature is normal. His blood pressure is remaining stable. His brain remains swollen from the impact. It has been only 70 hours. We are continuing to believe **1 John 5:14-15**. Pray for wisdom for the surgeons in the Sunday meeting with Dan.

Our god is sovereign and loves Dan far more than any of us do (**Psalm** 117).

FAX #3

To: All Overseas Fields

From: Paul Bubar

Date: May 10, 1996

Re: DANIEL BUBAR'S HOMEGOING

DANIEL RAY BUBAR

HOME WITH THE LORD...May 10, 1996

"I have fought the good fight, I have finished the race, I have kept the faith. Finally, there is laid up for me the crown of righteousness, which the Lord, the righteous Judge, will give on that day, and not to me only, but also to all who loved His appearing."

II Tim. *4:7-8*

Yesterday, we flew Daniel by Air Ambulance from Budapest to Munich to be under the observation of the finest doctors in Europe. After many tests, it was conclusively determined that our wonderful son, Daniel Ray Bubar, went into the presence of his Lord whom he loved so much at 1:00 p.m. EST (7:00 p.m. Munich time). His race is finished. He is finally Home.

It is very clear to us that it was Dan's time to go Home. Everything–everything about this incident was so specific–a crowded highway–a careening heavily loaded trailer out of the night–hitting Dan only–all the efforts to spare Dan's life, including an emergency Air Ambulance to the most credible Medical Center in Europe–the top neurosurgeons–all to hold on to Dan. We wanted to know before the Lord that we had done all we could for Daniel. But it was Dan's time to end his great ministry here on earth and enter into the presence of his Lord (**Psalm 139:16**). Dan was deliriously happy in his ministry. Bringing young people to his Savior was his delight, his food, his sleep, his dream time, his very life.

Shirley and I, with Don Johnson, return to Hungary tomorrow for a Memorial Service at Toalmas Castle on Tuesday night at 6:00 p.m. A Memorial Service is being planned for Monday, May 20, at 1:00 p.m. at Dan's home church, the Mountainside Bible Chapel, in Schroon Lake, New York.

We ask that you not send flowers, but if God should lead, you may contribute to the Dan Bubar Memorial Fund, which will be used to further the ministry of Bible Clubs to the Hungarian youth. We want all to know that God has been glorified through Dan's life and Home-going. We, as parents, have no regrets. Only those who have sent a son or daughter on ahead of them understand the hurt, but our God truly is sufficient in every situation (**II Cor. 3:5**).

Pray for Eric Murphy and the Hungarian ministry that this strategic ministry will have someone to fill Dan's leadership role. Eric will need much wisdom and help.

We truly are on the victory side.

—Paul & Shirley Bubar

This poem was written by younger brother, Jonathan while Dan was on life-support in Budapest. He was experiencing the agony of waiting to know if Dan would live or be taken home to heaven.

How do I begin to tell
The feelings in my heart, dear Lord?
For they flow deeper than the deepest well,
And time would not afford.

My brother's life is in the balance,
And teeters to and fro.
It all happened in sudden instance,
And so soon he could go.

My heart aches for I love him true,
But the aching is for me.
For if he goes to be with You.
He would be totally free.

He is my teacher and dearest friend,
Whose love was tough, yet tender.
He served You till the very end.
And all, to You, he'd render.
A testimony true and bright,
Lord, this does not make sense.
But then, with wisdom heavenly,
You truly know what's best.

I guess that I must not need
His words as I feel I do.

Maybe I need to really heed
The things he already told me to.

Things like, "Jon, listen to Dad.
He's wise and always right."
"Jon, don't let yourself get sad.
Get up and fight the good fight."

"And don't let turkeys get you down,
You're an eagle and meant to fly.
A turkey walks along the ground,
But an eagle, in the sky."

"Listen to instruction, Jon,
And always take advice."
"Don't listen to the foolish one,
But make friends with the wise."

"Lastly, Jon, Don't be afraid
of anything or anybody.
For that is a trap that Satan laid,
to turn you from wood to putty."

So if You decide his time is done,
And this his final day,
In my heart his **LIFE** still rings on,
Of one who did things Your way.

—Jonathan Bubar
May 2, 1996

A letter from Sarah, Dan's Sister.
Read at his Memorial Service, May 20, 1996.

Dear Dan,

It seems silly to write a letter I know will never be sent. But, I just wanted to express to you what you've done for me. It's partly because of you that I am who I am. I remember growing up as a child you wanted me to be a boy so you could have your even basketball team–2-On-2.

I remember, too, teasing I would get from you about being afraid of the dark. I was so afraid that the blackness would swallow me up like the monster in the closet did to my Barbie's minivan. You would calm me down with no sympathy whatsoever, reminding me that "I was such a baby"—imagine that at six years old.

I remember as a young teenager, barely in the eighth grade being made to start a quiz team at church. You supported me through, lying to me when you assured me that this was the "absolute funniest part of Teens Involved." You know that I never would have been on the Quiz team had you not been so enthusiastic about it. If you hadn't been there quizzing me on all 30 verses in the Word of Life Scripture memory verse pack, I would have never stuck with it. And we went to Nationals every year–even won a couple times, too! I did it just for you.

You pushed me all the time to be the best I could be (without going into the army). You were my own personal drill sergeant (how lucky for me!). But I want to thank you.

Because of you, I am not afraid of the dark. In fact, the room has to be absolutely black for me to get any kind of sleep. (I even have to turn off those little candles Mom has in all the windows–those dumb things light up the entire room).

Because of you, I love to run. I'm no marathon runner and I'll probably never bring home a turkey from a race I win. But you gave me a love for running.

Because of you, I got an A on my verses while at the Bible Institute. My friends would all be racking their brains trying to remember these verses for five hours, while I had them memorized since eighth grade–still do.

But I think, Dan, the greatest thing you've given me is my love for the mission field. It's because of you that at twelve years old I told God I'd go where ever, just like my big brother Dan. It's seeing your eyes light up when you see a young person responding to a message that has given me this desire. It's watching your perseverance and determination in learning the Hungarian language that has spurred me to that end. And it is hearing your testimony and reading of your love for the ministry that has cultivated that love in me. I don't know if Mom or Dad had told you, but I changed my major from Bible to Missions. And it's because of you!

Dan, there's one more thing that you've given me. You gave it to me the day you left us. It was a longing for Heaven. Before, I always loved life. I wanted to live till I was 100. I really truly wanted the Lord to tarry so I could live a long meaningful life, filled with great things done for Christ. I wanted to live the kind of life Sophie Muller did— live one patterned after our dear "Uncle" Jack. To be able to live life to its fullest capability. Now, I have a different point of view. Because of you, Dan, "For me to live is Christ"–but to die–that would be so much gain!

Till we meet again–I love you.

—Your sister, Sarah

In April of 1998 Shirley and I were back at Toalmas Castle. It was Shirley's first return since Dan's memorial service at Toalmas on May 14, 1996.

Without considering the emotions my wife would be experiencing, without thinking I left her in our room alone and went about the tasks I had come to do. Shirley penned the following as she sat alone in our room).

Reflections from the Castle

Toalmas, Kastely – Hungary

April 2, 1998

Tonight I sit in the same room where I spent one of the worst nights of my life–on May 13, 1996, almost two years ago–It was the night before Dan's Memorial Service here in Hungary–and I knew my life would never be the same again. When your child dies, there is a depth to the grief that transcends anything imaginable. I remember thinking my heart would stop from the ache–or surely I would die from the hurt.

But, amazingly, we've survived for almost two years–one day at a time, one hour at a time and one moment at a time–by God's grace. Two years ago, I thought I would never smile again–and I fought within my heart for a purpose and a reason. Here we are–two years later–and there is still no reason I can imagine and certainly no purpose I can see–but God gives a peace that passes all understanding and we have not only survived: we've even learned to shine–and yes, to even smile.

Our precious son was involved in a freak accident while serving the Lord as a missionary to Hungary's youth. He was here for six years–he was only 29 years old. Dan learned the language, started the camping program and began the Bible Club ministry in this land of talented, tender people. He loved serving in the ministry, he loved the Hungarians, but most of all, Dan loved the Lord with all his heart–and as his parents, we were terribly proud of him.

Why does the Lord allow such tragedy in our lives? There are some things we've learned in these two years:

1. *God makes no mistakes. Out God is in control–and He is sovereign. This alone is a necessary fact for survival–and one to appropriate when facing grief. I CAN trust that God knows what He is doing in our lives. Where would we be without this?*

2. *God loves us. John 17 tells us how Christ prayed for us. Our Bible says He makes intercession for us before the Father. What a wonder! The God of creation loves me–and He loves our wonderful Dan–even more than we could.*

3. *There are many people who have traveled this road before me–and many who will follow. Grief is no respecter of persons and I am not alone in sorrow. We have heard of many, many others who have been through our sorrow and much more. I am not unique in my suffering. What makes the difference is how I choose to let God use it–I can choose to question the Father's plan–to struggle and strive–to be angry and bitter–OR, I can choose to throw myself in His arms and ask Him to teach me to trust Him more–to learn all He has to teach me–to crawl into His lap and cry "Abba (Daddy), I don't understand. Please help me."*

4. *I have learned that there are worse things in life than having a missionary, servant of the Lord, son, go on to heaven before you—We know where Daniel is today—and we know his ship has arrived home safely in Heaven's harbor—Dan finished his race—he ran it well—he "did it right" and I no longer have to "worry" (as all mother's "worry") about Dan—what he is doing, where he is going, is he safe, is he warm, is he happy, etc. etc. Now my other three Children—that's another story! (My children always teased me, Mom, why pray when you Can worry?!")*

5. *I have also learned how fragile life really is: how to grasp and enjoy each day while you hold it; and how important it is to live life with eternity in view. This earth is so terribly temporary —none of us are going to get out of this life alive! Furthermore, this isn't REALLY living— yet how contorted is our view–this is just the classroom–we still have the test to take before we really get to know what it is like to REALLY live–eternally that is!*

People spend their lives saving for "retirement" when God's retirement plan is "out of this world!"